THE
You IN *You*

UNVEILING THE YOU THAT'S HIDDEN FROM VIEW

WILBERT HUNT, MSLS

About The Author

A T THE AGE OF 18, WILBERT HUNT, M.S.L.S., LEFT HIS home in Texas to join the U.S. Air Force. After completing his tour of duty, he attended Compton Junior College, California State University, Dominguez Hills, and the University of Southern California where he obtained a Master of Science in Library Science degree. Shortly after graduating, he accepted a position at the Los Angeles County Public Library System, later to be renamed the County of Los Angeles Public Library, where he held, at various times over the years, until his retirement, several library positions: Government Publications Librarian, Reference Librarian, and Community Library Manager of several libraries. Currently, he spends his time writing, reading the Bible, and praying.

THE
You IN *You*

UNVEILING THE YOU THAT'S HIDDEN FROM VIEW

WILBERT HUNT, MSLS

Wilbert Hunt

Published by

Charlton Park LLC

Published by Charlton Park LLC

PO Box 904, Hemet California, 92546

Copyright © 2016 by Wilbert Hunt

Print ISBN: 978-1-54392-087-1

eBook ISBN: 978-1-54392-088-8

For more information write the publisher at the address above or email: TheUNU@aol.com.

For:

My Mother, Amanda, who transitioned when I was about 2 years old.

My Father, the Reverend I.P. Hunt.

Emma Bryant, my Big Sister and mother stand-in.

David Hunt, my equanimous Big Brother.

Winston Hunt Sr, my twin, who accompanied me into this world.

Doris Pierson, my Little/Big Sister and lifelong protector.

Doree Joiner, my creative, God-fearing older sister.

Barbara Lynn, my multiple-lives companion.

Special Thanks To:

Albert Taylor, P H.D.

Neale Donald Walsch

Shirley MacLaine

Dr. Eben Alexander

Whitley Strieber

Joyce Sumbi

Sanford Rosette Jr.

Ada Branch Booker

CONTENTS

INTRODUCTION

For there is nothing covered, that shall not be revealed;
neither hid, that shall not be known.[1]

THERE'S YOU, AND THEN THERE'S *YOU*. THIS IS NOT A quixotic play on words, but a statement about who you really are: the possessor of two bodies, and not just a physical one, but a non-physical one—a *you* whom I will unveil in the pages of this book.

What would you say if I told you that the physical body that you're attached to is merely an inferior replica of another body, one more excellently constructed in every way—seemingly indestructible, exhibiting amazing properties? What would you say if I told you that your physical body is not alive, but is kept alive by another body, not unlike the way patients are kept alive with the use of life-support machines?

What would you think if I told you that you have lived perhaps hundreds of lives and, in addition to living in this world, you exist simultaneously in a number of parallel worlds? What would you think if I told you that you could see future events before they happen, that ghosts exist, and that extraterrestrials visit our planet regularly, revealing themselves to those fortunate individuals who were born with, or have developed, the requisite senses to perceive them?

---

1 Luke 12:2

What would you believe if I told you that God still talks to people in this modern age, just as He did millennia ago to Moses when He appeared to Moses in the form of the burning bush? What would you believe if I told you that it's possible to imitate the life of Jesus to the extent that your spiritual development allows—heal the sick, cast out devils, cleanse the lepers—as well as know the thoughts of others? What would you believe if I told you that you could influence the weather and converse with those who have crossed over to the other side that we call the "afterlife"?

No matter how you answered the preceding questions, before you finish this book, you will have to grapple with them again, as well as with others that you, yourself, may form as you read. You will either find yourself awestruck by humankind's latent abilities and wonderful capacity to be more than physical bodies with all the limitations we usually associate with that seeming reality—the breadth and depth of our intelligence, the limits of our knowledge, and the life-numbing restraints that circumscribe our day-to-day activities—or you'll find yourself dumbfounded by the sheer magnitude of the claims made herein.

Simply put, I will make certain claims in this book that will be so fantastical and mind-boggling that they will force you to take sides. Some readers will readily believe these claims, while others will dismiss them out of hand. Before I do so, however, let me make a confession. For the better part of my life, I have lived straddling two worlds: this world, and a world we don't normally see—existing seemingly with one foot planted in this world, and one firmly in another, what some have called the "astral plane." You see, I'm an out-of-body traveler and explorer. Where others see a physical world, I see one governed by our thoughts and subject to our beliefs and emotions. Where others founder, mesmerized by a world filled with one material distraction after the other, I'm keenly aware that our Earth, as seductive as it may be at times, is merely a refueling station, a brief stop on our return Home.

Why write this book?

My reasons are several, each of which I believe are imperative, if we're to escape the illusions of the past, the stolidity of the present, and embrace a future that could be grander in every way, breaking with hoary concepts that may have served us once, but which are now holding us back and holding us down when our potential as sons and daughters of God is skyward, a potential that's redolent with the majesty we associate with the heavens.

This account of my out-of-body explorations will add my voice to those explorers who have gone before me. Their journals, replete with answers for the uninitiated, fearlessly mapped the paths that they carved out of astral wildernesses. In addition, their journals chronicled the strange, but wonderful, sights that they encountered along the way, and the description of denizens of worlds that, until they wrote about them, existed only in our imaginations. I'm getting older, and if I don't take time to establish way markers and document my experiences, they will be lost to the world forever.

And that would be tragic. These way markers are of sufficient value to be preserved, not because of ego-gratification, but to build upon the body of knowledge that says that man is more than flesh and bone, that he's larger and more magnificent than we have ever dared hope. It is my wish, further, that my record will encourage future explorers to follow my path, and, where possible, to blaze new ones. It is my wish that it will inspire others to dig below the surface of their day-to-day reality and discover the infinite wonders and possibilities that await them there.

It is also my wish that once we as a species come to accept our grandeur, we will conduct ourselves in ways that hold every man, woman, and child as the marvelous creations of God that they are, and rouse us to put an end to the horrors that now mar our world. It is my wish that its message and revelations will hasten the realization that all life is precious, and that what we do to one, we do to all.

It is my firm belief that had humankind put as much energy and thought into its spiritual development as it has put into its scientific inquiries, then we humans would by now have created a New Eden. Rather than seeing Jesus' life of spectacular spiritual achievements as exceptional and "miraculous," we would now see them as commonplace and within the reach of all.

If I were to assign a purpose to this book, it would be this: I want to shake people out of their lethargy. I want to awaken them to their grand potential. I have seen intolerance. I have seen the damage that indifference, bigotry, hatred, and fear have wreaked, and will continue to wreak upon the people of this planet, unless a renewing of the heart and a changing of the mind become our lot. I have seen man's inhumanity toward those with whom he shares this world. It's time we put all this behind us and take an evolutionary leap that will reveal our full potential as creations of God. It is my hope that this book will serve to remind us all of who we are, who we've been, and who we can become again—children of God, aspects of the Divine, reflections of Deity.

Further, it is my hope that by revealing the particulars of my life, it will reveal something about your life—indeed, about the life of us all. It is my hope that you will come to see that the masterful life that was Jesus', His total dominion over the world, as evidenced by His *rebuking* the wind and *calming* a boisterous sea, knowing the thoughts of others, and healing the sick, wasn't just peculiar to Him and Him alone. I want to show that others can perform these so-called miracles to the degree that their spiritual development permits, that miracles don't set aside natural laws, but use them in ways that we don't yet fully understand.

The potential to become more than humans is ours, although our humanhood would insist otherwise. The Bible is clear on this. Jesus stated in part, "He that believeth on me, the works that I do shall he do also; and greater works than these shall he do."[2] I believe that the best way to impart this information, to promote my cause, and to remind others—to bring back to memory, to give others the remembrance of who they are—is to

2 John 14:12

write it down, both for posterity, and for those in search of their *real* self, their true identity. Regrettably, we live in a world that defines us in its own image, rather than in the image and likeness of God.

Not unlike the lives of millions of others, I haven't always lived a perfect life, not by my standards, nor likely the standards of others. Along the way, I learned many things about myself, things that caused me consternation, melancholy, and regret, but things which also gave me hope and a sanguine outlook; things which I believe, with the use of extrapolation, speak to the human condition, past and present, and provide insight into why some things are as they are.

There's a great deal here to digest. Largely, it will vie with much of what you have come to believe is true about yourself and the world in which you live. This will be true for most readers. Much of what I write here will not hold up to the scrutiny of science, unless it falls within the realm of speculative science, a thought-based approach, one not yet subjected to the scientific method, the centerpiece of science. Further, you'll find that science and scientific experiments cannot easily replicate certain astral-related phenomena to satisfy the strict rigors of relevant scientific disciplines.

My experiences are mainly anecdotal. For that reason, they don't provide the requisite level of proof or evidence to satisfy the staunchest critics. Notwithstanding the book's semi-autobiographical focus, the content of the book will follow a topical, rather than a chronological, approach. Biblical references and quotes—and there are many herein—are from the King James Version (KJV) of the Bible. Of the number of books I've read on the out-of-body experience, not one examined the phenomenon in quite the way that I will examine it herein. Although each book touched upon many of the same topics covered in this book, not one organized those topics into a cohesive whole. I seek to remedy that in this book. To do so, I've divided the book into four parts. Part One focuses primarily on the astral body, or the non-physical properties of ourselves, identifying some of its attributes, characteristics which I discovered while out of my body on hundreds of occasions. Part Two focuses on the astral body's preternatural abilities, several of which have been revealed to me, but which in no way exhaust the whole of this body's amazing nature. Part Three focuses on the negative forces that have arrayed themselves against humanity and against the evolution of the human soul, using our human energies for their own nefarious purposes. Part Four reveals the methods that I have used, sometimes knowingly, and sometimes the result of serendipity, to connect with my two selves: my non-physical self, and my Higher Self, or God Self, also known as the Soul. Throughout the book, I use the term *soul* rather liberally. I use the capital "S" Soul to refer to God, the God Self, or the Soul Self. I use the lowercase "s" soul to refer to humans or to our human senses, or to our astral, or spiritual self, or our spiritual sense. In most instances, the context will determine the use, and differentiate between the several meanings. The purpose of the four parts is to give you a more complete picture of who you *really* are, the *you* that's hidden from view, the *you* in you.

As I bring to light my experiences in the astral realm, you'll learn that the astral plane is highly personal. You'll learn, too, that it's a world that complies faithfully with our thoughts and beliefs. This shouldn't come as a complete surprise; the physical world that we occupy is similarly structured, and is also subject to our thoughts and beliefs, whether we recognize it or not.

Given the extraordinary life I have lived, you'd think I would have revealed it eagerly to all those who would listen—certainly to friends, or family, or spouses. But I didn't; perhaps because I believed my story to be so fantastical that few would believe it; or perhaps because I was afraid of what they might say, or think—that they would question my sanity, or even my grip on reality. Whatever the reason, I've only shared my story—and only a very small part of it, at that—in recent years, to my now companion and one family member. For those who thought they knew me, what I will reveal herein will surely prompt a recounting of our time together, searching for any hint of the *real me*, the one that I carefully shielded all these years, for fear that I would be misunderstood—or worse, repudiated.

For reasons that will soon become clear, let me reveal now that I'm black. Were it not for certain particulars to follow, this information would be irrelevant. Because of those particulars, the fact that I'm black—or, as some would say, African-American—will illuminate a portion of the information herein in ways that the absence of it would not—information that is critical to a fuller understanding of life, and our purpose for being here. That said, I will not reveal some information from my life. If I revealed everything, it might expose others to a glare that they haven't consented to. While I'll try to impart as much as I can—the good, the bad, and the ugly—I will do so without resorting to hyperbole, pandering to the bizarre or staking positions that I haven't fully tested, or carefully weighed.

A prophet is not without honour, but in his own country, and among his own kin, and in his own house.[3]

Wilbert Hunt

---

3 Mark 6:4

PART ONE:

WHO YOU REALLY ARE

ONE

HOW IT BEGAN

In the beginning God....
(Genesis)

U SING MY PERSONAL EXPERIENCES TO GUIDE ME, AND drawing upon my story to tell *your* story, to reveal who *you* really are, I will tell two stories: my story and your story. Growing up in Texas, there was little to distinguish my life from the lives of others. It was mostly uneventful until that fateful summer day when I went to bed early to use sleep as a sedative and an analgesic to subdue the daylong headache that raged within my head well past suppertime.

When you're eleven or twelve, a headache is a rare event. Sure, I had experienced headaches before, and when they were particularly bad, I sought the healing balm of sleep. As with previous headaches, when I awoke in the dark this time after a rather painful episode that lasted most of the day, the headache remained asleep. Thankful, I pulled the remaining cover over my body and settled in for what I thought would be a quiet night of sleep. I couldn't have been more mistaken; several hours in, I was awakened.

My sudden awakening signaled the awakening of something new, something alarming. After that night, everything changed.

A little after midnight, I awoke to an explosion—not an external blast, but one that resounded in my head. It took me a moment or two to realize that the explosion wasn't exterior to me, but had originated from within me. From what seemed a long distance, I could hear something falling. It whistled as it fell, the way that bombs released from a bomb bay of a World War II bomber whistled when heard from below. I had heard this sound before, emanating from the Saturday matinee war movies that I had seen over the years. My brother and I called them "war stories," and we preferred them to "love stories."

As the whistling—which was faint at first—grew louder, the closer the bomb seemed. When the whistling was at its loudest, the bomb exploded in my head. After the explosion, the whistling started again—once more heard from a distance, only to crescendo louder until it culminated as before into a large explosion.

I panicked.

I probably wouldn't have with one bomb exploding, but when they kept falling and exploding, and I couldn't stop them, fear gripped my mind. The terror that followed did nothing to break the grip.

For a preteen on the cusp of adolescence, the explosions augured the end of the world, if not the end of me. My father and mother were asleep several rooms away. I called to them, pleading for help. Rather than emitting an audible sound, my pleas rolled around in my head until they were drowned by the din of the bombs exploding, reaching no farther than my frantic mind. Summoning all my strength, I tried to cry out. Mentally, I called out again and again, while the bombs kept falling and exploding. Finally, the awareness set in—no one could hear my desperate cries, and no one was coming to my rescue.

It was then that I became aware of something more terrifying than bombs exploding. I was paralyzed. The paralysis was complete, covering the full length of my body, extending to all my body's extremities, seizing me the way a vise might. Hard as I tried, I couldn't break the grip. I now understood why my efforts to wake my parents and raise alarm had failed: I couldn't move any part of my body (and God knows I struggled long and hard to do so), and I couldn't make a sound, with my lips refusing to cooperate, as well. As long as I was in this muscle-restraining condition, I knew that my pleas for help would form like ice crystals, only to melt as soon as they touched the Earth.

In sheer terror and desperation, I fought the force that held me immobile. After a time, I gave up trying to reach my parents; I wanted to conserve my energy to break the chains that bound me, invisible shackles that made me an unwilling captive of my own body. With utmost concentration, I held my body in mind. It was as though it had sunk below my consciousness, leaving only the pinnacle of my mind in sharp focus, the way that capstones on pyramids—the ones pictured in my geography textbook—stood out, a feeling that would possess me again and again after that night and as the years came and went.

For what seemed a lifetime of immobility, my unseen captor released its hold, giving my body free range again. Relief and joy swept over me. At last, I was once more in control of my body, and I made certain of it by moving every part of me. And just as quickly as it had started, the paralysis ended, and the explosions ceased. Lying on my back, I wondered if any of it had happened at all—the paralysis, the bombs. Now that the crisis had passed and I could speak again, I resisted the temptation to alert my parents. After all, what would I tell them—that bombs had gone off inside my head, and that a strange paralysis had immobilized me such that it kept me from moving and crying out?

Later, I reasoned that the explosions had been the return of my pounding headache and that I had witnessed a physical manifestation from the inside out of how a headache might sound to someone witnessing it from inside my head. But I couldn't be sure. This was the end of it, I thought.

Whatever it was that had intruded on my sleep was over, as was my head-ache. I was relieved to find, too, that my reason for going to bed early that night—to use sleep as a balm—had worked. I had been clever. Nevertheless, the sheen of that initial cleverness wore off over time, as the paralysis con-tinued to visit me, during the interim, night or day, numerous times, but without the accompanying bombs falling and exploding inside my head that attended the first one.

Years later, I was to learn that night paralysis, or sleep paralysis, was the usual launching pad from which those who wished to could lift off into the astral realm, leaving their physical bodies behind. In the early days, I didn't initiate an out-of-body experience. That came later. There was the launch pad (the paralysis), to be sure, but rather than personally taking steps to lift off—usually by sitting up straight and swinging my legs over the side of my bed—I was placed on automatic pilot. Without any effort on my part, a mysterious force did the lift off for me, whisking me away at an incredible speed on a current of a sort, called an "astral current" in some of the literature.

My flight through space was from the reclining position, head first, supine. If I opened my eyes during the flight, I would only observe streaks of colorful lights, indicating that I was moving at an immense speed. If I slowed down while in flight, I could recognize lofts and upper floors as I traveled, sometimes peopled with startled humans. Most of the time, I observed nothing more than what you'd expect to find in those parts of the house.

While some out-of-body travelers merely reported a paralysis as a prelude to their out-of-body adventure, my out-of-body experiences were always accompanied by an additional element: an agitation (as I called it then), a vibration (as I would call it later) at a center point between my eyes (known as the third eye), and over my heart. The vibrations shook me so violently that I often thought my heart would stop. Of course, it never did.

VIBRATIONS

For many of my out-of-body explorations, the experience began with the vibrations and then the paralysis; or the paralysis, and then the vibrations. At any rate, the vibrations and the paralysis are an unwelcome condition for out-of-body travelers, but a necessary one, if they wish to travel in the astral realm. I find the vibrations more unsettling than the paralysis. The discomfort of the vibrations was either severe or transitory, lasting as long as I remained in the body and ending the moment I managed a separation. One out-of-body explorer, Albert Taylor, calls this leaving of the physical body the "disconnect," and the returning to the body the "reconnect." Both terms capture the sense of what occurs when the astral body separates from, and returns to, the physical body.

As for the vibrations, they may be localized, that is, limited to certain areas of the body such as the "third eye" (the area between the eyes near the middle of the forehead) or over the heart. Despite the discomfort the vibrations cause, the experience is pain free. I'm often reminded of pain during the vibrations, however, without actually experiencing pain. The vibrations are usually accompanied by no small amount of fear, generating concerns that the body is enduring a physical trauma. I have read of no explorer who has suffered ill effects from the vibrations, or as a result of repeated and frequent jaunts into the astral realm.

Although I've experienced pre-launch vibrations many times as a prelude to the out-of-body experience, they didn't always occur. Many a night, I have used "lucid dreams" as launch pads for my out-of-body experiences (lucid dreams are dreams in which the dreamer is aware, or becomes aware, that he or she is dreaming). Becoming conscious that I'm dreaming (waking up in a dream) allowed me to end the dream—to consciously stop it dead in its tracks—and to use the opportunity to lift out of my body.

On other occasions, the vibrations are mild or non-existent. I can recollect the first time the vibrations began, which was fairly early on. I never learned to tolerate them well, although they represented a doorway to a larger experience, one which I was eager to have. No matter how hard I struggled to end the vibrations while in their grip, they were practically impossible to break, except with what seemed to be a superhuman effort, if even then.

The vibrations were an irresistible force. This force would draw me deeper and deeper into its clutches, as a maelstrom might draw a swimmer into its vortex. These were scary moments. Resistance was usually futile, but I resisted, nevertheless. When I relaxed and allowed myself to go with the swirls, the discomfort that attended this experience wasn't half as bad. But the loss of control—brought on by the vibrations—worsened my fear of what was happening, or might happen as a result of my surrendering, and led to my resistance. My reading of the literature hadn't turned up much about the vortex I entered when the vibrations began. When the vibrations were at their strongest, so was the maelstrom. Although I put up a mighty struggle to extricate myself, I usually lost, and in losing, was forced to succumb to the unrelenting force.

When the battle for control had ended, with myself the vanquished more often than not, I found myself in a familiar, but unsettling, place, familiar because I had been there before, and unsettling because my con-sciousness was now fully entrapped in another state—a state where pos-sibilities were immeasurably expanded—supplanting my normal state of conscious control and awareness in the physical realm with another, one operating according to a different set of rules than the previous state.

The first time it happened is still clear in my memory. It was probably a year or so after my first nocturnal scare. The experience frightened me so badly that it etched itself permanently along the folds of my brain. I was asleep in bed. The vibrations woke me. At that time, I thought of them as "agitations." They had started as I slept. Now that I was awake, the vibra-tion in my head began to pull me under, take me deeper into what I later defined as a trance, the way a whirlpool, or a maelstrom, might swallow up a hapless swimmer. Invariably the trance state won out, leaving nothing of me but a mound of flesh that was once my body, now suddenly turned into an immobile stone statue—my mind aware of nothing but my concentrated consciousness, a pyramidal capstone, resting atop a noncompliant body that neither protested nor fought back. Not able to move, I lay there helplessly, my mind furiously seeking some remedy for my sudden and unwelcome dilemma.

The vibration over my heart synchronized in perfect rhythm with its counterpart between my eyes. If only I could move my hand, I thought, and touch the place over my heart where the vibration was strongest, the vibration would surely stop. This plan came from nowhere. It would take years before I would learn even the name of what was happening to me, let alone how to manipulate it. Yet, I had a certainty that it would work. With that in mind, I gathered as much willpower as I could muster and, with a Herculean effort, managed to move my right arm slightly, and aimed my right hand for the spot over my heart where the vibration raged, unabated. Persistence and what seemed like hours paid off; my right hand finally touched the offending area, and just as I had hoped and predicted, the vibrations stopped immediately.

Now released from the constraints of the vibratory trance, I faced another quandary. My right arm and hand—the one I used to extricate myself from this new restraint—rested, not upon my torso, where I might have expected, but at my side, as though it hadn't moved at all. What arm, then, had I used? What hand touched the spot over my heart? Years would pass before I received answers to these two questions, answers that posed new questions, even after learning of the existence of another body, another *me,* hidden from view.

As an out-of-body traveler, subjected nightly to sleep paralysis and violent vibrations, marriage proved to be a godsend, when my wife, on cue, would release me from my night-time paralysis, springing into action when my moans signaled my inability to disrupt my trance state. It only required the gentle touch of her leg against mine, or the light touch of her hand upon my arm. Her touch never failed, and neither did my gratitude.

My father, the pastor, and my stepmother, the teacher, would die years later without ever knowing the horror that visited me that night, when bombs fell and exploded in my head, or the special ability that ensued from the crucible of that fear. I never spoke of it to them. In fact, I never spoke of it to anyone for a long time thereafter. In retrospect, I attribute my strange baptism to the hormonal changes that were taking place in my soon-to-be-adolescent body. New stirrings in my body riveted my attention toward girls, as well as some women, with a renewed interest. I must confess, however, that when I was barely school age, I was already attracted to several girls my age from across our small community.

SEXUAL ORIGIN

There appears to be a sexual component to the out-of-body experience, a component which, I believe, contributed strongly to the beginning of my new experiences on the astral plane and the new abilities that came with them. On the physical plane, it appears that sexual energy draws undue attention to things physical, as well as a desire for material gratification. On the astral or more rarefied levels, the same energy may be used to explore the many regions of the mind (the past, present, and future), as well as transport the soul into the presence of God. One noted New Age guru has stated unequivocally that sexual energy is spiritual energy.

A few months prior to my life-changing headache, and the subsequent sleep paralysis, sexual stirrings were introducing themselves. Newspaper photographs of women in bathing suits fired my imagination with preadolescent passion. These stirrings were new, and relentless. From my early youth, the opposite sex had stirred my interest, but what I was now feeling went well beyond those interests, stoking a fire that unleashed a new energy, an energy that grew stronger with each passing day.

Now that I'm considered a senior citizen, and my sexual energy and passion have abated somewhat, so, too, have the out-of-body episodes. They don't occur nearly as often as they once did, the lessening coinciding with a decrease in sexual energy. I do miss my night-time peregrinations, and midnight flights, which facilitated my ventures into other worlds, my viewing of past lives, and the assurance that life outlives the body, as well as the sure awareness of the unity of all life. Although I don't explore the uncharted regions of the Soul as often as I'd like, I do explore them just enough to keep the wonderment alive. Not all out-of-body travelers have seen their out-of-body excursions diminish with age, some retaining their ability to leave their bodies well into their twilight years, experiencing rather robust vibrations and retaining their pre-launch paralysis.

THE GOD CONNECTION

I like to think that it was my early devotion to God—whom I never doubted existed—which accelerated my transformation, as much as, or more than, the hormones. Not a night went by that I didn't pray for my Earthly father who suffered chronically from ulcers. We lived across the street from a public school. A church with black congregants stood several feet beyond the school's boundary. On most nights, church hymns blended with the occasional shouting, blanketing my body and my spirit with its melancholy strains, as tears brimmed my eyes soon to dampen the pillow supporting my youthful head. I peered out of a nearby window at the brightly-lit church whence the singing streamed, and prayed to God for the healing of my father.

"Please God, don't let my dad die," was my nightly plea, which I repeated many times before falling off to sleep.

The fear of losing him was a burden that I bore, but not easily. One night, my stepmother summoned a neighbor to take him to the hospital. Wailing in pain, he uttered words that seared my soul like the red-hot potbelly heater had seared my backside as I attempted to pass behind it through a narrow passage.

"Oh God, I think I'm going to die," my father repeated as the neighbor guided him through the night to a waiting car, while I watched anxiously from a window on that side of the house, fiercely praying to God not to let him die.

And he *didn't* die.

My dad lived to be ninety-three, or perhaps older, depending on the documents used to ascertain his birth date, two of which conflicted by as much as two years. I'm certain that my humble, fervent, and innocent prayers added years to his life. Over time, we saw a marked improvement in his health, as he was able, well before his death, to pretty much eat whatever his appetite fancied, and to do so without the attendant pain brought on by ulcers. I can't tell you how much this pleased me, and swelled my heart with gratitude to God.

During the intervening years, from childhood to adulthood, nighttime was never the same. My out-of-body adventures numbered in the hundreds, if not in the thousands, and were always at their strongest, and most enduring, around full moons. A dream study found that sleepers sleep less and more lightly during full moons. It would be instructive to know just how many of these sleepers had an out-of-body experience when the moon was full.

I told no one about these nightly excursions into the unknown, and began to believe, after a time, that everyone was so afflicted. I was to learn later that only one in ten people, of the seven billion on the planet according to United Nations estimates, had, at one time or another, left their bodies at least once. How many had left their bodies frequently and consistently, or at will, are perhaps considerably fewer.

THE KEY

Once I had the key, I was able to exploit fully what had begun years ago, my new-found ability to leave my body. For the longest time, I didn't know how to refer to the phenomenon of leaving my body. This, in itself, precluded any serious research into the subject had I been so inclined. This changed one day during the seventies. I was in my late twenties, and was a student at California State College, Dominguez Hills. Two white students, both young women, perhaps a few years younger than I, approached me as I walked across the campus green. They were researching a subject and wanted first-hand accounts of those who had the ability to leave their bodies.

"Excuse me, but we're doing a research project on people who have left their body," one of the young women explained. "Have you ever left your body?"

Had I! So this was what it was called: "leaving the body."

When they learned that I was one of those for whom they were searching, their eyes lit up, and they bombarded me with enough questions to rival those on my previous Biology test. From her, I learned a *key* term, "astral projection," which led me to another term, OOBE, or OBE, which stands for "Out-of-Body Experience." At last, I had names for what I was experiencing. At the time, it was the biggest breakthrough of my life. It led me to the meager literature on the subject at the time, and the assurance that there wasn't anything wrong with me, a thought that I had occasionally entertained. I will be forever grateful to the two young women who selected me from the crowd. From them I received *The Key* to a storehouse of knowledge, and information, a meager one by today's standards, but for me it couldn't have been better stocked.

Today, there's no dearth of books on the subject, many promising to have you out of your body in short order. Publishers are publishing them with amazing frequency. This wasn't true in the seventies. Nevertheless, the books that were available at that time were some of the very best. Despite their age, they still enjoy a currency and a popularity to rival any of the new ones. An Amazon.com search turned up 6,673 results for the search term "astral projection," and 1,492 for "out-of-body experience."

"The Projection of the Astral Body" by Sylvan J. Muldoon, first published in 1929, remains both a classic and wonderful guide to the subject, as well as Oliver Fox's book, "Astral Projection: A Record of Out-of-the-Body Experiences." Robert Monroe's several books on the subject, "Journeys Out of the Body," "Far Journeys," and "Ultimate Journey," are still widely read and widely respected.

The elation I felt upon discovering these books and many others like them from the out-of-body genre eludes description. With each discovery, I was giddy with delight. I couldn't have been happier had I unearthed diamonds in my own backyard. The number of reprints of these books testifies to their popularity, and the on-going public interest in the subject of astral projection or the out-of-body phenomenon.

TWO

MYSTERY OF THE UNSEEN BODY

*It is sown a natural body; it is raised a spiritual body. There
is a natural body, and there is a spiritual body.
And so it is written, The first man Adam was made a living
soul; the last Adam was made a quickening spirit.
Howbeit that was not first which is spiritual, but that which
is natural; and afterward that which is spiritual.*[4]

TO UNDERSTAND WHO YOU *REALLY* ARE, THE *YOU* IN
you, we'll have to begin our story in an uncustomary way, using an
unconventional approach, that is, working our way from the inside out.
Unveiling the mystery of the unseen body begins not with the astral body
itself, but with its most mysterious aspect, the *silver cord*. Attached to this
non-physical body is what can only be described as a cord, silver in color,
luminous, and stretchable.

The literature I've read had little to say about the cord, but it's clear
that its function is indispensable to the out-of-body experience, enabling
humans to exist in two realms simultaneously—the physical realm and the

---

4 I Cor 15:44-46

astral realm—maintaining, while the body is viable, an indissolvable link between physicality and non-physicality, the astral body's more suitable environment. Thankfully, the Bible isn't silent regarding the existence of the silver cord, actually devoting two verses to it in Ecclesiastes, Chapter 12.

THE SILVER CORD

Or ever the silver cord be loosed, or the golden bowl be broken, or the pitcher be broken at the fountain, or the wheel broken at the cistern.

Then shall the dust return to the earth as it was: and the spirit shall return unto God who gave it.[5]

Some out-of-body explorers believe the silver cord to be more myth that reality, mainly because they've never seen it. Actually, the silver cord operates much like an umbilical cord, serving, essentially, a similar purpose. Unlike the physical umbilical cord, however, the silver cord exists on the astral plane. It's likely that it exists on several planes simultaneously. How many we may never know. On the physical plane we know that the umbilical cord connects the mother to her unborn child for the purpose of providing the fetus with oxygen and life-sustaining nutrients. On the astral plane the silver cord connects the astral body to the physical body for basically the same purpose—to give the body the sustenance it needs to exist—the life energy that pulses from the astral body to the physical.

Further, the cord regulates the many functions of the physical body through this life-giving conduit. Without it, the body ceases to be a vehicle to navigate within a physical environment. When physical death occurs, the umbilical cord connection breaks, and the body begins the process of decomposition. Fortunately for the newborn, the severance of the umbilical cord allows mother and child to exist as two separate beings, the newborn

---

5 Eccl 12:6-7

now doing for itself what Mom had heretofore done on its behalf. This is where the umbilical cord analogy breaks down. On the astral plane, the severance of the silver cord releases the individual soul from its connection with the physical, while dooming the physical body to certain death. At some point during the birth process, the astral body uses the silver cord to attach itself to the soon-to-be-born fetus, either before leaving the womb or shortly afterward, when it emerges as a newborn.

I discovered the "silver cord" purely by chance. For several days, I'd been suffering with a pain in my lower back, in the tailbone region. During this time, it so happened, I left my body; I had an out-of-body experience. I wasn't out for very long when I experienced a familiar sensation in my lower back, the one that accompanied the back pain, but this time the sensation didn't come from my physical body, but from my corresponding astral body. Although the sensation was the same in both bodies—the physical and the astral—in the astral, I felt the sensation without the pain.

Reflexively, I reached behind me to where the sensation emanated, and grabbed something the size of my wrist, perhaps two or three inches in diameter. I could feel the fleshiness of it. I've got a tail, I thought. My astral hand moved farther down the cord, and, as it did, I felt the tail extend several inches away from me. I reached up and felt a network of cords fan out from the base of the tail, the cords rising up my astral back like hundreds of outspread fingers, steel fingers attached to a steel hand and arm, the fingers reaching as high as my shoulders and the base of the neck.

Although the cords felt like flesh, they were, nevertheless, stronger than flesh, and appeared unbreakable. Each strand, and some were the size of narrow electric cords, while others were the size of fingers, felt stronger than steel. I strummed them, as one would guitar strings, and they didn't budge. These multiple strands—and there were many of them—bundled at the base of the spine, and became a cable, the cable that I'd first imagined to be a tail. Interestingly, the human tailbone is in the same location as the silver cable at the base of the astral back, imitating physically the astral cable, explaining, in part, its presence, although man no longer possesses a tail if, indeed, he ever did. I'm of the opinion that he never did, but that the vestigial representation of one, the coccyx, or tailbone, is merely a physical reflection of the astral cable.

I looked behind me and saw a bright silver ribbon lying flat against the floor. Was this ribbon the astral counterpart of Hansel and Gretel's breadcrumbs? Apparently this ribbon, the result of the cord thinning when it's stretched, is laid down as we walk or fly in the astral realm to keep us from getting lost and to keep our physical bodies alive and functioning. I reasoned that the cord, now a ribbon, ran back to the room where my physical body was asleep. As I walked, I laid down more ribbon. In the darkness it glowed brightly, and was unmistakably silver, albeit with a luminescent quality.

On an earlier occasion, I began to suspect that something peculiar was going on behind me. While in my astral body, I left my bed and walked about the room. When I was about two yards in front of the foot of the bed, the bedroom, bed and all, receded about twenty yards, and I was thrown off my feet. I was like a drunk. My astral arms and legs were no longer mine to control and command. As they flailed in an attempt to keep me upright, it was as though I was a kite trying to steady myself in a raucous gale; my feet, by turns, were now on the floor and now flying from under me. I struggled to keep my balance. I tried walking again, but something attached to the back of me was restraining me. At the time, I knew nothing of the cord, and didn't think to reach behind me to learn the cause of my restraint. I was too busy trying to steady myself. Had I done so, I might have discovered the cord then and there. I might have seen it as it whipped me about with great up and down loops, as though it had a mind of its own. And if this wasn't strange enough, I felt that I had been skinned from head to toe.

I had never felt so naked. It was as though all the nerves of my body were exposed to air. The whole of me felt strangely sensitive, and vulnerable. And covering my entire body was a fine hair. Since I wasn't within my physical body, my new hirsute condition puzzled me. This feeling of having been skinned the way that a captured wild animal might have, persisted, as though my flesh had been cut away, flayed, layer by layer. Combine that with my struggle to stay on my feet, and I was more than ready to end this out-of-body experience and return to my physical form. This was the last time I was to experience this kind of excursion out of the body, the experience of utter nakedness. It's possible that the astral form, during this one outing, had adjusted itself or had adjusted me, to our new environment, the astral plane, or that I had mentally adapted to the rigors of leaving my body.

It will be illuminating as well as instructive to share my interpretation of the several verses in the Book of Ecclesiastes, Chapter 12, verses 1 through 7, that discuss physical death and the role of the *silver cord* in that process. At the time of its writing, the author, referred to as the Preacher, chose imagery and concepts with which he was familiar, and which he knew would be familiar to those for whom he wrote. From the Preacher, we get a glimpse into the dying process (what precipitates our death), how it happens and why. His is a cautionary tale.

Remember now thy Creator in the days of thy youth, while the evil days come not, nor the years draw nigh, when thou shalt say, I have no pleasure in them (Eccl 12:1).

It's critically important to find God early and often, before the world has a chance to assert itself in our life, "while the evil days come not," that is, before we grow old in the world, battered by a plethora of worldly beliefs that rob us of our spirituality, even before we have a chance to develop it fully:

"Oh that I were as *in* months past, as *in* the days *when* God preserved me; When his candle shined upon my head, *and when* by his light I walked *through* darkness; As I was in the days of my youth, when the secret of God *was* upon my tabernacle."[6]

For a brief time after our birth, and into our youth, "the secret of God" is still remembered (giving us easy and immediate access to Him), requiring only our tender devotion—our continued expression and outpouring of love for God and neighbor—for that love to grow, and mature. If we wait too long to revere "his light" within, if we postpone the process until the "years draw nigh," until "his candle [no longer shine] upon [our] head," we put God's "light" and his "secret" further beyond our grasp.

> *While the sun, or the light, or the moon, or the stars, be not darkened, nor the clouds return after the rain* (Eccl 12:2).

The *sun* of our being is the "*secret place of the most High.*"[7] We came from there, and it's there where we feel the most at home, and not here in this world. As our "light" from the "*secret place of the most High*" is reflected by other heavenly bodies that surround us—Truth, Soul, Spirit—we exist beyond the darkness. Regarding my own light, my Inner Wisdom, in the voice of a woman, had this to say:

> "*The sun shone down on your face something terrible, taking away your sunset.*"

Her words didn't frighten me, as they were tailored just for me; it's almost as though she knew I would understand her words. I knew the word "terrible" was defined as "intense," not "dreadful," as in this passage from the Bible:

---

6 Job 29:2-4
7 Ps 91:1

THE YOU IN YOU   21

"A man of God came unto me, and his countenance was like the countenance of an angel of God, *very terrible*: but I asked him not whence he was, neither told he me his name."[8]

I can't imagine this angel of God possessing a "dreadful" countenance. Most likely it had a light surrounding it that was *intensely* bright.

The sun represents God's Light (the light of His Existence), which lights our countenance. It is written that Jesus had such an experience, described here in this passage from the New Testament:

"And after six days Jesus taketh Peter, James, and John his brother, and bringeth them up into an high mountain apart, And was transfigured before them: and *his face did shine as the sun*, and his raiment was white as the light."[9]

The *sunset* represents our death. We're born (our sun rises) and each successive day of our life, the sun approaches its zenith, and afterwards, begins its downward descent, until it culminates in our sunset (our death). I'm well aware that the sun has no zenith, and that it's the Earth's orbital path in relationship to the observer and a celestial object that is referenced. The meaning of the message: I would have died years ago, but for the Light of God shining down, in all its Heavenly brilliance, upon my countenance, keeping me as though I am still in the *Noonday* of my life, postponing, for now, my sunset.

Once the light is extinguished, *darkened* by our inattentiveness to the "*secret place of the most High*," and after our prodigal-son journey into a "far country," the world, and after we join our self to a "citizen of that country," the quickest path Home is to *come to our self*, that is, to remember who we are, sons and daughters of God: "How many hired servants of my father's have bread enough and to spare, and I perish with hunger!"[10]

---

8 Judges 13:6
9 Matthew 17:1-2
10 Luke 15:13-17

Rain is to be expected from time to time in our life, but to prevent the "clouds [from] return[ing] after the rain," the passing of some trial or tribulation, only to create new trials, the result of our losing sight of the sun because of the clouds we have gathered, it's paramount that we keep our focus on the sun and not the clouds.

In the day when the keepers of the house shall tremble, and the strong men shall bow themselves, and the grinders cease because they are few, and those that look out of the windows be darkened (Eccl 12:3).

All that we depend upon in this life to keep our earthly existence intact will, at some point, fail us, and precipitate our death. The "keepers of the house," our conscious mind's inner workings, shall, at some point, fail us, *trembling* at the prospect of being overwhelmed by the task of keeping our hearts pure, and our thoughts unsullied, in the face of the mounting challenge to keep the soul upright, and perfect.

And the "strong men," our greatest human concepts, and staunchest beliefs, those that proved themselves so dependable over a lifetime, and worthy of our praise and steadfast allegiance for their seeming invincibility, will fail us, *bowing* to a greater than they—death itself—*humbling* themselves before the inevitability of falling at the hand of a stronger, more powerful enemy.

The "grinders," whose task it is to separate the chaff from the wheat, the good from the evil, the pure from the impure, will fail us, as the "evil days" reduce their numbers, casualties of a war of attrition, unable to keep up with the demand placed upon them.

As our internal light begins to dim, "those that look out of the windows," those parts of us that seek to reinforce and reaffirm our hope in the outward, our trust in things seen, our beliefs in the puissance and supremacy of the external world, will fail us, "darkened," too, by the growing absence of light.

And the doors shall be shut in the streets, when the sound of the grinding is low, and he shall rise up at the voice of the bird, and all the daughters of music shall be brought low (Eccl 12:4).

Rather than the doors flung open when the "sound of the grinding is low," indicating an abatement of the grinding, our mental effort to separate the good from the evil, they are instead "shut in the streets," as the low sound augurs impending disaster. Once the "sound of the grinding is low" because the grinders are few, and our external sources of succor have been exhausted, suggested by the "doors ... shut in the streets," the "voice of the bird," the uplifting, soaring, still quiet voice, calling us home, initiating our *rising,* might be heard above the world's din—melodies provided by "all the daughters of music," a siren's song, haunting, and alluring.

The *voice of the bird* has always been with us, singing its still, quiet song deep within us, but it couldn't be heard until the ambient noise ceased, and our trust in worldly solutions to save us had also been "brought low." When all the internal chatter was hushed, resulting from our persistent effort to silence thought, the seeming endless mental chore of keeping our thoughts pure, and perfect, the still, small voice—the "voice of the bird," soft, innocent and sweet—allowed the man, referred to as "he" to *rise up,* to find the true source of his being while, at the same time, bringing low the "daughters of music," worldly music which had previously drowned out the still small voice within.

Also when *they shall be afraid of* that which is high, *and fears* shall *be in the way, and the almond tree shall flourish, and the grasshopper shall be a burden, and desire shall fail: because man goeth to his long home, and the mourners go about the streets* (Eccl 12:5).

A lifetime spent chasing what was thought to be *high* (of the highest value) is now seen for what it is: *low,* of little value, of little estimate, and substance, offering no pleasure. These *high* things are now met with "fears," as they will have little value in *man's* afterlife or his next incarnation, even as they had little value in his current life, but were, nevertheless, revered as though they did.

That which is *high*, signified by the *almond tree*, either leafing or in riotous bloom, will flourish prior to and when the time of our death draws near, and that which is *low*, signified by the *grasshopper*, will continue to "burden" us, as the "evil days" have now arrived and will now remain, as "the [worldly] years draw nigh," although they have lost a great deal of their luster, and their import for our lives.

Or ever the silver cord be loosed, or the golden bowl be broken, or the pitcher be broken at the fountain, or the wheel broken at the cistern (Eccl 12:6).

Using certain images from his own experience, The Preacher accurately describes how death occurs, expounding on the several elements involved. One expounder of the penultimate verse, which begins, "Or ever the silver cord..." believes that the "or" between the words "loosed" and the "the golden bowl," should be replaced with "and," yoking the two together to correspond with the actual material cord which is used to suspend the bowl—the lamp itself—whence the analogy is borrowed.

As it stands, the analogy, the imagery, is preeminently correct, "ors" and all. The *golden bowl* is the light which encompasses the physical. When seen by an observer, it appears as a bright golden light illuminating everything in its immediate surroundings, including the astral body, and shouldn't be confused with the aura of that body, which, I'm told, may alternate between several colors, some of which may be unique to each individuated soul. An astral body so viewed is not unlike a lamp, emitting a glowing light from its center outward, dispersing the darkness according to its reach.

The bowl *breaks* away from the physical once a decision is made to move to the non-physical realm. The *pitcher* at the *fountain* represents the life-giving astral body, a fount that never ceases flowing, but whose "pitcher," which collects and transfers the flow of life from the fount to the physical body, may break at the loosing of the cord, and thereby fail to sustain the body. The *wheel* represents the process that carries the flow of life-giving energy and intelligence (instructions) from the source (*cistern*) to the body.

Human life would cease at the moment that any one of these conditions were to prevail. The "silver cord [is] loosed," when the body is impaired to such an extent, either by accident, the ravages of disease, or old age, that it can't be sustained by the astral body from which the silver cord extends. Life in the body would also cease if the "golden bowl [is] broken," that is, break away from the physical body, at the behest of the Soul when it decides to move on, or the "pitcher [is] broken at the fountain" essentially separating the life of the astral body from the physical body, or "the wheel [is] broken at the cistern" ending the flow of life and intelligence to the body, so many instructions to keep the physical body properly functioning, and to channel the flow of life through the silver cord, animating the body, a life force which exists external to the physical body, surrounding the whole of it, finding its greater manifestation into the physical realm by way of the brain.

Using the imagery extant in our modern world, we might analogize the silver cord as an optical fiber cable, a cable that allows information in the form of instructions, and the force we call life, to flow from its source, along its length, to a terminal, the physical body, and return. We might, too, analogize the physical body as an *avatar*, subject to an unseen host that we refer to as the astral body, or a spiritual body, an avatar not unlike the one from the movie by the same name, operated at a distance by a human host, one who used an alien physical body without actually residing within that body.

> *Then shall the dust return to the earth as it was: and the spirit shall return unto God who gave it* (Eccl 12:7).

The statement above further corroborates the existence of man in both a physical (dust) and a spiritual state, suggesting that *spirit* is man's primary and ultimate state, and that *dust* returns to a state that existed before the advent of the spirit, and that spirit returns to the Source from which it came, God, Spirit. Jesus stated it this way:

"What and if ye shall see the Son of man ascend up where he was before?

It is the spirit that quickeneth; the flesh profiteth nothing: the words that I speak unto you, they are spirit, and they are life."[11]

All things proceed from the spiritual (our native state). Three of those things are mind, intelligence, and life, all of which allow thought (words, spoken and unspoken, as well as mental images) to exist on the physical plane, yet remain the sole properties of the astral body.

THE SEPARATION OR THE DISUNION

Almost as mysterious as the cord itself is the actual experience of leaving the body, the separation or disunion, and the subsequent feeling that accompany it. As the cord is needed to effect the leaving of the body without the body suffering injury or death, the ability to separate from the physical body is what makes an out-of-body experience possible. And since we're able to do so, this ability must have existed from the beginning, part of the original plan, whether we do so often, infrequently, or rarely.

It might sound hyperbolic, but at the point of my separating from my physical body, it felt as though I was dying. During the early years, when I was a teenager and a young adult, leaving my body meant enduring the sensation of dying. It was a high price to pay to enter the astral realm, but I didn't always have a choice. If I had never died, how could I know, then, what it felt like to die? The answer is rather obvious: It's because I have *lived* before, have *died* before. During each lifetime, we enter the physical realm

---

11 John 6:62-63

forgetful of the fact that it isn't our first advent in the flesh, our first incarnation, so that each birth and each death is as new as the first.

Early on, the death analogy was the only description that resonated. After all, what is death, if you believe in an afterlife, if not the separating of the soul from the body, a disuniting, but a permanent one? An out-of-body jaunt, although a kind of death, is not a permanent death. It's more like a near-death experience (NDE), a temporary dying and returning, which is the hallmark of an out-of-body experience. The only sensation that made sense upon leaving my body was that I had died. This was my mental and emotional realization without it having a foundation in physical reality. Nevertheless, the sensation of dying and being restored to life upon leaving and returning to my physical body during an out-of-body experience persisted for many years, and subsided only with age. For years, the sensation of dying accompanied most of my out-of-body excursions. The only exception was when I was swept away by what is termed the *Astral Current*. If you've died thousands of times, which is what an out-of-body experience was for me, you don't fear death. In time, you learn to live with it.

We have all heard the old saw attributed to Hemingway, which is possibly a borrowing from and a restatement of Shakespeare: "The coward dies a thousand deaths, the brave but one." Well I have died a thousand deaths, not in my imagination alone as is suggested by the Hemingway quote, but with all the seeming of the real thing, for which I didn't always do bravely. When I do die with finality, the "but one," I will do it bravely, and fearlessly, as death, even an out-of-body experienced death, heralds a new life, a rebirth, a returning to the body, to a state of physicality. If reincarnation is a fact (and I believe that it is), we have experienced death many times whether we remember that we have or not.

The separation from the physical body, occasioned by an out-of-body experience, occurs without fanfare—no choir of angels, no beings of light to mark the event. For years I discounted my out-of-body experiences because they felt as though I was taking my physical body with me, actually moving physically through space and time. It became more perplexing when I realized that I wasn't missed by anyone during my many absences. At no time during the early years did I know that I was leaving my physical body behind, that I was taking another body, not physical, instead.

Over time, as I became more acquainted with the astral body, I learned that it was this body, a non-physical body, which traveled outside the physical body, and not the physical body itself. It took a while, but after years of astral projecting, I realized, finally, that the body that I used to journey almost nightly into the astral realm was my true body, more real and more alive than the one I left behind. That understanding reinforced another conclusion: Contrary to appearances, my physical body wasn't really *me*; that me was nothing more than a physical substitute for the real *me*, the *me* that was using the physical me to exist for a time in the physical realm. Although the physical me appeared to be real, it wasn't real. Only the astral or the spiritual *me* was alive, real, and eternal, a point that the following biblical passage makes clear, as it reflects on what happens at the time of our death, the death of our physical bodies: "Then shall the dust return to the earth as it was: and the spirit shall return unto God who gave it."[12]

Our astral senses, then, exist independently of their physical counterparts. Nevertheless, our physical senses, which are nothing more than our astral senses employing physicality to experience the physical plane, are indispensable agents on this plane. Scientists need a microscope to view the world of microbes, but sight isn't obtained through a microscope, rather through the eye in conjunction with the brain. A computer, when programmed to do so, may perform sophisticated calculations, play chess with a world-class chess master and win, and we're tempted to say that it's intelligent. Yet, we all accept that sight is not in the microscope and intelligence is not in the computer, even if we might disagree as to whether intelligence is a creation of the brain.

---

12 Ecc 12:7

The Bible asks, "O death, where *is* thy sting? O grave, where is thy victory?"[13] At the moment of death, it may take you some time to actually realize that you're dead. That's because you cannot die. There's only life after life, not a state called death after life. Death is merely a process, the process that the soul uses to evaluate the physical life just lived. There will be no severance at death, no loss of who you are. The body that you leave behind, you will not mourn. To mourn it, you'd have to miss it and you won't. Notwithstanding the years spent here on Earth, you will find yourself in a realm that feels more familiar than foreign. Why? Because you have lived in this realm in the always even while, as you believed, you were living in a physical body. Besides, each night while you're sleeping, you enter this realm. You're accustomed to moving and living in this realm because you've spent one third of your physical life there.

---

13 1 Cor. 15:55

THREE

THE UNSEEN BODY

I F WE'RE ASKED WHO WE ARE, THE ANSWER USUALLY centers upon our physicality, a physicality seemingly bounded by the characteristics of our corporeal body, its physical and mental attributes. Because very few of us understand that the physical body is simply a counterfeit of another body, unseen, and hidden from view, the answer to the question is as incomplete, as it is inadequate, as it's restricted to what is seen with our physical eyes, or perceived by other corporeal senses, when so much more of us exists, non-corporeal, out of sight, just below the fleshly surface we claim to be us.

Were you to sift through the massive literature on the out-of-body phenomenon, you still might not compile a complete list of all the various aspects of the phenomenon. That would be equally true for the body that's used while exploring and navigating the astral realm, without which there would be no out-of-boy phenomena.

You've heard this saying before I'm sure: "There's more to us than meets the eye," or "there's more than meets the eye." Perhaps you heard it in a song, or from someone you know who's feeling a bit underrated, and undervalued. No matter what human insufficiency prompted the statement, the truth of it is *often* underrated. This chapter will correct that oversight.

Over a lifetime, I've experienced numerous out-of-body excursions. The number is in the hundreds, if not the thousands. During those excursions I used a large portion of my time exploring the astral plane on which they occurred, in addition to investigating the phenomenon itself—the astral body that allowed me to navigate the astral plane, the astral environment, and the countless aspects of the out-of-body experience.

You may think it's superfluous, but every living person has more than one body. There's the physical body, the physical you, that we see each day in our mirror with all its imperfections and blemishes, and then there's the one that very few have actually seen, the astral body, a body so perfect that it's startling for its beauty, with "the very hairs of your head...all numbered."[14]

Perhaps like me you grew up reading a parade of comics of your favorite superheroes. What inspired comic book creators to invent these superhuman characters, I know not, but you may be intrigued to know that your "unseen body" has many of the attributes associated with these superheroes, advancing the possibility that the *unseen body*, the astral body, might have been the inspiration, if not the model, for many of them. The unseen body is usually invisible to the naked eye. It can see through solid objects, wield incredible strength, is impervious to pain, possibly invincible, and can fly. Also, like another superhero, the astral body may stretch, shrink, and do what this superhero's body can't do: pass through solid objects.

ELASTIC MAN

I don't remember the first time I learned of the astral body's elasticity. However, I do remember that, on several occasions, while lying down, entranced, and immobile, I stretched my astral arm and hand clear across

14 Luke 12:7

the room, perhaps twelve feet from where I was reclining, and ran my astral hand along the surface of the wall, feeling, as I touched it, the wall's rough, granular texture.

I'm not the only out-of-body explorer to experience the elasticity of the astral body, whether in the out-of-body state, or the pre-out-of-body state, the state associated with the confining, paralytic trance known as sleep paralysis.

Spirited away on an astral current, I came to rest in a dark room. Immediately I shrunk from the height of an adult to the size of a small child. This was my first time shrinking, and, as a result, I was a bit bewildered. Despite the darkness, I could still make out a door to the left of me. If I wanted to know what awaited me beyond the door, I would have to open it. The doorknob was a foot or more over my head, almost out of reach. I reached up to open it, and as I walked out, my little feet began to run involuntarily, carrying me from the back of the house midway to the front. There I found three other children sitting quietly on a couch, behaving as though they had recently received a stern warning to do so. I stopped long enough to take in the scene before my little feet begin running again. Later, I will complete in more detail the outcome of this out-of-body experience.

The elasticity of the astral body serves two purposes, it allows the astral body to shrink, as well as to grow and expand, perfectly accommodating the size and height that the physical body might assume during its first year of growth, and beyond, when, as adults, we pack on a little weight or lose it. At times, while standing in my astral room, I have reached for the ceiling to initiate flight only to have my astral body stretch until my head ended up pressed hard against the ceiling, with my neck bent to one side, as it tried in vain to stretch beyond the limits of the obstructing ceiling.

INVINCIBLE MAN

On more occasions than I care to remember, my physical body has shown its vulnerability and its predisposition to pain—from a stubbed toe, accidentally cutting myself with a knife, to hammering my thumb, instead of the nail I was holding. The astral body, on the other hand, seems impervious to pain, although it can register a sense of touch and is sentient.

Several times, while out of the body, I've pinched my astral arm as hard as I could and felt nothing but the pressure of the pinch. Here's an answer to a question you may have posed: What does the astral body feel like? It feels like flesh. It feels the exact same way that the physical body would feel if you were to touch it or pinch it. The astral body mirrors the physical body so closely, that it replicates all the characteristics that we associate with that body: the body's soft flesh, its wrinkles, its curves and dimples. The only time I've felt pain on the astral plane was when I was attacked by non-physical, evil entities while I was still in my physical body and still under the thrall of a trance.

I reasoned, further, that it was this astral body that was sentient, that the physical body experienced sensations, not because it was sentient, but because the astral body that surrounded it was sentient. Let me illustrate: Many times, while in a trance state, I have lifted my astral hands to my eyes, and have seen the faint outline of hands that appeared more ghostly than physical. Indeed, I could see my physical hands resting at my side, which prompted the question: How was it possible for me to have two sets of hands, one visible and one mostly invisible? The perplexity only grew when I realized that the invisible hands felt more like my real hands than the physical ones. I pressed these non-physical hands together, rubbed them, and pinched them. Except that they were practically invisible, I couldn't tell these invisible hands from the physical ones resting at my side. Like the physical ones, they seemed covered with skin. They had wrinkles and folds where wrinkles and folds should be, as well as bone protrusions. The conclusion: These astral hands were my hands as much as, or more so, than the physical hands with which I was familiar.

I concluded further: When I touched my astral hands, I was touching my *real* hands. I asked, "If these non-physical hands are my real hands, then where did the physical ones exist in this enigma?" I reasoned that the physical hands didn't really have sensation. It only appeared that way, one of the many illusions that the physical body advances, when in reality it is the other body, the astral body which registers all sensations. I concluded, then: If I rubbed my physical hands together, or clasped them, it wasn't my physical hands that I was touching, but my nonphysical hands, my astral hands.

Further experimentation reinforced, to my satisfaction, that it was not the physical body that feels sensations, that was sentient, but the astral body that's hidden from view. When we touch our physical hand, or the physical hand of another, we're touching and feeling *our* astral hand, or the corresponding astral hand of another, and not our physical hand or their physical hand. From these experiments, I've concluded that the physical body, despite appearances, doesn't feel. Touch, or the sensation of feeling something, is the exclusive province of the astral body. As to pain, the astral body experiences pain only when it surrounds the physical, envelops it, subjecting itself to what the physical experiences. It's my firm belief that it's impossible for physicality, the physical body, to experience sensation, that sensation is an attribute of the astral, unseen body, which is the only body that's sentient.

Because the astral form has taken up residence in a physical, material body—that is, has surrounded it, as the two never really integrate—sensation is experienced through the intermediary called flesh, thoughts through the intermediary call brain, sight through the intermediary call eyes, hearing through the intermediary call ears, and taste through the intermediary called a nose and a tongue.

The illusion is so complete that, at no time during an astral projection does it feel as though I've left something behind. Everything that is *me* leaves with me—my body, my consciousness, and my identity. Further, while in the out-of-body state, I give little or no thought to my physical body, other than I might not be able to return to it. I suspect that upon my death (my final out-of-body experience, at least for this lifetime) I'll feel the same. Those who have had near-death experiences or have had out-of-body experiences have corroborated my own experience with the astral body: Other than the occasional concern for its safety while out-of-body, they hardly gave their physical bodies a second thought. You can't miss that which you've never had!

Unlike the physical body, the astral body is self-sustaining, not requiring food for fuel, existing exclusively on the astral plane, and other non-physical levels of existence. As a result of this sustainability, it's likely that the faculties of smell and taste are rarely needed, but dwell in abeyance, until such time as they're called upon.

As a small child, my multiple-lives companion underwent a near-death experience; it was after extremely hot, roofing tar splashed from the rooftop upon her tiny body below, causing her to immediately pop out of her physical body, and stand alongside it, while it writhed in excruciating pain, her small body continuing to respond to the last stimuli from her astral body. It's very likely that her experience is not uncommon. Faced with the unspeakable horror of burning to death, or hitting the ground after a high fall, the soul may opt to leave the body before the flames can consume it, or before it impacts the ground.

While we're in the physical realm, we're at the mercy of our physical bodies. It doesn't have to be that way, but until we advance spiritually to the point of having dominion over our bodies, that will be our lot. We enter life at birth reflecting whatever conditions are prevalent at the time within our physical body, as well as what our mothers passed to us while we were fetuses, during the gestation period, which is more than a physical gestation, but a mental and spiritual gestation as well, where the human or spiritual propensities of the mother are passed to the child. If the condition of the body is optimum for self-realization, and spiritual growth, then our lives will reflect that predisposition. If the condition of the body is less than optimum for our physical or spiritual development, then we shall experience what that condition dictates.

We can override these undesirable propensities, but only with great effort and dedication. Love for God and neighbor is always optimum, and can facilitate our transformation, and allow us to rise above the body's restrictions and propensities. Although some have considered it, eugenics is not the answer; the answer lies with the spiritual evolution of the human species, the result of parents maintaining spiritual wombs for their fetuses, allowing them, upon their birth and maturation, to exercise greater *dominion* [15] over their physical bodies and their material world. This can be achieved if the parents keep their hearts as pure as possible, and send love continuously to their unborn child, and when the child is born, wrap it in the swaddling cloth of God's Love. What I have learned as a sometime denizen of our non-physical world, the astral realm, is this: Our belief systems, singularly and collectively, determine our experiences. If we believe that the condition of our physical bodies can subject us to certain realities, then that belief will hold sway and manifest itself.

For a while, I was imbibing alcoholic drinks socially. From my Inner Guide came a strong warning: If I continued this behavior, the alcohol would impede my spiritual growth, and destroy, or severely limit, my spirituality. I quit drinking right then and there.

BI-LOCATION MAN

It's a bit unnerving to have your consciousness in more than one place at a time, or to have it alternate between your physical body and your astral

---

15 Gen 1:26

body. This happens when your astral body remains too close to the physical for a period before moving on. It's as though there's a magnetic field around the physical body that creates this bi-location of consciousness. The sense is that your body is residing in two places simultaneously, in the physical realm as well as the astral realm, in the physical body and outside of it. This usually occurs when I'm lifting my astral body from my physical body for the purpose of leaving it. During that time, I'm partly in the physical body, or near it, as I attempt to put distance between it and the astral body. Until I manage to do that, it's possible for my consciousness to alternate between the physical body and the astral body, and at times to reside in both bodies simultaneously.

To say that consciousness resides in the physical body or in the brain is a misnomer, and doesn't actually capture the whole of it. Nevertheless, this claim, that consciousness is a product of the brain, represents the usual understanding of the mind and consciousness that is held by most humans, and certainly held by many NDEers before they had a near-death experience, but who may now, because of their NDE, think otherwise. Contrary to their pre-NDE position, they now see consciousness as *external* to the brain, a conclusion drawn from their near-death experience.

MAGNET MAN

As I've stated, bi-location occurs because the physical body acts as a magnet, keeping the astral body aligned with the physical. You can imagine what might happen were this not the case: The astral body could drift away from its physical mooring at the most inopportune times—while we're driving, for example, or running machinery that require our utmost attention to avoid physical injury.

If you don't move far enough from the physical body while in the astral body, your physical body will act like a strong rubber band, snapping your astral body back into alignment with the physical, maintaining the illusion that you're your physical body, when in fact the astral body, more than your physical body, represents your true, natural self. Because the "real" *you* remain in the astral realm at all times, you're never actually here in the physical realm. If you've seen the movie *Avatar*, you'll appreciate what that is like. Your physical body is an avatar for the astral. It's a clever deception complete with seeming sensations from the physical body, and the seeming presence of other corporeal senses to round out the illusion.

Before the movie, I had to conjure other examples to illustrate the relationship of the astral body to the physical. Now, thanks to the movie, all those who have seen it can understand the concept of one body using another to navigate a foreign and more hostile world than the one from which it originated. Because of this relationship, the astral body gets to experience the physical realm, as well as interact with others in this realm. This was not by accident.

I call Earth the playground of the gods.

We gods get to create in matter—to extend ourselves into eternity—in ways that we could not in the non-physical realm. Although it's the belief of many that we live in a physical world, in reality, we live within a mental universe. In fact, both realms, the physical and the non-physical, are mental realms, subject to our thoughts, our beliefs, and our consciousness, individually and collectively, singularly and universally.

It's the material properties of the physical universe, where our physical senses seem to rule, that make this realm so seductive. Yet, if you're inclined toward spiritual sense more than physical sense, then cause and effect, intention and manifestation, narrow to such a degree that the time differential between the two is negligible.

The fact that most of us have forgotten that we're living in a mental universe, that we're more than flesh and bone, doesn't mean that it isn't so. Again, one of the purposes of this book is to awaken humanity to that possibility, and to remind us of who we *really* are. I'm hoping that, once we know who we are (Wasn't it written, "Man, know thyself?"), we'll act and behave accordingly.

Everything in this world has conditioned us to accept ourselves as physical, to believe the lie. Of the several illusions with which humankind contend, our supposed physicality is one of the most devastating, as this illusion leads inevitably to another illusion, that life ends with death. We've had a lifetime of conditioning that affirms our identity as physical beings. Yet, if we've never been physical, then, we are, by default, spiritual beings. As spiritual beings, we can't be imperfect, not even as beings believing that we are our physical bodies.

Because everything in our physical world correspond to a life-giving reality that we don't see, but which, nevertheless, gives life to all that we do see, we're living among the dead, and the temporal, among the unreal, and the illusory. This saying attributed to Paul, from *The Second Epistle of Paul to the Corinthians*, states it eloquently:

> *While we look not at the things which are seen, but at the things which are not seen: for the things which are seen are temporal; but the things which are not seen are eternal* (II Cor. 4:18).

And in another place, the thought is restated this way:

> *It is sown a natural body; it is raised a spiritual body. There is a natural body, and there is a spiritual body.*
>
> *And so it is written, The first man Adam was made a living soul; the last Adam was made a quickening spirit.*
>
> *Howbeit that was not first which is spiritual, but that which is natural; and afterward that which is spiritual.*
>
> *The first man is of the earth, earthy: the second man is the Lord from heaven.*
>
> *As is the earthy, such are they also that are earthy: and as is the heavenly, such are they also that are heavenly.*

And as we have borne the image of the earthy, we shall also bear the image of the heavenly (I Cor 15:44-49).

INVISIBLE MAN

For most, the astral body is invisible. I've seen my own astral body, and the astral body of another and the glory of her astral body surpassed anything in the physical realm. Sensing the presence of someone to my right as I lie in bed, I lifted myself up slightly and saw her sitting on the edge of the bed. It was a close friend and a fellow out-of-body explorer. She didn't seem to notice that I knew she was there, or that, at the time, I was watching her intently. She seemed to be lost in thought.

My friend's skin was flawless. Each strand of her blond hair was distinct and perfectly aligned with every other strand (not one was out of place). The experience reminded me of Jesus' statement, "Even the very hairs of your head are all numbered."[16] In the darkness (it was nighttime), her countenance and body glowed with a soft, but bright, light that filled the entirety of the room where I was sleeping. Were it not for her presence, darkness would have engulfed the room. From her, a light emanated. She was the light, golden and radiant.

Not threatened by her presence I returned to my previous slumbering position. This experience would have perturbed many. They would have mistaken my friend for a ghost, had she been seen at all, rather than the out-of-body traveler that she was. This is not to say that ghosts don't exist, or to say that those who present themselves in this manner are all out-of-body travelers. Be assured: Ghosts exist. I will discuss them later.

Let me restate what I said previously, but with a slightly different twist: While in a trance, I've looked at those parts of my astral body that I could see from a lying-down vantage point. With my physical arms and hands resting at my side (and within sight), I've lifted my astral arms and hands

---

16 Luke 12:7

to a position where I could see them. I could barely make out a faint outline of my arms and hands, and this was possible because I knew where to look. Had others been in the room at the time, it's possible they wouldn't have seen any part of my astral form, its invisibility the reason the astral body is hidden from view and its existence often denied.

Although I believed my physical eyes to be opened when I examined my astral hands, it's entirely possible that my physical eyes were aided by my astral eyes, which would account for my ability to see my astral hands then and not afterward with the use of my physical eyes alone.

As with my friend, I've been awakened many times by an unknown presence that entered my room while I was asleep. Were it not for the fact that it's happened to me several times over the years, the sensing of a strange presence in my room might have set off an alarm. On another night when I awoke, aware that I wasn't alone, I did what I always do: I asked for the presence's name. When the voice responded, it was male. The name he gave me was a strange one, neither English, nor Spanish.

I searched for the name on the Internet, and found it. A certain New Age writer had written rather extensively about the person who owned the name. On returning to work, I found the book among our vast library collection and in time had it in hand, reading it for the first time. The author of the book wrote about a man who had extraordinary spiritual gifts, one of those gifts clearly on display by virtue of his visit to me while I was sleeping. Other than connecting with a kindred spirit in me, I discovered nothing about his reason for visiting me. On that visit had he imparted knowledge or a spiritual gift? I can't say for sure. Since that first encounter, I haven't knowingly entertained his presence again.

Awakened by clothes hangers rattling, I didn't panic as I have had many usual experiences in and around sleep. As is my custom, I asked, "Who's there?" The answer came back, "It's me."

I knew who it was, it was my companion to be. At the time, she lived in a city almost two-hundred miles away, but because she didn't exit the closet, I never saw her in all her out-of-body splendor, a missed opportunity and a lingering regret. On the morrow, I called her and asked if she had visited me the night before. She said that she had. I asked her to tell me what she had experienced, wanting to hear her account first to see if it coincided with my own.

She said, "I saw that you were waking up, so I jumped inside the closet, rattling the hangers there. I was afraid that you might see me."

If the astral body is subject to time or space limitations or restrictions, I haven't, as yet, encountered them. While out-of-body, I have visited previous lives, several of which were lived hundreds of years ago, and have been privy to the unseen particulars of future events. I have visited these places and seen these events with as much ease as I have visited physical locations while out-of-body—some of which were close at hand, while others were hundreds of miles away. In addition, I have visited dimensions beyond our physical realm, the home to strangeness, and host to experiences outside of our daily norm. Were it not for these out-of-body journeys, my view of the world would correspond accordingly, it would be limited, and it would be bound by the limitations that the physical realm imposes.

UNBOUNDED MAN (PASSING THROUGH WALLS)

With the use of a nimble imagination, Hollywood, using special effects, devised one version of how the dead in spirit form might pass through solid, material objects, such as walls and doors. In a popular movie, the recently deceased protagonist, finding it impossible to turn the doorknob with non-physical hands, elected to exit through a door by walking through it. Gingerly he pushed his hand through the door only to find to his shock that his hand, and now his whole arm assumed the character of the wood, the process threatening to consume his entire body, as he looked on in horror.

Visually, this was a striking scene. Having passed through many material objects, walls and doors, I can inform you from experience that the astral body does not take on the character nor the substance of that through which it passes. The truth isn't as dramatic or as cinematically interesting as the fictional account, but it does offer, nevertheless, a substantive piece of information, one that I hope will fill in a hole extant in the literature. It's my hope to fill in several such missing pieces of information; such has been my extensive investigation within this little-known realm.

Initially, before I gave any thought to the possibility or impossibility of it, I walked through walls rather easily. When I did, my body didn't integrate with the wall, or the wall with my body, as in the Hollywood version; instead, it displaced the wall, the way that gelatin is displaced (pushed aside) if a finger is poke into a bowl of it, or the way that feet displace sand on a beach when walked upon, all this without changing the form or character of hands or feet.

I have walked to the nearest wall and continued walking, the wall giving way, the substance of it displacing as my body moved through it. This displacement and other salient features of the astral body, such as its invisibility and elasticity, are hallmarks of this body. This hallmark, then, delineates a definite distinction between the astral body and the physical body, placing it outside the physical realm, rather than including it as an integral part of it.

With the failure of the flying technique, I resorted, at times, to walking through walls, and then falling, drifting actually, to the ground below. I deployed this method until it, too, stopped working, again the possible victim of my belief system. Finally, I opened windows and leaped out. Always concerned that I might be sleepwalking I prepared myself for a hard landing. Yet, hard landings never came, much to my relief. I merely floated to the ground, and landed on my astral feet.

Confirmation of this difference between the astral body and seeming physical objects occurred rather dramatically when I left the room once by opening a two-story window, and jumping. A tree just below me stood in the way of an unobstructed drop to the ground and an awaiting sidewalk. On the way down, I drifted, not unlike a falling feather, the first clue that I'm out-of-body and not sleepwalking. When I reached the tree, my astral body seemed to pass around the tree's limbs, twigs, and leaves, as they became so many razors shredding small and large portions of my astral body. During the fall, I experienced no pain, only a severe discomfort. The discomfort was so unpleasant that I would, during subsequent out-of-body trips, find alternate ways from which to exit my home, usually by walking downstairs and using the front door.

Leaping from windows to exit a building was always fraught with risk. I was never certain if I were sleepwalking or had actually left my body, so complete was the astral experience of possessing a body, and using a body. Always, I threw caution to the wind and took the risk. (The risks I've taken in the astral realm find no parallel in my so-called real world, where I operate with a great deal more caution.) Had I thought to do so, I could have pinched myself to confirm whether I was in or out of my body, but it never occurred to me.

When flying through ceilings or walking through walls failed me, or when jumping out of windows wasn't practical, I used doors as alternate exits from within houses or buildings, although that approach delayed the leaving of whatever structure I found myself in. Invariably, my out-of-body experiences began within structures—a house, an apartment, a car, or some other enclosure where I had laid down to rest. In addition, it wasn't uncommon, especially when taken aloft by an astral current, to have as my final destination a structure of some sort, usually the interior of a house, or a large building. On rarer occasions, I've come to rest in fields, or alongside roads, or the exterior of buildings.

FLYING MAN

Much has been written regarding the implications of flying in the dream state. I have flown many times while out-of-body, and found the sensation exhilarating. Some believe that, when we fly in dreams, we're actually using the astral body to navigate the dreamscape. Others believe that it's a result of being slightly separated from our physical bodies during sleep, and that the sensation of falling happens when the body, on the verge of awakening, suddenly reenters the physical. It's their belief that during sleep the astral body automatically disconnects from the physical and that it's natural for both bodies, physical and astral, to separate at that time.

From a book I read years ago on the subject of astral projection, I learned how to initiate flight while in the astral realm. Because I hadn't tried flying, I was eager to employ the author's method. The closest I had come to flying was when I rode the astral currents. That was fine, but I wanted a way to initiate it myself. The author said that he simply extended his arms above his head and gave the command, "Go, mind!" and he flew, his body soaring through space as though he were superhuman. This simple technique worked amazingly well for a time. I would lift my arms over my head in the direction of the ceiling, and with the use of the command was rocketed through both the ceiling and the roof into the night sky at such an astonishing speed, the breeze rushing against my face and body, that I hardly noticed passing through what in our world would have been serious impediments.

After that I always looked forward to flying. Sometimes I would just stay aloft for what seemed like hours, allowing the breeze to lift my body upon its wings, floating at times, and at times soaring above the trees, the fields below, or through canyons, or over mountain passes and peaks. Having a fear of heights most of my life, the result of a fall when I was around 9 or 10 years old, flying that high above the terrain was at times unnerving. Yet, in my new body and in my new environment, with my now very special skill, my fear lessened, and was usually overcome. The thrill of flying was just too exciting to allow a little fear to get in the way of it.

Again, for no reason I could discern, the command that initiated flight stopped working. Once more, I suspected the intrusion of my belief system for my sudden failure. How was it possible, I thought, for me to pass through the ceiling, the roof, and into a waiting night sky? Rather than lifting off as I had done hundreds of times, my astral body remained stationary, stretching instead, until my head and shoulders pressed against the ceiling in an awkward manner. Had a witness stood near, I'm certain that my comical predicament would have elicited hearty laughter.

Outside my house, under the sky, it was easy to return to flying mode. I would just leap up, catch a breeze, and allow it to take me away. I was lighter than a feather. I maneuvered my direction and speed by using my arms and hands as wings, flapping them quickly to climb higher, go faster, or change directions.

My fear of heights should have been a serious determent to my flying, and from time to time it did interfere. Yet, the simple thrill of leaving the Earth for the heavens always won out. All I had to do to take flight was to jump up. Once aloft, I could fly, either by staying close to the Earth—soaring over fields, towns, or mountains—or by leaving Earth altogether. Once, flying extra high, seemingly beyond the Earth's stratosphere, a huge tongue came out of nowhere and licked me as I passed over what seemed to be a large gaping mouth, or opening. Later I thought of the hellhound that guarded the gates of hell or the underworld, the three-headed Cerberus, as the tongue was unmistakably that of a dog.

On another off-planet flight, flying blind as I couldn't see where I was going, I suddenly felt hands seize both my arms, near the armpits, and my speed abruptly accelerated. I had never known such speed before. One of the two holding me said to the other, "Let's take him to the Father of Lights."[17]

---

17 James 1:17

As promising as that sounded, I worried about getting back to my body, and just as quickly, I was back in my bed again. I can only imagine the shock of my two fellow travelers and helpers as I was *there* and then I wasn't. I can only surmise that they saw something in me that attracted them, and wanted to bring me to the attention of the Father. Or they believed me dead, and, because of something that interested them, believed that the Father of Lights would find it interesting, too.

Many years later, upon reading Dr. Eben Alexander's book, *Proof of Heaven: A Neurosurgeon's Journey into the Afterlife*, I recalled this experience. In his book, Dr. Alexander related how he found himself, after a near-death experience (an NDE), in the presence of God. When I was told that I would be taken before God, The Father of Lights, I often wondered if the entities, whoever they were, would have actually taken me there. If I'm to take Dr. Alexander's experience at face value, then the answer is an unreserved Yes.

Yet, we don't have to die, or nearly die, to go before The Presence of God, or engage Him in a heart-to-heart talk. In truth, we can't leave His Holy Presence or be separated from Him, not even for a nanosecond, for He's the very essence of who we are—our life and our mind. To the degree that we seek Him with all our soul, with all our heart, and with all our mind, to that degree do we find ourselves in His presence—to that degree do we experience our never-ending oneness with Him.

PART TWO:

WHAT THE *YOU* IN YOU CAN DO

FOUR

HAVE A CONVERSATION WITH GOD

HEARING OF A *YOU* IN YOU, YOU MIGHT BE TEMPTED at first to say, "So what?" When you learn, however, that this *you* in you can perform some rather amazing feats, at times imitating, if only in small measures, the miraculous deeds attributed to Jesus, you're inclined to be less dismissive, compelled, as it were, to take notice.

To be sure, this *you* in you is only limited by your spiritual growth, the degree to which you have developed your spiritual sense. Once this sense is honed, there's no limit to what the *you* in you can do. Not yet a spiritual powerhouse myself, I have, nevertheless, emulated Jesus' works in small measures, suggesting that we can *all* do more as we gain more.

If you always thought it impossible, think again: The *you* in you can have a conversation with God, and not just in dreams or visions. As did the prophets of old who spoke on behalf of God with so many repetitions of "Thus saith the Lord," a large number today are having a personal conversation with God. A book, published just before the beginning of this new century and new millennium, titled, "Conversations with God: An Uncommon Dialogue, Book 1," by Neale Donald Walsch, has inspired many of its readers to accept the *uncommon* notion of a conversation with God, and many have struck up conversations of their own.

I learned of the *Conversations with God* book a few months before I was scheduled to retire. One day, a woman approached the reference desk and asked if the library had the book in its collection. After checking the library's catalog, I informed her that it didn't, to which she replied, "I'm surprised. It's been on the New York Times Best Seller list for weeks. You really should get it."

At the time of the woman's inquiry, the library was experiencing a severe shortfall of operation and materials funding, owing to a loss of revenue. The books that would have been in the collection, simply for their popularity, or by virtue of their bestseller standing, were missing throughout the library system because of that shortfall, a system composed of more than a couple of dozen libraries, including the one where I was then working.

After retiring, I used gift certificates, several of which were given to me by those with whom I had worked over my long career as a librarian, to purchase a number of books, among them the book that I had first learned about from the aforementioned library patron, *Conversations with God*.

Now before you exclaim that "conversations with God" seem highly unlikely, let me offer my experience with the book. While reading it for the first time a number of correlated questions came to mind about the book's content that begged for answers. I would ask God to explain. The explanations came in one of three ways: (1) I would hear the answer; or (2) I would see the answer; or (3) I would just know the answer, and would have to summon words to give verbal shape to what I knew. I received enough additional information by asking God follow-up questions that I could have written a book myself. It was, as I read, like having a running dialogue with God.

Even now, I receive sporadic information from this internal source— usually after I pose a question, or after facing a dilemma. If you're not careful, you, too, may find that you're having a conversation with God. Does this sound unimaginable? That's why so many ignore Him, or, if they do engage Him, they talk *to* Him without expecting a response; they can't imagine, not in their wildest imaginings, that God talks with them (note the tense).

I asked God, why He would talk to us, thinking that we weren't worthy of this highest of honors: to have a conversation with God. God's answer: "Why wouldn't I talk to myself?"

The answer suggests many things about our relationship to God, His nature, and our nature: We're not just one with God, but actually an aspect of Him, a part of Him. This aspectual relationship says that God is us, and we're God, although God with a little "g" as we're not the whole but a part of the whole.

I purchased the *Conversations with God* book perhaps days leading up to an automobile accident that left me injured and in severe pain, the pain running the full length of the left side of my upper body—my neck, arm, and torso—for more than a month. It was the site of an old injury, one sustained while falling off a ladder and, at the same time, adjusting my body on the way down to minimize the impact of the fall. The pain was incessant, vexing me throughout the day, and interfering with my sleep at night. Often I would awake in pain, and spend hours searching for a pain-less sleep position but with little or no success.

Because I was between health plans at the time of the accident, I had no health coverage and I couldn't afford to see a doctor about my complaint.

While lying in bed one night, reading my newly-acquired book, *Conversations with God*, the pain reached a new intensity. I asked God why I was having such difficulty healing the injury. Through prayer alone, using nothing more than my understanding of God and my relationship to Him, I had experienced over the years many remarkable healings, but this injury proved to be exceedingly stubborn. I knew what I needed to do to effect a healing, but I wasn't getting very far.

We had talked at length, before I realized that I was talking with someone (the conversation taking place within). At the end of the talk, and after I had been directed to a Bible verse, the pain just disappeared. The conversation that followed after my asking God why I wasn't able to heal my injury went something like this:

God asked me: "Do you know what the secret place of the most High is?" I realized that the "secret place" was a term used in a passage from the Bible with which I was conversant, which had long resonated with me, and which was one of my favorites, the 91st Psalm.

I told Him that I didn't.

He said, "It is love."

I said something to the effect of, "It doesn't say so in the passage."

He said, "Read it again."

I retrieved my Bible, thinking, "I don't remember any such words. God has to be wrong here."

I found the Psalm that had been referenced, and read the following:

Psalm 91:

He that dwelleth in the secret place of the most High shall abide under the shadow of the Almighty.

I will say of the Lord, He is my refuge and my fortress: my God; in him will I trust.

Surely he shall deliver thee from the snare of the fowler, and from the noisome pestilence.

He shall cover thee with his feathers, and under his wings shalt thou trust: his truth shall be thy shield and buckler.

Thou shalt not be afraid for the terror by night ; nor for the arrow that flieth by day;

Nor for the pestilence that walketh in darkness; nor for the destruction that wasteth at noonday.

A thousand shall fall at thy side, and ten thousand at thy right hand; but it shall not come nigh thee.

Only with thine eyes shalt thou behold and see the reward of the wicked.

Because thou hast made the Lord, which is my refuge, even the most High, thy habitation;

There shall no evil befall thee, neither shall any plague come nigh thy dwelling.

For he shall give his angels charge over thee, to keep thee in all thy ways

They shall bear thee up in their hands, lest thou dash thy foot against a stone.

Thou shalt tread upon the lion and adder: the young lion and the dragon shalt thou trample under feet.

Because he hath set his love upon me, therefore will I deliver him: I will set him on high, because he hath known my name.

He shall call upon me, and I will answer him: I will be with him in trouble; I will deliver him, and honour him.

With long life will I satisfy him, and shew him my salvation.

Foolish me! Of course it was there! When I read the line, "Because he hath set his love upon me, "I immediately reached out to God with all my love, and the pain that had been my constant companion for over a month, instantly disappeared. And, for the first time in days, I slept through the night without pain and without it interrupting my sleep. You can't imagine the fullness of my joy. I still rejoice for the freedom I found after reading the Psalm. This experience taught me several things:

First, it taught me that the "secret place"—love, when consistently applied—protects us from:

the snare of the fowler

the noisome pestilence

the terror by night

the arrow that flieth by day

the pestilence that walketh in darkness

the destruction that wasteth at noonday.

Second, it taught me that the "secret place"—love, when consistently applied—gives us certain assurances:

no evil [shall] befall thee

neither shall any plague come nigh thy dwelling

Thou shalt tread upon the lion and adder:

the young lion and the dragon shalt thou trample under feet.

Third, it taught me that the "secret place"—love, when consistently applied—will elevate us, and set us apart from those who don't "dwelleth in the secret place of the most High":

I will set him on high, because he hath known my name.

He shall call upon me, and I will answer him:

I will be with him in trouble;

I will deliver him, and honour him.

With long life will I satisfy him, and shew him my salvation.

All of this and more shall be ours, just by doing this one simple thing: set our love upon God and dwell in the "secret place."

Jesus cites the law of protection, the law of assurance, and the law of elevation ("I will set him on high") this way, as he answers a lawyer who is seeking to tempt him by asking the question:

Master, which is the great commandment in the law?

Jesus said unto him, Thou shalt love the Lord thy God with all thy heart, and with all thy soul, and with all thy mind.

This is the first and great commandment.

And the second is like unto it, Thou shalt love thy neighbour as thyself.

On these two commandments hang all the law and the prophets (Matt 22:36-40).

Our prayers, then, stand a greater chance of manifestation if we have love towards God and our neighbor, than if our heart is bereft of love. Obviously, dwelling in love is the key. And this is where the going usually gets tough. We'd rather indulge many other states of mind (fear, hatred, worry) than dwell always in a state of love. Of course it doesn't have to be a big hatred; it can be a little one, such as unwarranted prejudice, dislike, and contempt.

It doesn't have to be a big worry, or a big fear; it can be a little one, such as concerns about failing, getting sick, having an accident, or not making the grade in some other way.

When we love the Lord our God with all our heart (as our greatest treasure), and with all our soul (with all our senses), and with all our mind (with all our thoughts, attention, and awareness), then there's no room for anything unlike love to dwell in our heart, soul, and mind. With a mind always on love, expressing it, thinking it, meditating on it, practicing it, we don't have to fret about the three "deadly" negative states of mind: fear, hatred, and worry.

This healing wasn't my first encounter with the 91st Psalm. In Rudolf Flesch's book, *The Art of Plain Talk*, he prescribes a punctuation method consisting of pauses. Following his method, I recorded the 91st Psalm, and listened to it for hours one day while I busied myself with chores. For years, I witnessed those who were supposedly taken with the Spirit, who were under its spell, as it were, raise church roofs with their shouting, wondering if, someday, I would be so taken. While listening to my recorded voice recite the Psalm again and again, I felt only what could be described as the Spirit of God descending upon me, enveloping my whole being, but that envelopment didn't transform me into a human dynamo, suddenly able to run at breakneck pace up and down church aisles, or walk the top of church pews with amazing ease and protection, but rendered me so physically weak I could barely stand. Overtaken by this unexpected weakness, I was constrained to put my chores aside. I'm not mocking those who manifest the Spirit by shouting or otherwise demonstrating amazing physical agility, but to contrast my experience with theirs, to describe how the Spirit impacted me differently than it impacted them. Since that time, the 91st Psalm has held for me a special meaning and a special value.

Recently, The Voice imparted additional information regarding the power and efficacy of love. After recounting the many troubling things that we might face while in this world, The Voice offered a remedy, a way to render them all null and void, and harmless—to do the following when they show up: "Know the complete and irrevocable Truth: Love is all there is." Although I understood the potency of love, this new revelation regarding love elevated it further, making it the only requirement in our life, the only panacea for a world-weary people eager to find heaven, and the harmony that it bestows.

For a time, I thought about love in this new light. If Love is all there is, I concluded, then evil, and all its related aspects, didn't exist, not sin, sickness, nor death—as there was no place in the totality of Love for them to exist. Further, if Love is irrevocable, then it is irreversible, unalterable, unchangeable, permanent and final—the Alpha and the Omega. "I am Alpha and Omega, the beginning and the ending, saith the Lord, which is, and which was, and which is to come, the Almighty."[18] I realized in that moment that the whole of our human history, replete as it was with

---

18 Rev 1:8

man's inhumanity towards man, replete as it was with pain, suffering, and destruction, replete as it was with "wars and rumours of wars,"[19] was merely an illusion, an assortment of events that were illegitimate, and powerless, illegitimate because they took place outside of the domain of Love, and was, for that reason, impossible, and non-existent in the grand scheme of things. I realized, further, that the entirety of our sullied history might be swept away in one fell swoop, reversed completely, provided a sufficiency of Love—its full recognition and realization—could be brought to bear. As difficult as it might be for us to apprehend such Love in our human state, I understood that we had the means to do so, that we could use that Love to do away with our dark past, bringing it into the Light, into all that truly exists, banishing forever all that is unlike Love, as *Love is all there is*, then as now.

As a follow-up to the revelation, "Love is all there is," The Voice instructed: "Love a thing into existence." I understood that, in addition to general instances, this creative aspect of love could be applied to specific things, too. This advice came as I pondered how I would praticalize the revelation I had received from The Voice. I knew that, with this new revelation, I could love into existence whatever things I chose—Peace, Harmony, Good, Joy, Justice, Perfection, Health, Abundance, as well as Love—merely by contemplating them with love and sending them forth under the auspices of love, infusing them, as well as other desired conditions, with as much love as I could gather within my heart and soul. As long as they went forth on the pinions of love, these desired conditions would be given flight, that is, brought into existence.

Not long after experiencing the *Secret Place* healing that ended the pain occasioned by the auto accident, I met the author of the book, *Conversations with God*. At the time, I didn't know that the person I met was the author. You see, I met him before I met him—first, in a vision, and later, many months later, in person. As with visions, it was presented through a lens of

---

19 Matt 24:6

vibrant colors, and with a sharpness and clarity never seen in our every-day world. We were sitting on what seemed like a bench. He was sitting to the right of me, a middle-aged white man, bearded, and casually dressed. The setting was the beach. The sun was shining, but not too brightly. We didn't speak to each other at the time, just sat there in silence. Revisiting the vision later, I wondered who the man might be. I didn't recognize him as someone I knew, not even casually. I wondered, too, why I was given the vision. What was the purpose of it?

It would be months before I had an answer. As it turned out, the person of my vision was none other than the author of *Conversations with God*. Meeting this modern-day guru, this messenger, would take place, not face to face, but in person, nevertheless, on Friday, February 11, 2000, from 7:30-10:00 p.m., just a few days from my birthday on February 15, at the Miramar Fairmont Hotel in Santa Monica, California, well within walking distance of the ocean, and the beach, during an event titled, *Empowerment Week 2000*, where Neale Donald Walsch would kick off the event by speaking before a packed house. Once settled in our room for our week's stay, we searched out and found the auditorium, a converted ballroom, where Walsch would be speaking. My companion and I stood at the rear of the auditorium, along a back wall near the entrance to the Miramar Fairmont Starlight Ballroom, as all the seats had previously been taken, due to our lateness braving Los Angeles City's Friday evening traffic, a challenging task on any evening, but Friday was the worse of the worse. The letter I received prior to the event detailed that week's schedule, and began in this promising fashion:

"Dear Friend,

"Congratulations! You have just taken a step toward activating spirituality in your life. We know that your participation is this exciting event is going to call forth the next grandest version of the greatest vision you ever had about yourself. During Empowerment Week 2000, Neale Donald Walsch and ReCreation Foundation will offer opportunities for you to really *get* how the message of Conversations with *God* can be proactive force in your life."

Several days into the event, I went to the front of another large room reserved for smaller gatherings and spoke about my encounter with The Voice, and how that encounter had resulted in a much-desired healing, one that brought me great joy at the time. I spoke extemporaneously but with some preparation, as I had mentally rehearsed, at the last minute, what I would say, although I hadn't planned to speak. After walking to the front of the room, and taking a deep breath, I told the audience there about how I came to need a healing, the automobile accident I had been in, and how The Voice had come to my rescue, and healed me, and about the Bible verse that The Voice had directed me to, the 91st Psalm. Later, a young man stopped me as I walked from one venue to another. He wanted to know the number of the Psalm that The Voice had referred me to. Apparently he hadn't heard it the first time I gave it, or he had forgotten it soon after hearing it. If the young man's interest in knowing the number of the Psalm was any indication, my brief talk before the rather large crowd had been well received, and perhaps bore some fruit.

FIVE

TAP INNER WISDOM

The Lord thundered from heaven, and the most High uttered his voice.[20]

T HE *YOU* IN YOU CAN TAP INNER WISDOM. TAPPING
Inner Wisdom is similar to having a dialogue with God, but without
the verbal exchange that usually marks a conversation between two inter-
locutors. Because the answers to my questions came from within, from
a presence having the characteristics I would associate with God, it was
natural therefore to attribute the answers to Him, although it's possible that
the answers came from what some have described as one's Higher Self,
one's Soul, or one's God-Self. Either way, these experiences have had a lasting impression.

I place the following experience into the out-of-body category because
of its similarity with that experience. Properly, it should be placed in the
category of revelation. The revelation came after many months of meditation, and a prayerful study of spiritual literature, including the Holy Bible,
which had been my constant companion, as well. During these hours of
prayer and meditation, I searched my soul for an answer as to how I might

---

20 II Sam 22:14

live out the remainder of my days—in service to God or a human endeavor. My life at the time had entered a new phase. I was recently divorced from my first wife, and was unsure of the direction I should take my life now that it had been painfully interrupted. I wanted direction. I want to know where I should go from here. Divorced, heavily in debt, I was facing a bleak future. This question of what I should now do with my life was uppermost in my thoughts, although I didn't give voice to it. It was like swimming in a pool, where you're concentrating so hard on the act of swimming that you're unaware of the water. This was my state of mind, when I was suddenly lifted out of my body.

It was nighttime. I was reclining in bed, sleepy, but still lost in thought. At some point, my astral body became unmoored from the physical. Floating free, I drifted about a couple of feet upward. It was a short distance spatially, but a memorable one. It reminded me of this passage from the Book of Ezekiel, Chapter 3, Verse 12:

Then the spirit took me up, and I heard behind me a voice of a great rushing, saying Blessed be the glory of the Lord from this place.

And Oh My God! I knew immediately that this was not going to be my usual out-of-body experience. From the moment that I was lifted from my body, "taken up," as it were, I found myself within the presence of another, someone or something that had incredible power, a power so vast, so pervasive, and so irresistible, that it felt like the fullness of God's power, God's omnipotence. I wasn't afraid: The presence presented no threat. Although I could feel it all around me, I couldn't see it, not through the darkness that enveloped us both. And to the presence that resided in the darkness, surrounded by a seemingly infinite power that emanated from it, a power that permeated the full depth of my being, so that I and the power seemed as one, I prepared to ask my question.

Somehow, I knew that if I asked the unseen presence my question and asked it without ceasing, I'd receive an answer. The question that I had felt

often, but which hadn't taken form, began to take shape, all four words of
it:

"What must I do?"

I asked the question repeatedly, directing it towards the presence in
the darkness, and to that incredible power that resided there. Instantly, I
knew that I could ask for anything I wanted, and it would be mine, or I
could pose any question I wanted, and an answer would be given. In that
moment, within the fullness of that power, I could have asked for riches,
and King Solomon's legendary wealth would have been a pauper's sum by
contrast. I could have asked for a great intellect, and I would have surpassed Einstein. I could have asked for great physical strength, and I would
have put Samson to shame. In short, I could have commanded a mountain,
"Be thou removed, and be thou cast into the sea,"[21] and it would have been
done. And the shocker, I didn't need faith to make it so. Within this power,
I felt that all things were possible. I could have raised Lazarus from the
dead. I could have called out, "Lazarus, come forth,"[22] and Lazarus would
have come forth.

And did I ask for any of these things? No. I asked, instead: "What must
I do?" All I wanted at that moment was the answer to a simple question.
Not wealth. Not a great intellect. Not great physical strength. Not to raise
Lazarus from the dead. Not the power to heal. None of these things. I
merely wanted an answer to a question that had preoccupied me for some
time, albeit not consciously. The answer didn't come right away, but I knew
that it would. I was in the center of this mountain-moving power and I
wouldn't be denied. So I asked the presence again and again.

I could tell that the presence didn't want to answer the question that
I had posed, and was peeved with me for having asked. I could feel the
presence grow agitated.

---

21 Mark 11:23
22 John 11:43

I felt what can only be described as a *great wrath*[23] emanating from the presence. This surprised me, because I was now associating the Presence with God. I didn't think that it would harm me, but that it didn't like the idea that I had asked a question that it didn't want to answer, but couldn't avoid answering. And answer it did. The voice of God has been described as rushing waters, and the rumbling of thunder. It was all of this and more. The Voice was a deep bass. It was a voice that I had heard only once before, and have never heard again. With what seemed like profound reluctance, The Voice finally spoke from the darkness, and from within this all-enveloping power. It said,

"You must do what you must do."

The words were stated deliberately, distinctly, slowly, and with great majesty. The Voice was like that of thunder and rushing water, or a "rushing mighty wind." The following biblical passage captures The Voice perfectly:

And I heard a voice from heaven, as the voice of many waters, and as the voice of a great thunder. (Rev 14:2)

Immediately I protested: I wasn't satisfied with the answer; it was inadequate. I wanted something that was unambiguous, something with the brilliant clarity of the sky after a rain. Something that would guide me, direct me, as I moved forward in time. So I asked, again: *"What must I do?"* By then, I could feel my astral body descending, returning to my physical body, and to the physical realm. Although I kept repeating the question, I was no longer within the Shekinah of power where all petitions are satisfied, and all questions answered.

Try as I might, the enigmatic words yielded no understanding which satisfied me. I was now as much stupefied as I had been before asking the question, and just as disappointed. I went over the answer again and again

---

23 II Kings 23:26

in my mind. I said the words silently and then out loud. I rearranged the words hoping for insight. Nothing came. Finally, I reasoned that I knew unconsciously, if not consciously, what I had to do, and that I should get on with the doing. I didn't feel that my free will had been violated, but that I had already decided, perhaps before coming to the Earth plane, what my life work would be, what it was I *must* be doing.

For days afterward, the presence of unlimited power, the omnipotence that was conferred upon me, that permeated my being for a short time in the darkness, clung to me. It lingered in the air, became an aura around me that faded after a few days. For a time, I felt as though I could have done anything that I wished, could have had anything that I desired. I felt that I could have moved mountains. I had only to command it.

Looking back, I wondered why I didn't ask for something other than the answer to a question. I could have asked for anything—for knowledge, wealth, the power to heal, or wisdom, as did Solomon. Perhaps I felt so complete within that power that I didn't feel that I lacked anything. Moreover, the answer that I did receive haunted me for years. One day it all became clear. I'm not sure of the events that led up to the answer, only that the answer was finally in hand. All humans, I came to know, are subject to these "must do's." The "must do's" are the things we're compelled to do, relentlessly driven to do. I call these compulsions the "must do's." I've wrestled with many of these "must do's" most of my life, giving in to them more often than I've bested them, if indeed I did. In all these instances, these "must do's" marked watershed events in my life. Writing this book is one those "must do's."

This experience taught me that faith, the belief power to manifest things into our physical reality, becomes superfluous, an unnecessary requirement when we're in the center of the awesome power I felt. The power was all-powerful. It was a power that nothing could deny. It was a power that could heal the sick, cleanse the leper, raise the dead and cast out demons. What, then, is the value of faith, when this incredible power makes it seemingly useless? Jesus talked about a grain of mustard seed faith, referring to the quantity, or the quality of faith needed to move mountains.

This point is driven home further during an exchange between Peter and Jesus, establishing the importance of having *faith in God* to do what otherwise might seem impossible to mere mortals:

> *And Peter calling to remembrance saith unto him, Master, behold, the fig tree which thou cursedst is withered away.*
>
> *And Jesus answering saith unto them, Have faith in God.*
>
> *For verily I say unto you, That whosoever shall say unto this mountain, Be thou removed, and be thou cast into the sea; and shall not doubt in his heart, but shall believe that those things which he saith shall come to pass; he shall have whatsoever he saith* (Mark 11:21-23).

Jesus seems to be saying that we need only believe that God has the power and the willingness to answer whatever prayers we offer Him; it's not necessary, therefore, that we have the faith, ourselves, to move mountains, but that we believe that God has the power to give us whatever we ask. This puts faith in a new light. Faith, then, isn't something we use apart from God to work miracles on our own, but something we use when we pray, when we make our request known to God. We need no more faith than this. The power to bring about our request is already His to use as He sees fit.

"The Son can do nothing of himself, but what he seeth the Father do: for what things soever he doeth, these also doeth the Son likewise."[24]

My first suspicion that there might be an intermediary, a Higher Self, between God and us, came to life during this event. From this experience, I learned that we're also guided by our Higher Self, our Soul Self. I believe that it was my Soul Self that answered the question, rather than God Himself. It's my firm belief that the gods (our Higher Self) direct the

---

24 John 5:19

seminal events of our life, maneuvering into our world many of the people, and events, with whom we must interact.

If it's true that I have a Higher Self, it follows, by way of extrapolation, that all humans possess a Higher Self. This Self, I knew, had been with me all my life. On many occasions, he spoke to me, and shared knowledge with me about people, places and things, things past and things to come.

And the Lord God said, Behold, the man is become as one of us, to know good and evil: and now, lest he put forth his hand, and take also of the tree of life, and eat, and live forever: Therefore the Lord God sent him forth from the garden of Eden, to till the ground from whence he was taken (Gen 3:22-23).

Taken at face value, it's hard to deny what this Scriptural passage reveals: the existence of more than one god, and from the mouth of Lord God no less, when He says, "man is become as one of us [gods]." The title "Lord God" can also be taken to mean the God that is lord over other gods, a king, or, to state it another way, the "King of Gods." In the Book of Revelation, the white horse rider is described this way: "And he hath on his vesture and on his thigh a name written, KING OF KINGS, AND LORD OF LORDS."[25]

These gods, then, are representations of our Higher Self, the Soul Self, or the God Self. The Lord God, then, is the God that exists in an exalted state, much like the god Zeus, a supreme deity in Greek mythology. The god, Kronos, the son of Quranos and Gaea, fathered Zeus, who, himself, also fathered men as well as gods, suggesting a hierarchy of gods.

Perhaps Our Higher Selves are the source of these mythologies around gods, deities not unlike the twelve gods of Mount Olympus, headed up by Zeus. The one difference is that we, ourselves, are the gods, separated from them in belief only, and as a result of our human condition. Responded

---

25 Rev 19:16

Jesus, "Is it not written in your law, I said, Ye are gods."[26] The Soul is God, nevertheless, and becomes our connection to the Sublime God, the one Who is forever perfect, and Holy, the one to whom Jesus prayed and referred to as "Our Father, which art in heaven."[27] This God remains always at the pinnacle of perfection and eternal harmony, and is not the relative and individuated God to whom we usually communicate and who communicates with us. This is not to say that the Sublime God never talks with us; there's ample proof to indicate otherwise.

I believe that I connected once with the Absolute and Sublime God. While in prayer, I was told: "You're my beloved Son. Hear me." The Voice was Love itself—gentle, tender, and sweet. The beauty of that moment and the tenderness of the words stayed with me for days, contrasting sharply with the Voice of Thunder. The idea of various Gods in One shouldn't seem all that strange since Christians already accept God as a trinity, that is, as the Father, the Son, and the Holy Ghost.[28]

I admire Shirley MacLaine as much for her writings as for her acting. It was in one of her books that I was first introduced to the concept of a Higher Self. What stands out now for me from her writings are the conversations that she had with her Higher Self, an exchange detailed in her book, *Dancing in the Light*. In the book, MacLaine recounts her first meeting with her Higher Self. She described this self as very tall, with blue eyes and auburn hair. Several years after reading the book, I recalled that MacLaine had been able to contact her Higher Self. Intrigued, I set out to do the same. One night, as I meditated before falling asleep, I asked to see my Higher Self, curious to know whether my Higher Self would be similar in appearance to that of MacLaine's, although I was black.

That night, I left my body in the usual way, and walked from my bedroom into my living room. Standing at the window overlooking my driveway, apparently peering out, stood a dark figure. It was dressed in black,

26 John 10:34
27 Luke 11:2
28 Matt 28:19

with a black cape extending from its shoulders. I knew immediately that this was my Higher Self, my Soul Self, and my God Self. I will refer to my Higher Self as "He," but I could just as easily refer to this entity as "She," such was its appearance. He turned to face me, projecting a decidedly masculine presence, but rather than walking towards me, he walked into the kitchen to his left, a short distance from the window. I followed. I wasn't afraid, just curious. He was as tall as MacLaine's Higher Self, but without the white features—blue eyes, for example. My Higher Self was distinctively Negroid in appearance. When I drew close enough to see the details of his face, I recognized the features of several women with whom I had been intimate over the years. Their faces seemed to meld into one visage, yet I could still make out certain individual features of each of them, as each feature was instantly recognizable.

The appearance of my Higher Self was a surprising twist on MacLaine's experience with her Higher Self. What could account for *his* difference in appearance? Could it be that it was because I had been black in several lifetimes, and that my intimates had also been black? For several lifetimes, I too had been white, as were they. Yet, my Higher Self gave no indication of that in his appearance. It was only recently (during the past three or four lifetimes) that I have reincarnated as a black person. I say this, not out of disappointment, because I'm quite happy to be black in this or any lifetime, my blackness having contributed substantially to the advancement of my soul, but that you might appreciate my quandary.

I was now standing in front of the figure. It had stopped abruptly, seemingly to allow me to catch up. Standing next to the figure now, my head came up to his midsection, which I could see because it was uncovered. From this vantage point, I could tell that my Higher Self was unmistakably black, with strong, broad, masculine shoulders, but with clearly identifiable feminine characteristics and features, a description akin to, but not the same as, the androgynous appearance of MacLaine's Higher Self.

He said, finally, "If you don't go out tonight, something exciting will happen tomorrow."

Divorced at the time, I would go out on weekends in hopes of finding someone with whom to share quality time, or perhaps even to marry. Although twice divorced, I was not opposed to marriage. The next day was Sunday. As promised by my Higher Self, something "exciting" did happen: I spent part of the day in a trance, one longer than usual. It was surreal, as I was able to look about the room with ease, but, as with the trance state, I wasn't able to move a muscle.

This meeting with my Higher Self sealed my understanding regarding a Higher Self, the existence of an intermediary between God and His Creation, Man. That understanding only grew more firmly when I recalled another experience from years earlier.

We think of ourselves as solitary units, discrete, and separate from everything else, rather than the unified energy that we are. But it doesn't have to be this way. The You in *you* that is your Soul, your Higher Self, is as much a part of you as you think your physical body to be. In fact, it is you. Were it not that we believed otherwise, we would know ourselves as one with it, integrated and whole.

A meeting with my Higher Self—a Self which I had no knowledge existed at the time—surfaced earlier in an unexpected way. It happened while I was visiting my sister who had recently undergone surgery and was recuperating in her hospital room. Concerned about her health, I asked if I could pray for her, and she consented. The night before the visit I had spent some time in meditation, realizing the omnipresence of love and light. As I prayed for my sister in her recovery room, I did so by realizing anew the omnipresence of that love and that light. Well into my prayers, I experienced a new sensation. It was as though the doors and windows of my mind were flung open—wide, fully—and all the love of the universe rushed in to replace the stale air that was my human consciousness, immersing me in a love I had never before felt.

In that love, I sensed a presence, another being, another entity; this presence had entered along with the rush of love that now infused my consciousness, as though my consciousness was a house, my home, and I was now entertaining and unexpected visitor. It was as if another person now occupied the same space that I had previously occupied alone.

Referencing my sister, I spoke to the presence: "She is spiritual and perfect, and you know it," I said, challenging the presence to give her back her full health. After a few minutes had passed, my sister asked, "Are you still praying for me?"

Her question startled me at first, grounding me once again in physical reality.

"Why?" I responded.

"There's a funny feeling in the pit of my stomach," she said.

After spending a little more time with my sister, believing that I had done all I could regarding her health, I left. In the hallway now, walking towards the exit, something had changed. I had experienced this change while in the hospital room, but here in the hallway the change was unmistakable. Everywhere I looked things sparkled with a brilliant light, as though the world and everything in it were suddenly transformed into resplendent diamonds.

It gave new meaning to this passage from Revelations: "And I saw a new heaven and a new earth: for the first heaven and the first earth were passed away."[29] Even the most mundane objects now shone brightly, each one possessing a beauty unsurpassed, a splendor not of this world. I marveled at this new reality, and was struck by a fascinating realization that in this light of love, nothing was ugly, nothing was ordinary, and nothing was insignificant. And in that moment, I knew that this was how God saw His creation, as I was now seeing it, resplendent with love and perfection.

---

29 Rev 21:1

GOD'S HAIKU

The *you* in you can impart its Inner Wisdom in many ways. Haiku is a Japanese lyric verse, usually a reflection upon nature, consisting of three unrhymed lines and a measured number of syllables, or morae. The haiku which have come through me aren't traditionally structured, nor do they adhere to strict Japanese haiku either in form or substance. They are more properly a shortened version of a Tanka, rather than haiku, as haiku usually comment on nature or the seasons. Nevertheless, in keeping with Western tradition which, at times, has taken great liberty with the form to approximate Japanese haiku, I have called those verses that I have been given, God's Haiku.

I'll let you decide the source of the haiku, whether from God, my God-Self, or from the Inner Wisdom that we all have access to, provided we seek it out, and allow it to manifest Itself through us without interference from our ever-present storehouse of beliefs.

Remembering that one of my professional associates wrote haiku and had published a collection devoted to his creations, I set out to learn more about this art form. Because of its specificity to the Japanese language, I learned that the English language wasn't suitable for the writing of haiku, but that the incompatibility hadn't stopped English writers from dabbling as dilettantes or wading into the professional depths reserved primarily for haiku experts. Satisfied that I could, as had many intrepid adventurers before me, commit the sin of writing English haiku, I resolved to try my hand. That evening while in meditation, I received my first haiku. It wasn't one that I composed myself, but one which was composed for me. Without further study, I hadn't planned to write one of my own, nor did I anticipate receiving one from my Inner Wisdom. It came, all at once, from The Voice that had been my companion for years. In the quiet, the stillness, I heard these words spoken:

Say a prayer:

Put a word

Into the mouth of God

Let me offer my interpretation of the haiku, as I believe its message to be both timely and instructive. Whispered to me as I was meditating, this haiku exemplifies what prayer means to me. I use "whispered" not because I didn't hear the words clearly spoken, but because they have an ethereal quality. It should be the aim of every supplicant to evoke the power of God on behalf of his or her prayer. When one's prayer becomes a "word" in the mouth of God, to be spoken by Him, that prayer goes forth with God's full authority, with an omnipotence that "calleth those things which be not as though they were."[30]

> *Man shall not live by bread alone, but by every* word that proceed-
> eth out of the mouth of God.[31]

Our jobs, our bank accounts, our investments—those which pro-vide us material subsistence (food, clothing, shelter)—are at best variably reliable, unless they proceed as "words" (spiritual assurances) from "the mouth of God."

Here's the answer I received when I asked God how He healed me of a certain affliction: "As My Thoughts touch your thoughts and your thoughts My Thoughts, together We shall keep you in perfect health."

When God's Thoughts touch our thoughts and our thought's His Thoughts, what does that say about the quality of thought required, in the first instance, to touch the Thoughts of God? Nonetheless, it's always the Mind of God that's operative, that is, indispensable in effectuating an answer to prayer, whether to obtain a healing, or to be blessed in other

---

30 Rom 4:17
31 Matt 4:4

ways. The key is to align our thoughts with God's Thoughts during the healing process, to know what He knows and only what He knows.

Given my spiritual nature, and my contemplation of things spiritual, I wasn't surprised that my first haiku was about prayer, or about God. The next time I received an unprompted, fully-developed haiku from my Inner Wisdom, the process was more a meandering than a direct path.

While waiting in the outer office of a business, I read a woman's magazine to pass the time. One of the articles offered advice on how to use laughter to reduce stress, and to achieve other health-giving benefits (low blood pressure, for one).

The writer, a woman, told of a neighbor who dressed impeccably, maintained a perfect house, and never seemed harried by life's daily routines. Since her neighbor had it all together, and she didn't, she always felt intimidated when the neighbor came to visit. On one such visit, the neighbor perceived the woman's anguish, and told her: "Lighten up!" Rather than allow her feelings to be hurt, the woman took a closer look at the woman's advice. Perhaps, she reasoned, it was through the use of humor that her neighbor had learned to cope with life's many stresses. The article detailed what science had learned about laughter, and the benefits that one could derive from a mere thirty minutes of laughter daily. Comedy, of all sorts, it concluded, could bring amazing health benefits into our life.

And the article ended by repeating the words again: "Lighten up!"

In the days that followed, the words showed up again and again, so often that it ruled out the possibility of chance. I heard them on television, and read them on the Internet. The words "stalked" me for days. That's when I realized that more was going on than mere coincidence.

On the morning of July 30, 2008, as I spent time, as is my custom, in meditation, the haiku was "whispered" to me, and I repeat it here:

Lighten Up!

When you can see the Truth

In Everything

There it was. *That's* where all of this was leading. Contextually, the haiku had expanded the meaning of the words *lighten up*, from the casting aside of one's worries and cares (not to take things too seriously) to the illuminating and brightening of all things with the radiant *light* of Truth. Later, as I thought over the possible meaning of the haiku, the following words from Jesus' teachings came to mind:

Ye have heard that it hath been said, Thou shalt love thy neighbour, and hate thine enemy. But I say unto you, Love your enemies, bless them that curse you, do good to them that hate you, and pray for them which despitefully use you, and persecute you; That ye may be the children of your Father which is in heaven: for he maketh his sun to rise on the evil and on the good, and sendeth rain on the just and on the unjust....

Be ye therefore perfect, even as your Father which is in heaven is perfect (Matt 5: 43-48).

Still, I wasn't making a full connection. And that's when it was shown to me: The light from His sun was His Truth which did not distinguish between "the evil" or "the good," but could be found dispelling the darkness of the lie with the Light of Truth. And the rain that He "sendeth" was His love, and it fell on the "just and the unjust" alike.

Have you ever been caught in the rain? Remember how drenched you were when you finally found shelter? Remember how soggy the Earth, and glistening the grass, and how wet the leaves on trees, and other plants, after days of a steady downpour?

Our Father, then, is always sending a torrent of Love upon His children, so much so that we are always drenched, and soggy, and glistening. We may not always be aware of this downpour of Love, but it's there, nevertheless.

We, too, can follow Jesus' advice and be "perfect, even as [our] Father which is in heaven is perfect." We, too, can shine the Light of Truth upon Everything, dispelling the evil in our heart, and in our world. We, too, can allow our love to rain down upon the Earth, and upon our neighbors, for all are our neighbors, whether they dwell on the other side of the world, or on the block where we live.

It's been said: "It's always raining somewhere." Let me reassure you: "It's raining all the time, everywhere." We need only eyes to see, and ears to hear: God's Love falls all the time, steadily, on the rooftops of our being, and against the window panes of our soul.

In the manner here described, I have collected several haiku, at times providing the first line, and then allowing my Inner Wisdom to fill in the next two, forming in the process a complete haiku. When I had enough to fill a book, I thought I might publish them, along with an explanation of how each individual haiku was obtained, and an exegesis that would unravel the meaning of each. Most have a surprising twist and an unexpected impartation of wisdom that is refreshingly insightful.

SIX

READ THE THOUGHTS OF OTHERS

A S UNLIKELY AS THIS, TOO, MAY SEEM, IT'S POSSIBLE
for the *you* in you to read the thoughts of others. To be sure, these
others don't always cooperate with our desire to know what they're thinking. To prevent others from knowing their thoughts, people erect a shield,
or a barrier. This is not a conscious decision, but an unconscious one, and
under certain circumstances, these same people may drop their guard and
allow their barriers to be breached, or, more likely, give us permission to
access their innermost thoughts. Most of the time, the barriers are quite
effective. Only a few adepts have had the requisite spiritual know-how
to bypass those mental barriers and lay bare our souls, and our private
thoughts. Jesus was one of those adepts:

> *And Jesus knowing their thoughts said, Wherefore think ye evil in*
> *your hearts?*[32]

When a friend of mine hadn't called in several days and I failed to
reach her by phone, I asked her son telepathically, "Where's your mother?"

---

32 Matt 9:4

He replied, also telepathically, "She's in the hospital." After a little persistent digging, I learned that her son was right, my friend was in the hospital, and had been there for several days, confirming the accuracy of the information I had received, and the reason I was unable to reach her or to receive a call from her.

On another occasion, I listened while my neighbor, a renter of the house next door, explained that she had no hand in her landlord's complaint from the previous day. Her landlord wanted to cut a tree limb that overhung the driveway and a portion of the house she was renting, fearing that it might break and cause damage. The tree stood in my yard but not far from the property line that divided our properties.

As she walked towards me, I could hear her mental plea, "I had nothing to do with the business of the tree," she said, "It was all their idea." She was referring to the landlord and to his wife who had accompanied him.

When she finally spoke, voicing word-for-word what she had been thinking, I smiled, knowing that I had already heard her thoughts on the subject and for that reason knew the sincerity of her words. Where conflict is likely, knowing the thoughts of others can come in handy. It can placate and defuse potentially explosive situations.

My companion's sister lived with us for a time, while she searched, evenings and weekends, for a new home in the area. She had moved in with us after landing a job nearby. While returning to bed after a trip to the bathroom early one morning, I heard her say, "I'm so sick!"

The voice had originated from within and was unmistakably the voice of my companion's sister. For a moment, I was tempted to walk to the other side of our house to inquire about her health, but thought better of it, knowing that she would come to us, if her health warranted it.

That evening, after she had returned from work, I asked her, "You were sick this morning. How do you feel now?"

Clearly a little taken aback, apparently because I knew something I shouldn't have known, she asked, "Who told you that?"

I said simply, "You did."

She didn't inquire further, and I let the matter drop. We often hear the saying, "He or she won't open up." The saying takes on a new meaning when the "opening up" is one's actual thoughts, rather than one's willingness to divulge what they're thinking.

I've had the tables turned, as it were, where one person seemed to know my thoughts, or what I was thinking.

Having spent time in a previous life as a captive, I find being alone a painful and unwelcome situation. Between marriages, I found myself alone many times. For that reason, I got out among people wherever they might congregate to escape the ache of that aloneness.

Although I found it intolerable to be alone, I have never been lonely, as I enjoy my own company, and don't mind keeping it. When I was out and about on these occasions, because I didn't wish to be alone, I would spend my time mentally sending thoughts of love to all who were present in my space.

One evening, a young black man who I had never before seen at my then location, walked up to me and said, "I know why you're here."

"Sure you do," I thought, knowing that this young man couldn't possibly divine in a million years my concealed purpose for being where I was.

Puzzled, curious, and thoroughly amused, I smiled and said, "Okay. Why am I here?"

"You're here loving everybody."

Without saying anything more, he walked away, leaving me stunned and suddenly flooded with questions, "How did he know that? Who told him that?" questions that would remain unanswered. He clearly discerned my purpose for being there, if not my thoughts. He walked away with the assurance of one who knew he had hit his mark, made his point and had no need for further conversation, or to entertain follow-up questions.

While in meditation, I often hear what others are thinking. They share with me what they're feeling at that moment. Most of the time they convey thoughts as well as feelings, usually thoughts of a positive and loving nature, but they can also send thoughts and feelings of dread or impending danger, prompting me to send, on their behalf, a prayer or two.

SEVEN

INFLUENCE THE WEATHER

THE *YOU* IN YOU HAVE NO LIMITATIONS, EXCEPT THOSE that you impose, and can, if you develop a strong connection with it, influence the weather. This *you* in you can turn on the spigots of nature at will, or turn them off. Native Americans used rain dance for the same reason that modern-day rainmakers use cloud seeding, to coax rain during times of drought, or unseasonably dry spells.

BRING RAIN

The first time I influenced the weather, it was not to make it rain, but to see if I could make it stop. I prefer the phrase, "bringing rain," rather than the more familiar one, "making it rain," since I exercise no control over the rain-making process, merely whether it rains during a given time of my choosing.

We were in the middle of a hard downpour. At the time, I was living in a three-room apartment, one of two apartments in a duplex. Not counting the bathroom, a kitchen and a small bedroom filled two of the rooms. The first room, a living room, had a large picture window that looked out over a porch and provided a clear view of nearby apartment units and a grassy area that had to be crossed to reach them. Bordering the units was a long driveway that ended at a row of garages, one for each tenant.

Although my unit was furnished, not all units were. In front of the picture window of my unit a well-used couch rested, consuming most the area in the small living room. And if I looked over my left shoulder while sitting, after shifting my bottom to my extreme left, my left arm resting over the top of the couch's back, I could watch the rain as it fell on roofs, pattered the paved driveway, and pelted hard against the porch.

The sun had long retreated and, with its departure, a sweltering pall hung over the scene. It was then that the thought took flight, like a bird hiding in my porch's eaves might take flight if startled. In that moment, I wondered what would happen if I knew that perfection, and only perfection, ruled. Could I stop the rain? As I contemplated this perfection, the rain soon broke, and a stream of sunlight shattered the pall, leaving a sparkling shine on the driveway, and crystalline beads of water on plants and grass.

But there was something more going on as well–the rain hadn't stopped everywhere. It was still falling on the apartment units farthest from the driveway, not more than fifty feet away. I felt like Moses, as he studied the burning bush from a distance and said, "I will now turn aside, and see this great sight."[33]

I walked outside and looked up. The clouds had formed a perfect circle directly over my apartment unit. Through it passed the clear light of day, illuminating everything below the circle. Outside the circle, the rain continued to fall on nearby apartment units, seemingly oblivious to the one exception: my unit.

I returned to my vantage point on the couch, and, after a brief interlude, the clouds returned as they were and the rain continued as though

---

33 Ex 3:3

it had never stopped. Years later I learned of hole punch clouds that leave circles in certain stratiform clouds, but hole punch clouds require a certain temperature to form, and the temperature above and below were not at a below-freezing point so that ice crystals might form. In addition, the circle above my house didn't resemble any of the pictures of hole punch clouds that I was able to find in books or on the Internet.

On another occasion, I pulled back the clouds, as though they were heavenly curtains. It had begun to rain, and I was waiting outdoors in a long line to register for college classes at a nearby community college, and I didn't want to get wet. Praying as before, I contemplated the perfection of all things. Soon a large circle opened in the clouds allowing it to rain everywhere but where I was standing. The other students hardly noticed.

From that time to now, I have been able to either stop it from raining for long periods—sometimes drying up naturally-forming lakes—or entice the rain, filling the lakes again. When I have stopped the rain from naturally occurring, it wasn't because of malevolence on my part, but because I had, unconsciously, held it back for fear that inclement weather would spoil an outdoor project on which I was working, or because I had holes in my roof in need of repair. There are positive side-benefits to bringing rain as well: I have helped extinguish at least two, perhaps more, major wild fires that had charred thousands of acres. To extinguish the fires, I first brought cloud covering and, in time, rain, usually after three or four days.

When I'm at my spiritual best, I need only desire the rain to bring the rain. At other times, I can bring rain by seeing the rain, imagining it in my mind's eye, or feeling the presence of it. When I feel the presence of it, I need do nothing more. It's as though the rain comes in answer to the feeling, to give the feeling an existential reality.

There are always risks associated with this kind of interference, as rain in the form of thunderstorms can expand, rather than subdue, fires, generating lightning strikes that can cause more fires, or whip up winds which can spread them further, aggravating an already bad situation. For this reason, I wait a spell to see if fire fighters can get the upper hand, and only act when it's clear that not acting will do more harm than acting.

It was late in 2013 that I learned for the first time that California was experiencing a drought. Governor Brown was calling for water conservation, and although he hadn't placed the state on mandatory rationing, it was clear that it was being contemplated. Further highlighting the urgency, President Obama, on a trip to the state in mid-February, 2014, surveyed drought-stricken areas, especially farm lands. Perhaps unknown to many, California is an essential provider of agricultural products to the nation.

Beginning New Year's Day, 2014, I endeavored to bring rain to California, and was rewarded near the end of January with rain. It was a good showing, but it fell short of the relief that I sought. To focus even more attention on the drought, and the resulting damage, a local television station showed pictures of several California water reservoirs in various stages of distress. It was clear that unless rain came, and came soon, these reservoirs would be nothing more than dried up holes in the ground.

Usually, I can bring rain within a week. During the previous year, when it hadn't rained for a while, I brought down varying degrees of the wet stuff. The rain I brought was usually for my local area, and not the whole state, although many times the entire state was blessed with it. With climate change, the weather patterns have grown more erratic throughout the length of the country. The West coast is experiencing drought conditions, while the East coast, and certain states in between, are being saturated with rain, or blanketed with ice and snow. As if the changing weather patterns aren't challenging enough, I'm now aware of a new impediment to bringing the rain.

When I attempt to bring rain now, I can feel a resistance to my efforts, but rather than capitulate, I redouble my efforts, and I usually succeed. (As an update, I've managed to beat back this resistance, this blockage to my effort to bring rain, as my sensitivity to weather conditions has been restored, allowing me, simply by thinking about it, to bring rain almost at will.) Because the whole state of California is experiencing a water shortage, it seemed that anything short of a whole-state solution would be ineffective in stemming the drought that was inflicting so much harm on farmers and crops, and ranchers and livestock.

So beginning the first week of February, I set out to bring rain to the full length and breadth of California and snow to the mountains. I didn't work for a little rain, but for several inches, as one meteorologist had called the previous rain "a drop in the bucket." California, he said, would need fifteen inches just to catch up with its normal rainfall output. Before the month was out, rain would be in the forecast again, and not just rain, but a great deal of rain. By Friday evening, February 28, several areas in Southern California had experienced at least one inch or more of rain, with some areas collecting two inches or more, the level of rain alternating from light, to moderate, to severe.

On Saturday, March 1, 2014, more rain was forecasted, rain that was expected to last well into Sunday, with the hope that it wouldn't spoil the Academy Awards on Sunday evening, and the expected red-carpet parade of stars. One television channel's Weather Doppler Radar captured and tracked band after band of storms forming offshore and moving on land as a massive cyclone sent them onshore as though it was an extraterrestrial weapon spinning off one Earth-drenching storm after the other. It was precisely what I had hoped for, and had worked toward.

If you're wondering whether I have failed to bring rain, the answer is No, not even when my efforts were met with an unusual resistance for a time, or when I have doubted my abilities. Similarly, I have never failed to stop the rain in my area, whether for a short time, or for several years. After praying for rain, it's not unusual—during future meditations—to be alerted to its impending arrival. Often I'm given a visionary preview, a precursor, actually seeing the rain falling in my mind's eye, the rain wetting—with a glistening sheen—my sidewalk, driveway, and street. The message: The rain that you have prayed for is in the offing; your work is done. Going about my work, I'm keenly aware of the downside to so much rain falling during a brief open window, in this case during a four-day period. Burned areas could be severely impacted, mud slides being the major hazard, as well as threats from rock slides, and flooding. I agonize when rain is finally in the forecast. Unfailingly, meteorologists detail the possible danger to inhabitants in certain areas, before and afterward, as news cameras visually record dangerous fast-water rescues, and the extent of damage to houses from mud slides and flooding.

For some time, I've employed a new tactic to combat California's drought. Rather than pray for rainfall over a period of months, I prayed for an end to the drought. Ending the drought, I felt, was a better use of my prayerful efforts. Previously I was ending one dry spell only to find it necessary to end the next one. The El Niño now facing the state is poised to do just that, end the drought, if California can continue to receive, year after year, the same levels of rain expected in 2016. Beginning Monday, January 4, 2016 through Friday and possibly Saturday, the forecasts for Southern California is rain measured in inches in some areas, while, over the next sixteen days, Northern California is expected to receive around fifteen inches of rain. At least two feet of snowfall are estimated in some mountains throughout the state.

My biggest concern is this: Who will bring the rain after I've passed over. Our salvation on this planet is predicated on our spiritual growth and development. I see nothing to say that we're making progress in that regard; rather, we're in a spiritual drought, a spiritual decline, fueled by our obsession with alcohol, marijuana, illegal drugs, and our material pursuits at the expense of our spiritual advancement. If we don't spiritualize our existence, and soon, our material preoccupations will continue to define us as children of this world, instead of Children of God, of Spirit. Because most of us have never tasted the sweet nectar reserved for the Gods (our Souls), the endless bliss of Spirit, we pursue the inferior joys of the flesh, which never satisfy, dispensing more pain and misery than fulfillment.

STILL THE WIND

When a violent storm rose on the sea, a storm so great that Jesus' disciples woke him from his slumber in the "hinder part of the ship," pleading for his intercession lest they perish, Jesus, using spiritual means alone, rebuked the wind. Uttering the simple words, "Peace, be still,"[34] Jesus, we are told, caused the wind to cease, and brought calm to the sea, allowing the ship and those aboard to arrive safely at their destination.

For hours, the winds are known to blow fiercely in my parts, wreaking all kind of damage on houses, apartments, and other man-made structures. My home was no exception, finding itself in the path of howling winds more than once, the winds uprooting trees, felling fences, and gates and ripping tiles from the roof of my two-story abode.

It was this concern that consumed me—the potential wind damage to my house and other structures, resulting in costly repairs—when one night I was awakened by a roaring, raucous wind that buffeted windows and exterior walls. As I peered out of one of those windows, my upstairs bedroom window, I watched as the wind juddered and tossed the trees in my neighbor's yard with such ferocity that I feared their uprooting.

I returned to bed and began to pray, determined to evoke the perfection of God's creation. I hadn't been praying for very long when a loud whoop sound brought complete silence. The ferocious wind that had only a moment ago threatened to rend my house in two, front to back, was now as still and as quiet as the unexpected eerie calm one experiences for the first time, when in the tranquil eye of a hurricane.

I leaped from bed again, and from my window I watched the trees in my neighbor's yard, reachable by crossing the cul-de-sac that separated our yards, a short distance by any measurement, swing and plunge violently, while the trees in my yard were stock-still. As with the rain on a previous occasion, I improved my situation without improving the situation of those

---

34 Mark 4:39

around me, unless, as with the rain on class-scheduling day, they were in proximity to me. What if I had wanted the wind to stop everywhere nearby, would it have stopped. My guess: It would have, in the same way that I have brought the rain to areas outside my locality, or have stopped the rain generally by stopping it specifically.

As I have stopped the wind, I have caused the wind to blow. Living in Southern California, it snows mainly in the mountains and rarely in lower elevations. On certain hot summer days, I have evoked the wind, by visualizing the presence of snow and ice as far as the eye can see. When I have experienced the cold within, I have experienced a cooling down without, "as within, so without," as nature turns on her powerful fans affecting the wind chill factor if not the external temperature. In short, it feels cooler on windy days even when the temperature remains unaffected. Why is it, then, that I don't bring snow and ice when I visualize it, only wind? I suspect it's because my spiritual abilities aren't that refine yet, operating, therefore, within the spiritual parameters that currently exist, as well as the physical limits I can't exceed without having at my command the requisite spiritual abilities to do so.

I don't do this often, that is, bring the wind, as I do the rain, because of the ensuing damage that winds cause, notably the Santa Ana winds. These winds impact my local area, as well as other areas, extending over many square miles, uprooting trees, overturning trucks, ripping off roofs, producing power outages—all the damage usually associated with strong winds over a period of time.

In seems that our prayers take on the character of our desires, or the strength of our beliefs, neither going beyond our wishes, nor giving us less of what we desire, provided we can tap the *Source of All That Is* in the first instance.

EIGHT

COMMUNICATE WITH THE DEAD

THERE'S NOTHING TOO HARD FOR THE *YOU* IN YOU, A fact clearly established by its ability to talk with the dead. Although they are gone from sight, it's not impossible for the *you* in you to communicate with the dead. From my experience, to talk to the dead, the dead must be willing to talk, as you can't force them—or so it seems—if they're unwilling.

Occasionally, I have conversed with the dead while I slept, or while I was in and out-of-body state, or while in meditation. It was during a re-reading of the Seth material, consisting of several books channeled by Jane Roberts, that I found an obituary for her at the end of one. If I had been punched in the stomach at that moment, the shock wouldn't have been greater, a shock that quickly became anger, anger that Seth, the entity that Jane had channeled, had allowed her to die so young. What a loss her passing would be for the New Age movement, as Jane had, by channeling Seth, contributed volumes of information to our understanding of the nature of reality. Additionally, she revealed how we might manipulate that reality, clearly establishing its malleability.

Later that night when I turned in, anger still seethed inside me, threatening to become a gushing, hot geyser. The following morning, while awakening and beginning my daily meditation, I heard a woman's voice speak, not into my external ears, but my internal ones. The voice said simply, "Seth tried to get me to see through it [presumably the illness that took her life]," she assured, "but I couldn't."

Without needing to ask, I knew the voice belonged to Jane, and that she had used the moment of my awakening to exonerate Seth. Her words were magical: As quickly as the anger had exploded within, shattering my inner peace, it just as quickly dissipated, turning fire into ice. I tried to reach her husband, Robert F. Butts, with the news that I had made contact with Jane, but my early efforts yielded no results, and I soon abandoned all attempts.

In time, the souls of those who have departed seem to move out of range of those on Earth, making contact difficult or impossible. Jane had been deceased for years before I discovered that she had died. Either she was remaining close to those here on Earth, or the pain of my grief was strong enough to shatter any barriers that existed between us, invoking a response.

Reputations don't always die with us when others are willing to speak out on our behalf, although dead.

After a brief illness, my older brother died suddenly, making my fraternal twin my only remaining brother of five. Shortly before dying, this brother's eyes, as did a brother who had died before him, became fixated on the TV, staring at it as though mesmerized, as though he'd never see one again, not once diverting his eyes as he watched with total absorption.

It was an unnerving thing to watch.

Not long after he had died, I visited him in an out-of-body state. I don't recall whether the visit was intentional or not, but I don't think so. Perhaps missing him had been the ticket to transport me to his final destination.

When I arrived at his new location, he was in front of me, a short distance away, moving rapidly towards me, actually gliding in space. He was instantly recognizable, his appearance unchanged from what it had been in the physical realm. His surroundings were nondescript, similar to a blank white canvas waiting for the sure strokes of an artist to paint on it.

Near his heart, I saw what could only be described as flesh in the final stages of decay, appearing as a large wound, as though his body was still in a transitional state, a transformational phase that conflated for a time his physical reality with his now nonphysical reality.

He appeared not to notice me as he floated over my head and came to rest at the scene of an outdoor restaurant or grill. I followed him. I felt that the restaurant should have been enclosed, but that appeared superfluous, this feature taking a back seat to others, ones more central. My impression was this: It was more important to establish a place from which to eat than to have it enclosed.

He sat down at a counter on a high stool, while a chef, in a chef's hat, along with other restaurant workers, all in proper attire, set out to feed their new guest. It seemed to have been a place that he, himself, had created, rather than one that was created for him.

While he ate, I asked, mentally, if he had seen his wife (his surviving spouse) today. I heard him say, No, also mentally.

He then asked me if I knew a certain person, and called him by name. At the time, I didn't remember that I did. He said, finally, "He's standing in your door!"

I had heard that statement once before, years before. My then wife and I had decided to ask her previous employer and friend, now living alone since the death of her husband, if she would live with us. We had recently moved into a larger house with an accompanying bungalow off from the main house that we were considering offering to her as a home, provided she was willing to move West.

While in meditation, I saw a man in my mind's eye. His head was as bald as Yul Brynner's had been in his later years, and then I heard The Voice say, "He's standing in your door."

Although I had never seen the man before, he did fit the description of the woman's now deceased husband. I took it to mean that he wasn't happy with our decision to ask his surviving wife to move to the West Coast, which meant she would be leaving behind the house that they had shared while he was alive.

Why would someone, whether alive or dead, stand in my mental door, if not to influence my thinking, or my thoughts, thoughts coming in, or thoughts going out?

Shortly after dying, my oldest sister appeared in a dream with the question,

"Do you pray?"

"You *know* I pray," I replied.

She then asked that I pray for my sister-in-law and my twin brother. As it turned out, the order of the prayer request was significant: My sister-in-law was soon to be diagnosed with a serious condition that came to light soon after the prayer request.

Shortly after passing, Michael Jackson, one of the celebrities I had been asked to pray for over the years, came through during one of my daily meditations, with this revelation about his death: "Propofol stopped my heart," he said. I don't know if that was the case, but Michael said that it was.

Before the death of her husband, I think I may have visited my friend and her husband twice. I was happy to have her as a friend, with or without her two special gifts: She was able to write mirror image with both hands simultaneously (one hand would have been remarkable in itself), and she was blessed with the gift of astral projection, able to leave her body in the same way that I did, perhaps with greater facility. Right away, upon first meeting her husband, I could tell that his was an amazing soul—exceedingly kind, good, and pure. Even when he knew that he was dying, he used his last hours comforting others—nurses and other medical attendants—who agonized because they could do no more for him

Sometime after the death of her husband, my friend revealed her brother's struggle with drugs, and asked that I pray for him, which I did, using my evening meditations to intercede prayerfully on his behalf. While in prayer, a dark form of a man, his torso and head, moved towards me as a shadow might pass along the surface of a wall, but the shadow had substance and could be recognized as a man, although I couldn't identify him.

His sudden presence might have startled others, but I was certain that his intentions were harmless, he merely wanted to give me a kiss, which I found exceedingly strange, and although I resisted internally, he continued to move towards me and placed a kiss on my left cheek. Before and after the kiss, he didn't speak, or identify himself. With the kiss, the moving form disappeared, but not my bewilderment. The dark form had receded into the blackness behind my eyelids, the blackness that preceded its arrival into my awareness, leaving in its wake a number of questions: "Who was this man? Why did he wish to kiss me?" The kiss was that of a friend, harmless and innocent, a friend whose only wish was to use the kiss to acknowledge that friendship; it was an act of gratitude, kindness, and friendly affection.

The next day, my friend and I talked by phone. I told her about my experience the evening before, the kiss that I had received from a stranger, a man, during my prayer for her brother—the kiss occurring within my mind's eye, but no less real because of it. Using her husband's name, she said that it was he who had kissed me, that he had come to her that morning and kissed her, as well as another family member. The kiss, she explained, was his way of identifying himself; he had used it on other occasions for identification purposes and to express his love. I guess it was his calling card of a sort.

Although I didn't need it, her husband's visit was additional proof of an afterlife and the fact that we survive death. I already had ample personal evidence of that. Nevertheless, I was grateful for the proof and thanked him for it, believing that he could hear me. And why not? If he could communicate non-verbally with a kiss, certainly I could communicate with him by using the connection that had long been established between kindred souls—a connection provided by God Himself, His Love, and His Omnipresence.

NINE

SUPPORT OTHERS WITH PRAYER

FROM WHAT I'VE SAID SO FAR, YOU MAY BE TEMPTED TO believe that the *you* in you is self-centered, primarily concerned with itself, and not concerned with others, but that conclusion would represent a misapprehension of the facts—the *you* in you can, and does, support others with prayer, as the following out-of-body account reveals. The out-of-body incident could have easily been placed under the heading, "Communicate with the Dead," but for the unexpected inquiry that followed, revealing once more that the *you* in you may be employed in many capacities.

A woman who volunteered for the organization I worked for died suddenly. I attended her funeral, but what was more memorable than the hours we spent together over the years in our official capacities, was our meeting in the astral realm after she had died. The meeting occurred during an out-of-body excursion, and was of such import that it set me on a new spiritual course.

The site for the meeting was outdoors, a park-like setting, but inside a structure. The structure was raised off the ground, and where windows might have been on both sides, it was open to the air. Near these openings, tables and chairs were placed, arranged to seat four per table, two on either side, which ran the full length of the structure. People I didn't know sat in chairs around the tables, chatting and playing games.

At the entrance to the structure, steps were erected, about five or six levels high, providing ingress. I mounted them and walked down the aisle which divided the structure midway, and separated those seated at tables. I stopped at one table. Believing that I was in heaven, and that those who were seated at the tables were dead, denizens of the next world, I turned to a man on my right and asked the question: "What is heaven like?"

He stopped playing and stared at me, clearly in thought, as though he had never been asked that question before, and wanted the answer to be as precise, and truthful as he could express it. He said, simply, "Happiness." With that, he continued his game with his fellow players.

Years later, I thought, If *happiness* is the same as being in heaven, then we don't have to die to experience heaven, we can have heaven, "happiness," right here on Earth: We have only to decide to be.

As I was leaving, descending the steps, the erstwhile volunteer followed, although I hadn't seen her in the structure. I was delighted to see her. At the base of the steps, she asked the question that has kept me busy for a couple of decades praying for numerous disparate souls—for those I knew (friends and family members) and those I didn't know (celebrities, as well as presidents).

"Would you like to be a Sentinel," she asked, using the French pronunciation of sentinel, that is, *sentinelle*.

The volunteer had a French last name, but I didn't know if she was of French extraction, or had merely married into the name. Without hesitation, I answered, Yes, and she promptly proffered a piece of paper, a certificate designating my new status, and I accepted.

Little did I know at the time what a Sentinel was, or what I was required to do as one, but, after a few days, that all changed. It started with the phone. I receive calls at all hours asking for people I didn't know. This was strange as I rarely received calls at all, and hardly ever from callers who had reached a wrong number.

Instinctively I knew that I was being asked to pray for these callers, to respond to their telephonic call for help. Before long, I was hearing these calls for help internally, an inner voice calling out their names. I would hear these names spoken in my mental ear. Because I didn't know the specifics for which I should pray, I merely sent them God's Love, or, on occasion, God's blessings, or God's protection, as I was moved at the time.

Some of the celebrities for whom prayer was requested were Michael Jackson and Whitney Houston, not once, but many, many times, with an uptick for Michael during his 2005 court trial in which he was a defendant.

During one of my meditations, Michael came to me and spoke at length. This was doing the trial. He said that he had invited the family, who later accused him of child molestation, into his home and into his heart, and he felt that they had, with their false indictment, betrayed him and his benevolence.

It was this betrayal that seemed to hurt him the most, as he had given his home and his trust, and for that he was on trial to prove his innocence, not a fair recompense for an act of kindness, an act of caring, and an act of love.

From time to time, while out of the body, I hear a voice speaking to me. I don't always see the one speaking, but I can feel his presence. When I was in my twenties, these discourses seem to last for hours, and rarely did I remember them. Sometimes I did and in great detail. For weeks my stomach had been the source of pain and discomfort. I prayed for a healing, but the pain persisted. During a session with my unseen discourser, The Voice said at the end of it, "You shall say to your stomach move to the right and it shall move." To my amazement I felt my stomach move to the right of my midsection.

The Voice continued, "You shall say to your liver move to the right, and it shall move."

As with my stomach, I felt my liver move to the right. It was then, that I returned gently to my body and The Voice ceased speaking.

But something was seriously amiss. I was lying there on my bed with my stomach and my liver pressed hard against the right side of my body, no longer in their customary place. I panicked a bit at the possibility that my stomach and my liver would remain in this new position indefinitely. The thought came: "If you can tell your body's organs to behave in a certain way, you can certainly tell them to return to their natural position."

I said in my mind, "Right yourself!" As quickly as my stomach and liver had shifted to the right, they snapped back to their usual location, but not without a complaint: I could hear noises emanate from my stomach, the sounds it makes sometimes while digesting food. It was as though my stomach had been startled and had responded thus: "This has never happened to me before, and it shouldn't have."

I knew then the level of control that we might exercise over the body, provided we were spiritually equipped to do so. Until this out-of-body episode, I had struggled with ulcers. This episode ended the struggle and the pain.

At one point, while out-of-body, The Voice referred to me as Vishnu. "You are Vishnu," it said. This was perplexing on two levels: first, because I had never before heard the name Vishnu; and second, I didn't understand why I was being addressed in this manner.

The Voice said further, "We will give you what you need to carry out your mission."

I thought, "What mission?" I had the impression that the giving would be in the form of an energy exchange of some sort. Later I learned that Vishnu was one of three Hindu gods and was known as the preserver (or protector), as well as the restorer, and that according to Hindu lore would make one more incarnation.

No, I don't believe that I'm the reincarnation of Vishnu. Vishnu is more likely an all-pervading spirit that infuses our world, perhaps with the help and cooperation of many in the world devoting themselves to prayer to preserve and restore when necessary the Light in our world, a Light that would be extinguished without them.

I wrote the preceding observations weeks ago. Since that time, I've revised my thinking about Vishnu, and my relationship to this god. Recent events indicate that if I'm not the actual god, Vishnu, then I am a possible a stand-in for him in this age, either because I was selected, or because I returned as an avatar in human form. According to one account, Vishnu will return to Earth in human form as himself. This return will be his final one, a return that will fulfill his tenth reincarnation. Vishnu's final reincarnation certainly coincides with my own likelihood of reincarnating, as I have long felt that this incarnation will be my last.

One morning while meditating, I asked God, "What would you have me do for you today." He responded, "Feed my family." I didn't take this request literally, that I should actually "feed" God's family, no more than the words from the Lord's Prayer, "Give us this day our daily bread," is a supplication for physical food only, but something on the order of Jesus' statement to his disciples when they implored him to eat, "he said unto them, I have meat to eat that ye know not of."[35]

I knew that I was being asked to feed God's *family* with Love and with Truth, the bread and the meat which sustain the soul—those which come down from Heaven—and to give drink to all who thirst from the well of "living water,"[36] a libation prepared by the Christ. Just before the "Give us this day our daily bread" in the Lord's Prayer, is the following passage: "Thy kingdom come. Thy will be done in earth, as *it is* in heaven."[37] Here then was my *Vishnu mission*, to prepare the way for the Kingdom of God (the Kingdom of Light), to declare that God's kingdom is come, and that His will is done in earth as in heaven.

---

35 John 4:32
36 John 7:38
37 Matt 6:10

As I affirmed this, again and again, the emotional intensity of it became almost too much to bear, but I didn't give up; I just redoubled my efforts to acknowledge the existence of the Kingdom of God, both within and without, to recognize a Holy and divine presence pervading all things, and, by my effort, offset the world's darkness with Light, the world's evil with Good, the world's illusions with Truth, and the world's fears with Love.

By affirming the Scriptural passage from the Lord's Prayer in the present tense, and not as a petition, "Thy kingdom [is] come. Thy will [is] done in earth, as *it is* in heaven," the affirmation released an incredible energy. I can't emphasize enough the awesome power of the energy in the *energy exchange*. It's as The Voice promised. The energy that was released (the power) during the exchange was amazing, it was the stuff of creation, quickening the vibratory rate of every cell of my body. I have only experienced this power—this energy burst—during the creation of one other thing, and that's rain, but the energy released during the bringing of rain never rose to the level that I was now experiencing. Even as I write this the release of this creative energy at this very moment is almost unbearable, requiring a stamina borne of sheer determination to manifest the Kingdom of God (God's Light) among men.

It was as if I had been on standby during the intervening years, in a state of quiet readiness, to be called up, enlisted, at a moment's notice when the situation warranted it. The call up lasted about a week or less. The first indication that the energy exchange would be short-lived was hinted at in a dream that I had about five days before its cessation, in which, my daughter, now grown, was an infant of two-years-old again.

"I'm two," she said, "but in five days, I'll be twenty-two."

With each passing day, I could feel the nexus that existed between me and the energy exchange grow stronger, a behind the scenes reminder that it was still with me, as I could activate it seemingly with little effort. The sense of it, the presence of the energy exchange continued unabated until the fifth day. Upon awakening the morning of the fifth day, the first words I hear from The Voice are these, "Twenty-two inches of snow on the ground."

There was the number twenty-two again—11 + 11. I reached for the energy that had been with me for several days only to find a diminution of it, a near emptiness, where it had once filled me completely, making itself known by its presence. For now, the energy exchange was on hiatus. How long I didn't know, but I felt that if the need arose again, requiring the infusion of Light, the Kingdom of God, into the world, to balance the light and darkness, it would signal its willingness to continue where it left off, using the precursor that marked the beginning of the first exchange.

Curious about the number twenty-two, I searched it out on the Internet. I discovered that the number 22 numerologically is a Master number, a number that is special in many ways, ways which resonated with my experience with the Vishnu energy exchange. Although the Master number 22 is only one of several—the others being 11, 33, and 44—they generally have meaning only within a person's numerology chart. From the fifth day onward, the energy exchanged began to diminish until it was much less than 22, closer to 11 in strength and creative energy.

There's an update to the *energy exchange* I previously experienced. As I continued to use this passage from the Lord's Prayers, but changing it, as I did formerly, from a petition to an affirmation, in this manner, "Thy kingdom [is] come. Thy will [is] done in earth, as *it is* in heaven," the energy exchange returned in full force, vibrating every cell of my body with an energy that's difficult to bear. Nothing had changed, the intensity of the energy exchange was remarkable for its power, and its impact upon my physical body. It's as though my physical body would explode from the energy that infused it from within. As it built, it was released into the ether, but the release didn't lessen its strength but actually increased it. I felt as though I was replacing one energy (a dark energy) with another, one more salutary and beneficial than the one I was displacing, the dark energy with the Light energy. It was as though these words from Job was coming to fruition in our day:

> *Yea, the light of the wicked shall be put out, and the spark of his fire shall not shine. The light shall be dark in his tabernacle, and his candle shall be put out with him* (Job 18:5).

Subsequent revelations suggest that the energy in the *energy exchange* I'm experiencing is, indeed, what Jesus referred to as "living water." After asking a Samaritan woman who drew water from Jacob's well for a drink, and was rebuked because he was a Jew, Jesus answered her thus:

> *If thou knewest the gift of God, and who it is that saith to thee, Give me to drink; thou wouldest have asked of him, and he would have given thee living water.*

Believing the living water to be as material as the water from the well, the woman replied with skepticism as to Jesus' ability to deliver on his claim.

> *Jesus answered and said unto her, Whosoever drinketh of this water shall thirst again:*
>
> *But whosoever drinketh of the water that I shall give him shall never thirst; but the water that I shall give him shall be in him a well of water springing up into everlasting life"* (John 4:13-14).

In the Book of Revelation, we encounter the notion of living water again, but this time it's referred to as *water of life*, with rather clear instructions as to how we might avail ourselves of this living water:

> *And he that sat upon the throne said, Behold, I make all things new. And he said unto me, Write: for these words are true and faithful.*

*And he said unto me, It is done. I am Alpha and Omega, the begin-
ning and the end. I will give unto him that is athirst of the fountain
of the water of life freely.*

*He that overcometh shall inherit all things; and I will be his God, and
he shall be my son* (Rev 21:5-7).

Again revealing the source of this *living water*, this *water of life*:

*And he shewed me a pure river of water of life, clear as crystal, pro-
ceeding out of the throne of God and of the Lamb* (Rev 22:1).

The *well* has, indeed, proven to be a "fountain," from whence living
water flows, and if I remain relatively pure in heart, that is, not steeped
too much in the ways of the world, I can draw "freely" from this fountain.
Because I'm drawing from the *fountain* on behalf of the world, I have from
time to time questioned the impact that the energy exchange is having on
the world, whether it's as salubrious as I would hope. Taking the thought
to bed one night, I woke up the next morning with a vision of the Internet
symbol (an Emoji) used to indicate approval of a particular comment in
the comment section of a site, the thumbs up image (a fisted hand with the
thumb up), and with the symbol came this assurance from The Voice, that
my efforts on behalf of humanity was bearing fruit, "You have a million
ups," The Voice reassured.

TEN

HEAL MYSELF AND OTHERS IN NEED

T HE YOU IN *YOU*, YOUR SOUL, CAN PERFORM AMAZING works, what we often refer to as miracles. One of the Soul's powers is the ability to heal. There was a time when I was a wonderful healer, when I could connect rather easily with my Soul's energy, a connection that allowed me to readily heal myself and others, but that was before the world broke through and despoiled my house. Alas, the time for healing has past. I've become an old man in the ways of the world, and am no longer the Little Child,[38] that I once was, not in chronological age, but in spiritual timelessness. I still miss him. He was close to God, and God was close to him.

Nevertheless, I was shown in a vision recently, in a rather dramatic fashion, that it's never too late to achieve our spiritual goals. Rather than give the full details of it here, I will summarize the vision, thereby yielding to a tactful telling of it. It featured the *Mission Impossible* star, Tom Cruise, and another person. The message: It's never too late to achieve one's mission in life. There are no *missions impossible*, and that applies to those spiritual missions we believe are now impossible, or any other. It took me some

---

38 Mark 10:15

time to sort through this vision. Visions can foreshadow events to come, or they can impart a message, in this case a symbolic message.

What I learned is this: We can become the *Little Child* in spirit that we once were, that we can be reborn, as well, but it requires our utmost devotion to Sprit, and that we stay the course until we're fortified my Love, and are wearing the mantle of spiritual sense, a sense which may be used to rejuvenate ourselves with Soul energy, the only true Fountain of Youth, and restore to the "old man, and full *of years*,"[39] the lost years of childhood.

I credit a college class for giving me what was then a unique view of our birth, our childhood, and the years that followed. It came from the unlikeliest of sources, one replete with new insights into the human condition. My college major was English Literature. Among the many English writers I was required to read was William Wordsworth. Wordsworth was described as a Romantic English poet, but I think that he was a great deal more than that. One poem in particular reveals Wordsworth to be a mystic as well a poet. In his *Ode: Intimations of Immortality*, from *Recollections of Early Youth*, Wordsworth captures poetically *our birth*, and our transition from childhood to adulthood, and its attendant outcomes. Only one line from this Ode has stood out over the years, one which I committed to memory because of its resonance and sheer beauty: "But trailing clouds of glory do we come / From God, who is our home." For those of you who would like further insights into how the soul, more often than not, progresses in this world, from infancy to adulthood, I highly recommend this Ode by Wordsworth.

Children, and childhood, were given a special place in the teachings of Jesus, as well. Jesus rightfully responds to the question of *"Who is the greatest in the kingdom of heaven?"* this way:

At the same time came the disciples unto Jesus, saying, Who is the greatest in the kingdom of heaven?

---

39 Gen 25:8

And Jesus called a little child unto him, and set him in the midst of them,

And said, Verily I say unto you, Except ye be converted, and become as little children, ye shall not enter into the kingdom of heaven.

Whosoever therefore shall humble himself as this little child, the same is greatest in the kingdom of heaven (Matt 18:3).

Had I taken Jesus's advice, I could have been more of a heavenly blessing to the world, a wayshower to those weary of the human burden that comes with each incarnation into the flesh. "Come unto me, all *ye* that labour and are heavy laden, and I will give you rest,"[40] was Jesus's invitation. In the Parable of the Sower, Jesus reveals the human shortcomings that despoils us, and deprives us of God's Kingdom, as well as the fullness of our spiritual prowess:

Behold, there went out a sower to sow:

And it came to pass, as he sowed, some fell by the way side, and the fowls of the air came and devoured it up.

And some fell on stony ground, where it had not much earth; and immediately it sprang up, because it had no depth of earth:

But when the sun was up, it was scorched; and because it had no root, it withered away.

And some fell among thorns, and the thorns grew up, and choked it, and it yielded no fruit.

And other fell on good ground, and did yield fruit that sprang up and increased; and brought forth, some thirty, and some sixty, and some an hundred (Mark 4:3-8).

---

40 Matt 11-28

Unless we can commit ourselves fully to a spiritual life, we forfeit the wealth that's derived from the possession of a spiritual sense. Knowing this, Jesus admonished, "No man can serve two masters: for either he will hate the one, and love the other; or else he will hold to the one, and despise the other. Ye cannot serve God and mammon."[41] When I obeyed one master, my spiritual selfhood, I wrought several healings.

REMOVED WARTS

My wife discovered several warts growing on her left hand. They hadn't been there for very long, but were unsightly. I decided to pray for her, and spent about fifteen minutes sitting in a chair, eyes closed, as I prayerfully acknowledged her spiritual perfection. The next day upon examining her hand, I found that the warts had disappeared: The flesh of her left hand was as clear as the right. Warts, I later learned, have been known to disappear on their own over time, but that it might take years for that to happen. Given the choice of their going away on their own in eighteen months or more, or resorting to potentially harmful treatments, or in a day, or sooner, with prayer, I believe that most people would opt for prayer.

HEALED INFLAMED GUMS

Sitting down to eat after work one evening, I struggled to open my mouth wide enough to permit food. All that day I nursed inflamed gums on the right side of my mouth. The swelling was so great that it made eating practically impossible, although I could drink water and other liquids.

Concerned that I should take steps to ease the swelling, if I wished to eat that evening, I again resorted to prayer. With a spiritual magazine in hand, I relaxed in my recliner and began to read, devouring page after page of words that reminded me of my spiritual perfection and my exemption

---

41 Matt 6:24

from anything unlike God, good. My reading was soon interrupted by an oozing in my mouth on the side where the gum was sore and swollen. Touching the area with my tongue, I was happy to learn that the swelling was gone as was the pain. I walked to the restroom where I rinsed my mouth, and expectorated. A further test of the gums assured me again that I was free of the swelling, that my gums were no longer infected. Opening my mouth as wide as I could several times, I found I could open it with ease, and could eat if I chose to. I sat down and ate, and that was the end of it.

ASSAILED TOBACCO HABIT

My oldest sister, a heavy smoker, had lived with me for several weeks when I asked her if she'd like for me to pray for her, to use prayer to end her tobacco addiction. She consented, but more from curiosity than her trust in my ability to remove, what, for her, was a long-standing habit, years in the making. As she reclined on a couch, I sat down in a chair placed about six feet in front of her, and began to pray. After about fifteen minutes, I stood up, replaced the chair to its previous position, and she lit up.

On her first draw, she complained, "That tastes awful!" And then she said, "Well, I'm going to keep smoking until I like them again."

Had she consented to more prayers, I believe that I could have, in a day or so, ended her desire for cigarettes, have ended her enslavement to tobacco, notwithstanding the pleasure she believed that she derived from smoking.

HEALED KNEE INJURY

One day into the job, the tractor operator I had hired to assist with the landscaping of my front yard asked me to lift a rather large and heavy boulder into the tractor's shovel. As I lifted it, I injured my right knee. I didn't know I had injured it at the time, as it took several hours for evidence of the injury to surface. When it did, I found that I couldn't lift my right leg to get in bed, but required that a mattress be placed on the floor, the family-room carpet, upon which I would sleep. Even then, the pain was so intense that I wouldn't have resisted death had it come calling. Despite the pain, I continued to walk on the leg, limping if necessary, to remain ambulatory. Walking and standing on the leg seemed to intensify the pain, signaling that something was amiss in the knee, and since it was never x-rayed, or examined by a physician, I never knew the extent of the damage, or the particulars of the injury.

After spending several days sleeping on the mattress, rather than in my bed, enduring great pain all the while, and continuing to work through the pain, not willing to use my sick days to stay off the leg, I did manage to sleep in my regular bed for a change, although lifting the injured leg onto the bed's mattress to lie down still presented a painful ordeal. Later that night, on the way to the bathroom, limping from the pain and dreading having to lift my leg again to return to bed, I mentally recited words from a spiritual book I was reading, words that assured me that the pain I was then experiencing in my leg and the accompanying limp were illegitimate. Halfway to the bathroom, the pain ceased as did the limp. The leg was completely healed in that instant. Returning to bed, I climbed in without difficult and without pain, rested through the night, and went to work the next morning, not missing one day as result of the injury.

HEALED HAND AND WRIST

After the Paris terror attacks of November 13, 2015, I accelerated my prayers for the world. On Saturday, November 14, 2015, while sitting up in bed, my back resting against the headboard, I focused my attention first on Paris, and then on the whole world, immersed for a time in deep contemplation and realization that *Love is all there is*, and for that reason, *Love is irrevocable*, that Love was fully expressed before the terrorists attacked in Paris and afterward. As I prayed in this manner, seeing the omnipotence and omnipresence of Love, I turned my attention to my right hand and wrist. While working in my yard the day before, unbeknownst to me at the time, the hand and wrist had sustained a painful injury. There was a deep soreness in the hand and the wrist, and on the hand, a swelling could be seen and felt.

While I prayed for Paris and the world, I also prayed for my hand and wrist, knowing that *Love is all there is* for the injury, as well, that Love existed before the injury and after the injury, and therefore an injury couldn't take place within Love, omnipotence, as Love can't be recalled, can't have lapses in Its infinite expression of Itself, as *Love is irrevocable.* While meditating in this fashion, I felt a warmth pass over the injured area of my hand and wrist, much like a warm waft of air. Preceding the warmth, I felt a surge of *exchange energy, living water energy.* The healing began in that instant. For an injury of this nature, it usually takes a week or two for the healing to be realized. Whereas before I could barely lift a cup or a glass with the injured hand without experiencing sharp pains, and a severe weakness in the wrist, I now had almost full use of it, as much of the pain and swelling had dissipated in that moment of healing, returning ninety percent of use to the hand. The flow of what seems to be a warmth over an affected area at the time of a healing isn't uncommon. I have experienced a similar warmth during a previous healing, as has others. During the remaining day of the healing I used the hand to lift and carry heavy buckets of water, water salvaged to reduce our water usage in the midst of California's persistent drought. When I did, the pain and the soreness in the wrist and hand were barely perceptible.

On Sunday, November 15, 2015, ninety-nine percent of use was returned to the hand. I actually wrote this account of the healing in longhand with my right hand and did so without pain or difficulty, something I wasn't able to do for part of the previous day without the presence of a prohibitive pain. It wasn't quite Sunday evening yet, but late afternoon when, after checking my right hand and wrist for any evidence of the injury, I found that the healing was complete. Searched as I might with my left hand touching and pressing down on the erstwhile injured area, I could find no evidence of the pain or the swelling, they had simply disappeared. It was though the injury never was. With the healing, I went about my chores effortlessly, lifting heavy buckets of water with my right hand without pain, or discomfort, or any hint that, only a day before, the injured hand had made lifting water buckets a painful and impossible task.

What I've learned over the years is that Love and Perfection go hand in hand, that Perfection is the handmaiden of Love, eternally one in substance and manifestation. During my prayer for the world and my hand, I knew the Omni-Perfection of Love, that one marked the presence of the other, that Love knows only Itself, knows only Perfection, Good, Life, Spirit, and Soul. I further learned that he who heals best loves best. Jesus called upon *all* His disciples, those living in His day, and age, and those living in all ages to follow the only commandment that He left them, a New Commandment:

> *A new commandment I give unto you, That ye love one another; as I have loved you, that ye also love one another.*
> *By this shall all men know that ye are my disciples, if ye have love one to another* (John 13:34-35).

A few years back, I healed an obstinate pain in my hip, and an irregular heartbeat, an arrhythmia, one that I was aware of, but which was also detected by a nurse during a medical checkup. To effect a healing of these two conditions, I spent several hours one afternoon contemplating Love and Love's Perfection, realizing that Love and Perfection were the only reality where these two unwanted conditions seemed to exist, actually directing love to the two areas in need of healing. To be sure, where you find one (Love), you'll find the other (Perfection), but until our spirituality, and our level of understanding advance to the point where we see Love and Perfection as One, it's important to direct Love as well as Perfection to the area in need of healing, acknowledging at the same time the existence and the presence of both, Love and Perfection. We need to acknowledge and know, too, that we're always dwelling in the Kingdom of Love, that "in him [divine Love] we live, and move, and have our being; ... For we are also his offspring."[42]

After praying in this manner for several hours, I arose from by bed, where I had been laying for a time, totally healed—no pain in the hip, no irregular heartbeat. The painful hip, which had made walking difficult, and the irregular heartbeat were now things of the past, appearing as though they had never existed, which was the Truth of the matter, as Love is always Love, never surrendering its omnipresence or omnipotence to a supposed physical or material condition or existence. The challenge, then, is to know this Great Truth, the Allness of Love, that Love is the only reality, before, during, and after a supposed evil event, or act, has occurred.

---

42 Acts 17:28

ELEVEN

REVEAL PREVIOUS LIVES

When Jesus came into the coasts of Caesarea Philippi, he asked his
disciples, saying, Whom do men say that I the Son of man am?
And they said, Some say that thou art John the Baptist: some,
Elias; and others, Jeremias, or one of the prophets.[43]

O F ALL THE THINGS THAT THE *YOU* IN YOU CAN DO,
having it reveal certain events of previous lives is perhaps its most
important achievement. These revelations disclose more than who we were
during those lives, they offer insights into our current life, and how that
information may be used to resolve conflicts carried over from previous
lives. Further, they allow us to incorporate into our current life the knowledge gleaned from previous lives, and to use that knowledge to evolve the
soul. At some point, out-of-body experiences have the power to convince
the most skeptical explorer of the validity of reincarnation. It's hard to deny
the existence of reincarnation, that it's merely the creation of an overactive
imagination, after experiencing lives in other times, and other places.

---

43 Matt 16:13-14

In retrospect, I found that many of my out-of-body excursions weren't happenstance, but were orchestrated by the ME in *me*, especially those that revealed a previous life. When these lives were woven together, and not taken singularly, they revealed an amazing tapestry of information and knowledge. Some excursions explained phobias that still haunt me today in my current lifetime, phobias that had their genesis in previous lives: the fear of dolls (pediophobia), the fear of being alone (monophobia), and the lesser fear of the three, the fear of public places or open areas (agoraphobia).

PRISONER IN THE BOWELS OF A SHIP

The last two phobias are probably related. In a previous life, I spent years in the bowels of a ship. The occasional visit of a guard who slipped food under a cell door, was my only human contact. When I heard the guard approaching, as I could hear his footsteps drawing nearer and nearer, my heart began to race, and panic set in. Perhaps I feared his coming, not because I might be punished, but because it might represent my last meal, after which I would be taken and killed, a death sentence for a crime, real or fabricated, that I had no knowledge of committing, as none was revealed.

The knowing was of less importance, it seemed, than the knowledge that I had been incarcerated during that lifetime. Incarceration, then, became one of the themes that have shed light on some of the events that have occurred within my present life, the light enhancing my understanding of these events. There are other themes, as well.

My research turned up only one instance where someone was imprisoned within the bowels of a ship as punishment. It was from a fictional account titled, *The Man without a Country*, by Edward Everett Hale. The protagonist of the short story, tried for treason, denounced his country and was subsequently sentenced to ships at sea, never again to set foot on his native soil or to hear the name of his country spoken again.

The story is supposedly fiction, but perhaps it was based on a real-life character. This theme of incarceration was reminiscent of another lifetime where I served as a Union officer who was captured by the enemy, fated to serve time as a prisoner of war. I learned the location of the prison with no small amount of serendipity.

INVENTOR–LIGHT DISPLAY

I'm standing before a long table. A painter's canvas on an easel is positioned at the end of the table near me. I'm in a large hall, a massive room. In front of me the windows extend the full length of the wall. They're placed so high that they don't provide an opening on the world without, but serve only to let in the light. Homes in England were outfitted with glass windows in the seventeenth century. Nobility certainly had them before commoners. Spectators are seated at an even longer table in front of me—men as well as women. They're dressed in clothing that I would associate with the Renaissance, but I can't be sure, and I don't know either the century nor my location, only that I'm white, and those at the table in front of me are also white.

I recognized one person at the table because, for a moment, her likeness was superimposed on one of the women. She's my longtime companion in this lifetime, the one with whom I've spent many lifetimes. She's seated at the table with the others, and I can tell by the way she's dress that she's a member of nobility. Along with others at the table, she's taking a keen interest in my experiment with light, as we wait for the sun to position itself so that its rays will slash through one of the windows, and strike the canvas just right to transfer the image there to another surface. As the observer in the out-of-body experience, I don't know the theory, nor the method, behind the light transference or how the image on the canvas is to be projected, using sunlight, but we're all eagerly awaiting the light show as soon as the sun's rays are in place.

I have always had a keen interest in light, and how it's reflected on glass. The barbershop where I once shined shoes as a teenager had a large window facing the sidewalk and the streets. When the light was just right it would capture surrounding images, cars parking, or people passing by, reflecting them with such faithfulness that I was reminded of movies, and, until the light shifted again, was treated to my own private viewing. Showing me this lifetime seemed to serve three purposes: It reinforced the number of times that I had incarnated, the period in which I had incarnated, and that I had incarnated with a person with whom I have spent many lifetimes in one capacity or another.

UNION OFFICER

During one of my out-of-body episodes, I found myself on the first floor of a multi-story structure, in a small room with bare walls, and a dirt floor. The room's only furnishing was a small mirror on a wall facing the street. I looked into it to see who I was in that lifetime. Staring back at me was an unfamiliar face, a white face, one mostly covered with an opulent, bushy, red beard that hadn't been trimmed for a very long time, and on my head a mound of red hair, unkempt, and uncombed, giving it, and the beard, a disheveled appearance.

I'm a Union officer, wearing a blue Union uniform, the uniform fading and a little worse for wear. I looked behind me and saw a door. Somehow I knew that I was a prisoner in this building. Suddenly the desire to escape overwhelmed me—my thoughts and my body—as I bolted out the door that faced a walkway, where men and women walked to and fro on personal and private business. Sailing ships moved along the waterway just beyond the walkway. This I found curious, ships so close inland and on what seemed a river, or perhaps a canal. I made a dash for the river in an escape attempt. I desperately missed my wife and children and other family members.

When I reached the river, I dove in and swam with all my might away from my prison and the walkway, swimming as fast as I could, as though my life depended on it, which I soon learned was the case. As I swam, I could hear bullets whiz over my head and plop in the water to my side and just ahead of me, barely missing me, spurring me to swim faster—actually swim for my life. I hadn't been hit yet, but I was afraid that, any moment, I might be. I felt my arms and hands reaching out to cut through the water and pull it back behind me, the strokes propelling me through the murky water, the strokes taking me to freedom on the other side of the river.

This experience as a prisoner of war during this nation's Civil War stands out as my most convincing proof of a past-life existence. Of all my out-of-body experiences, I've thought about this one often. It was because I could connect it to an actual place and time in history, that of the U.S. Civil War and my confinement as a POW during that war. At first, I never thought to research my experience, to determine, for example, if the prison in which I was held captive actually existed. I had tucked away this out-of-body experience in one of the recesses of my memory only to have it returned rather abruptly one day while leafing through *Chase's Calendar of Annual Events*. One of the entries jarred me upright. It was a historical entry, briefly discussing a daring escape that had occurred during the Civil War from a Confederate prison known as Libby Prison. Something deep within me told me that this was the Confederate prison in which I had been held prisoner, and from which I had attempted to escape. It told of a Civil War prison that housed Union military officers.

What startled me at the time, shaking me to my core, was an engraving of the channel that depicted the scene from my out-of-body experience: ships on a waterway with a walkway, or a road, next to a prison that I learned housed, at one time, Union officers only, known as Libby Prison. The prison was as I had seen it, and knew it to be: multi-floored and housing POWs. The prison had seen one daring escape that resulted in a large number of Union officers making good their flight from captivity to freedom. More than one hundred men escaped through a tunnel that they had excavated, the tunnel ending in a shed next to a warehouse. It was their third tunnel attempt, and the third proved successful. Depending on which account you read, four attempts were made and, instead of the tunnel ending in a shed, it ended in a nearby lot.

After my rather serendipitous discovery, I began my research in earnest. I knew that I had been a Union officer during the U.S. Civil War. Could this prison be the one where I had been held? Using library resources, I sought to find pictures of the prison and as much information as I could about Libby. I wanted to document my out-of-body experience. The books I found had a great deal to say about Andersonville, the notorious Confederate prison for the common soldier, but had little or nothing to say about Libby, the object of my search. It was not until I turned to the Internet that my search came to an end. A popular Civil War site confirmed what I had hoped: that Libby was the prison where I had been taken upon my capture.

To corroborate my previous life experience as a prisoner of war, the prison where I was confined had to meet several criteria: 1) it had to be near a waterway on which ships could sail; 2) it had to have a walkway that could accommodate pedestrian traffic; 3) the rooms of the prison had to be sparsely furnished; 4) it could not be escape proof; and 5) most of all, it had to house Union officers. In all these particulars, Libby fit the bill. The picture that I found was of a three-story building. The building seemed to have a fourth floor, but this was because the first floor was a basement which extended well aboveground on the south side of the building, the side facing the James River. The building was erected alongside a wide canal, so wide that ships could navigate its breadth. Indeed, the picture showed a ship anchored not far from the docks that ran beside it, and the walkway and street upon which pedestrians and horse-drawn wagons and drivers went about their daily business.

I learned, contrary to my first impression, that prisoners did not live on the basement floor, but could use it during the day. Prisoners, according to one account, were allowed to cook in an interior room on the basement floor. How I was allowed to be in this part of the building, I know not. Yet, according to my out-of-body experience, I escaped from the basement of the building through a door that wasn't guarded. That my escape was eventually discovered by military guards was substantiated by the gun fire and the many bullets that were sent in my direction. Several accounts agreed that Union officers were imprisoned in the building, and that escape attempts were not uncommon. Accounts also agreed that furniture and furnishings were sparse and living conditions challenging.

I found one instance of a prisoner of war escaping after trading his brand-new clothes to a guard for the guard's frayed Confederate uniform, his coat and pants, using the swapping as a pretext to acquire money with which to purchase supplies, actually walking out of the Camp in the bartered clothes, passed guards, and, while fleeing, assisted on his way to freedom by several blacks. I've found no record of anyone escaping by swimming the canal or the James River that ran next to the prison, but I suspect that many such escape attempts are lost to history.

SURROUNDED BY WHAT APPEARED TO BE MACHINES

My first out-of-body experience transported me to a factory where machines occupied a large part of the visible space. Each time I was transported to the factory—the experience having happened more than once—I hid among the machines, large metal boxes that appeared to be machines, as I feared detection. Although I have experienced hundreds of out-of-body trips, this journey among the machines was the first of only two out-of-body experiences that have recurred over the years. These out-of-body recurrences were probably the result of past-life events that left my psyche so scarred, so plunged into an irresolvable conflict—an emotional struggle seeking resolution—that I used the out-of-body experience to resolve the conflict. The oft-repeated machine experience fits that dilemma perfectly. The experience never changed. Again and again, I found myself in the same place, a room with large machines. I'm hiding behind them to keep from being discovered by the workmen in the plant.

From my hiding place, behind one of the metal boxes, I watched while white men in heavy work boots, shirtless, powerfully built, wearing pants held up with belts or suspenders, mercilessly pound something on the plant floor that remained out of sight. They used what seemed to be large mallets to do the pounding, lifting them high above their head with each up swing, and then allowing them to smash what rested on the floor below. They did this repeatedly.

Oddly, I was drawn to the thing that they pounded, wanting to move in closer to the knot of men in hopes of seeing the object of their pounding, but something more than the fear of detection held me back. I feared what discovery would mean if I were detected. A part of me understood that this "something" being pounded was me. What had I done to these men to meet such an ignominious end, to die in such a horrific way as to be beaten to death?

Recurrently, I've gone to this dreadful place only to experience the fear yet again, and to look on in horror as the massive mallets rose above the men's head only to come crashing down upon something they took great delight in pounding. Despite the recurrence of this experience, I never saw the thing that the men pounded, or understood why. After all, the structure was a plant where things were built, or maintained, and this kind of thing wasn't out of the ordinary. What stood out were the large metal-like boxes that gave the impression of machines, metal boxes that snaked their way through the plant, the cold, stark metal only adding to the horror of the experience.

In this lifetime, I've had only a few male friends. I suspect that this previous-life event where I worked among machines and likely died at the hands of angry men, explains my preference for befriending women, primarily, with this predilection constituting yet another life theme.

A LIFE AS AN APE-LIKE CREATURE & OTHER EARLY LIVES

If the recurring out-of-body experience among the machines represents my first out-of-body experience, it doesn't represent my earliest known lifetime, or reveal just how far back I've been able to go in time. My first lifetime was that of a creature more beast than man. As the creature, I emerged into an opening, perhaps from a cave. I was biped, huge, and incredibly strong, as evidenced by a surprising current of strength coursing throughout my entire body. For a while, this flow of power held my attention. It was immense. I felt incredibly powerful. I felt that I could break trees as though they were twigs, that I had no equals to match my physical strength. I knew that if I growled, my roar would be heard for miles, scattering lesser creatures, as they cowered and trembled in fear.

To my left was my companion of today, a female, but also beastlike, chatting with others of our species, while our son—her son of today—played in the dirt to my right. Even today, I emit a low, but discernible growl when perturbed. And until this pre-lifetime out-of-body experience, I didn't understand why, but simply wrote it off as belonging to one of my several idiosyncratic behaviors without a known source.

Once, I found myself on an ancient street where a cart with wooden wheels was being drawn by beasts of burden, oxen perhaps, when one of the wheels broke away and rolled directly towards me, striking me hard. During this prior life review, I didn't feel the impact of the wheel, or the ensuing pain, yet I knew that the blow from the runaway wheel had ended my life. What this event showed, as well as the others, is the number of lives I've lived, and how far back they go, one in particular placing me at the time that Jesus lived, finding me at a table, partaking of a meal, reclining at the table as was customary during that time.

MAN LEARNING FROM HIS ELDER

After my divorce, the end of a relationship that had lasted almost two decades, I met a young woman. At the time of the meeting, I didn't know that I had known her in a previous life. What I've learned since is that many of those with whom I've had an intimate relationship in this life, I knew in a previous life—another theme that runs through many of my past lives. This meeting up again with previous lovers, or close friends, or family members from a previous lifetime, is probably true for most people, whether they're aware of it or not.

Early in our relationship and after a moment of intimacy, something stunning occurred—I experienced a life review, one focused primarily on the two of us from a previous life. I had always heard the expression, "My life flashed before me," not quite sure if, indeed, such a life review was possible.

As I watched, I wanted to respond to what I was seeing, but found it difficult as the scenes in front of me rushed by faster than I could focus on them, as though they had been images flashed on a movie screen so fast that the images merged. The scenes were important, but I couldn't hold them in mind long enough to make sense of them. All I could do was respond with an, Oh!

I repeated, Oh! several times as the scenes raced by, each with greater rapidity than the previous one.

In another out-of-body experience, I was able to visit one aspect of our life together, and to do so in slow motion, or more specifically, at a pace I was accustomed to seeing. I was a young white man, and she a much older, seasoned elder, also white, and also a man. In this previous life review, I was looking through a door's opening at a rugged-appearing, older man sitting at a table eating. To reach the door, I had to mount several steep steps. As I entered the building, I couldn't tell if it was a public or a private accommodation. Seated at the end of a long table was a lone, bear of a man.

A scraggly beard and long unkempt hair only added to his rough, bearish appearance. My first impression was that he was a mountain man or a trapper, and extremely proficient as such, with all the requisite knowledge of the wild to assure his survival under the harshest of conditions.

I also knew who this person was in my present-day lifetime, because, for a brief moment, her face and body were superimposed upon the figure of the rugged mountain man. This superimposition had happened before as a way to identify who a person had been during a previous lifetime.

After entering the building, the scene shifted suddenly and I was now below the high steps that led to the door, and, looking underneath them, could see to the other side. From nowhere a horse jumped over the highest step and over me, as I ducked to avoid being hit. It was the rugged mountain man now atop a horse, clearly an expert horseman, to which his equestrian skills, recently on display, attested.

In the final scene, I'm walking alongside the mountain man while he's mounted on his horse, presumably because I didn't own a horse, and possibly because I couldn't afford one. I knew that I idolized this older man—his vast experience, and his skills, skills I wished that I possessed.

I adored him, wanted to be just like him, admired his skill with horses, and his knowledge of how to survive in a hostile world. He had the confidence of one who had taken on all that life could throw his way and still remained upright. What stands out about this experience is the degree to which I revered this man, my desire to be just like him, and my willingness to follow him, unquestioningly, wherever he might lead.

What we have today is a reversal of this previous life. In the previous one, I was the younger man, awestruck by the knowledge, experience, and skills of this older mountain man. In this lifetime, I'm the older man. The *older man* then is now the younger woman of today—reversing our age, and changing the gender of the elder man. We parted in time, yet I know that no matter how we may have experienced our life together here this time around, we're bound together in ways that will reunite us in death, and possibly in future lives. This prior-life connection is not necessarily unique to her; I'm connected to several persons in this lifetime, mainly because we've experienced life together in previous lives.

WHITE MAN PAINTING NATIVE AMERICANS

Having experienced a life together in a previous life was certainly true of my first wife. Interestingly, no gender reversal took place with the two of us; she was, in a previous life, as much female as I was male. In this lifetime, however, we're both black. What was different then in our previous life is that she was an American Indian, and I was white. I don't know the tribe, or the Indian nation, to which she belonged, but since she was born in Oklahoma in this lifetime, she might have been a member of one of the tribes that live there now, and who call Oklahoma home.

During that lifetime I was an artist who spent years among this nation's native people drawing and painting them. Even in this lifetime, I draw from time to time, after realizing at an early age that it was a talent that was natural to me. I just knew that I could do it, and this without drawing one picture. In one out-of-body scene, the Indian maiden is sitting for me, as I paint her. In another scene, I'm pleading with her mother to intercede on my behalf. I loved her but the feeling wasn't mutual, as she rebuffed my overtures and spurned my advances.

Other than bringing a girl child into the world together, I've often wondered why we were united in marriage, if only briefly, in this lifetime. I never felt that she loved me, that we had bridged the emotional chasm that existed between us. And it wasn't because we were destined to be together always in this lifetime. It would have precluded my being with others with whom I spent time in previous lives.

I feel I did my best to hold our relationship together for the sake of our daughter, who I loved dearly, but the more I tried, the more it slipped away. I don't blame my then wife for the breakup; it was inevitable that our Souls would set us both on different paths. During our marriage, I can't say that I was a sterling example of a husband, although I was prepared, after a time, to devote myself to her and to my daughter, that eventuality predicated on our ability and willingness to salvage a marriage gone awry.

I believe we were drawn together in this lifetime to resolve previous life business, so that I might come to terms with what I considered the loss of a lifetime: my greatest love. My feelings for her in this lifetime, however, didn't match those in the previous one, underscoring the folly of exclusively loving anyone—whether with human love or spiritual love.

He who loves greatest loves broadest, as love's not a narrow street and neither does it end in a cul-de-sac.

A JEW RUNNING FROM NAZIS

I believe that we all should walk in the shoes of others, to experience things from their perspective. It keeps us humble, allows us to understand their positions, and to empathize with their conditions. In another out-of-body experience, I'm in a train station, hiding in the shadows, attempting to elude those who would arrest me on sight and take me away, as they have taken away so many of my fellow brothers and sisters.

I am a male Jew.

I don't know my location, neither the city nor country in which I find myself, only that I'm hoping to evade detection and capture by the Nazis, or German soldiers. What I do know is that I mustn't be caught; I must find a way out of the city, and out of the country, my life depending on it. Once again, I'm confronted with the theme of detection and the possibility of harm if I'm discovered or captured. Because I'm hoping to board a train that will take me to safety, I'm in a train station. My enemies are all around me. People are moving with purpose all around me. I'm standing in the middle of the station reading train schedules, studying the destinations of departing trains.

The train schedules are appended to a kiosk. From them I'm hoping to learn the departure and arrival times of trains that enter and leave the station, so that I might travel to safety, as I fear that my life is in jeopardy.

In another scene, I am outside of a small white church, apparently a Christian church. I'm the same man, a male Jew, still afraid of detection and capture, but this time, I am burying something on the church grounds, near the church's foundation, so that those who find it in the future will know that I was there.

What I remember most about this experience is the tremendous fear that I felt. In this lifetime, I haven't felt a comparable fear. In this lifetime, I haven't felt so close to death at the hands of others, as I did then; felt that my freedom was hanging in the balance. I've lived, for a time, within a world where my freedom was severely restricted, but this was different. A person striving to elude the long arm of the law couldn't have felt more vulnerable.

This experience reminded me that, despite our current circumstances, or impediments, our contemporary race, or ethnicity, or our present religion, or beliefs, we all return to this world as members of many races, ethnicities, and religions, and under varied circumstances, and we do so to either satisfy a karmic debt, or to advance the interest of the Soul. The theme here is simple: The Law of Reciprocity (The Golden Rule) governs our existence. In the Bible, this Law, this Rule is stated in many ways, and in many places. My preferred statement of the Law comes from Galatians which reads: "Be not deceived; God is not mocked: for whatsoever a man soweth, that shall he also reap."[44]

To be sure, God is not responsible for setting the Law in motion for better or for worse, for good or for evil, for justice or for injustice. We are. The Law is as implacable as it is omnipresent. In the Middle East, I'm brutally reminded of this truth: If it's in the Soul's interest, Israelis become Palestinians and Palestinians become Israelis in a continual reversal of

---

44 Gal. 6:7

roles, until their souls advance to the point that they see the futility of violence by virtue of the incarnational swapping of sides, realizing, finally, that Jew and Palestinian aren't two people, separate and apart, but are, in reality, one.

Similarly, Native Americans become the white interlopers, and the white interlopers become Native Americans, just as slaves become the masters, and the masters become the slaves; the oppressed becomes the oppressor, and the oppressor becomes the oppressed. At the Soul's behest, we may become members of any racial group. Irrespective of the racial group we belonged to in previous lives, it will have no bearing on who we will become in future lives. At some point, we all view life from many different perspectives. I'm reminded, too, of John Dunne's observation regarding our oneness: "any man's death diminishes me, because I am involved in mankind, and therefore never send to know for whom the bell tolls; it tolls for thee" (from *Devotions Upon Emergent Occasions* MEDITATION XVII).

The path of the soul may be rugged or it may be smooth, but very few of us live an unchallenged life. In order for the Soul to carry out its purpose for us, it can take into account many things, not the least of which are race, social conditions, or any number of human or physical characteristics. This the Soul does when race or any other human characteristic promotes the growth of the soul, or contributes to its evolution in some measurable way.

ASIAN MAN

To illustrate, let me share this experience. Out-of-body, I saw, in one scene, this horrific, possibly deadly, accident in a desolate area. In the second scene, I'm an Asian man, my sense of my racial identity, and I'm standing on a hilltop overlooking a valley, next to a towering, large sign. I'm looking up at what seemed to be billboards suspended on wooden structures. Upon them are written symbols which I could neither read nor understand, because they represent a language not my own in this lifetime.

In the next scene, I'm looking down into the valley, where there's a sprawling tenement building.

Suddenly, I began running in the direction of the building, calling out what appeared to be a woman's name, again and again, the name sounding like: Ra Ta Ta! Ra Ta Ta! Ra Ta Ta! I believe that the name belongs to my wife. She's the woman whom I left behind. The pain of my violent and unexpected departure from this world, my death, is driving me forward, driving me to find her.

This recently deceased Asian man was me. By some means, I knew that; in that lifetime, I had died in an accident of some sort, and I wouldn't be returning home from my long absence, at least not while I was alive. Although the man acted independently of me, I could, occasionally, direct his actions. This has happened before, during several out-of-body experiences. It's as though for a time I'm the actual person in whose body I now reside, at times knowing that person's thoughts and that person's motivations.

The tenement was approached by large steep steps, several of them, perhaps a dozen or so, steps spanning the full length of the building. After bounding the long steps, and entering the building, all the while calling out my wife's name, I ran down a long hallway that had rooms on either side. Doors opened to the rooms were nothing more than strings of beads suspended from the door's top, as though the tenants needed nothing more to protect their property or their privacy.

I looked into each room, a quick glance, as I moved rapidly down the hall. Apparently, in my new state, I couldn't identify the room in which I had lived with my wife. It was as though my new, unfamiliar perspective—that of one dead—now affected my bearings in the physical world. I continued running from one room to the next, throwing the beads aside, peering in quickly, and when I saw no one, pressed on, my desperation to find my wife consuming me, my fear growing, fueling the possibility that I may never see her again, and that I couldn't bear.

Flinging aside the beads to one of the rooms farther down the hall, I saw her. I entered an area where a woman busied herself with housewife duties, oblivious to my presence. She was preparing food in a kitchen just behind a larger anteroom, which wasn't much larger than the kitchen. I drew closer trying to get her attention. She ignored me as though she was unaware of my presence. At some point, I, *my* consciousness, took over. I asked her the questions I always ask during these outings: "Who are you? Where am I? What is my name?" The answers are usually what you'd expect: "You know your name. You know who you are, and you know who I am." I persist, but usually my persistence is met with silence, or a quizzical smile, or outright anger.

When I take over, replacing the consciousness of the man with my own consciousness, it's as though I'm communicating with another part of the woman's being, perhaps her Soul, and not the unsuspecting woman before me who is unaware of my presence, not the woman who has just lost her husband, and who has yet to be informed. No matter how hard I tried to attract her attention, to connect with her, she seemed not to notice. It was clear that we couldn't communicate as husband and wife, because I was now dead. We were in two different dimensions, and I didn't know how to overcome the barrier that stood between us.

Sadness welled up inside of me, replacing the tears that I might have shed, had I not been in my new state. Other than giving me insight into the reincarnational process and who I had been in a previous life, this peering behind the incarnational curtains didn't seem to serve a definitive purpose. One thing I took away from this view of a previous life as an *Asian Man* was the knowledge that we reincarnate, not on a linear path, when we consider our physical lineage, but on several disconnected paths, an understanding that the *Asian Man* brought home.

I'd like to say that this out-of-body experience provided me with the means to identify who I might have been in that lifetime, but it didn't. The experience frustrated me; I couldn't reconnect with my wife, nor could I learn who I was during that life. What I gathered from this experience is that each past-life episode provides essential knowledge for a fuller understanding of the life that we're now living. I'm not sure what was going on in my life at the time of this episode, but the experience left me with a greater appreciation for life, and for those who're living this life with me. I learned that life is too short, too precious, not to cherish the moments I share with those I love; that it is our many relationships that enrich and strengthen our lives, and not the things we accumulate, not our material possessions, nor our human achievements, whether large or small.

WINDWAGON SMITH

On another out-of-body excursion, I found myself inside a barn pouring over plans, diagrams that I had meticulously drawn that I hoped to use to revolutionize transportation, plans that detailed the construction of a new form of transportation, a transportation method used by ships on the high seas, but not on land, plans for a wind wagon, a wagon with sails that would use wind power to traverse this nation's vast prairies, transporting both cargo and people.

As the inventor of land ships, I'm proud of my plans, and pleased that my idea will transform transportation. I'm looking over my plans to determine if I've overlooked some small, but important detail, because there in my barn stood my brainchild, a wagon that will hoist sails to the wind, and use the winds of the prairie to propel it from one location to another. I'm envisioning a fleet of these prairie schooners, some covered and some opened to the air. I am excited about my idea and can hardly wait to see it realized. In the next scene, I'm in the sailing wagon speeding across land towards an unknown destination.

My research turned up several persons who bore the moniker Windwagon Smith, making the task of narrowing down the one who carried my soul an almost impossible task. Windwagon Smith is the moniker for a historical figure, or a folklore hero, who, in all likelihood, is a composite of several persons who either originated the idea independently, or built upon the concept of others. My out-of-body experience left me with the impression that I, as Windwagon Smith, originated the idea, not only originated the idea, but was eager to give my invention of a wind-driven wagon to the world. I'm convinced that in a previous life I was that person, perhaps the one that gave rise to this American folk hero.

The story would end here, but for a rather interesting twist or two, explaining, in part, why I was shown this particular lifetime as Windwagon Smith. I didn't know of Windwagon Smith before this out-of-body excursion, but, with a little research, I was able to ferret him out. The notion of using sails on wagons as a transportation device made my task easier because of its irregularity.

Years later, after having met my now companion, we both decided, early in our relationship, to go our separate ways. Our relationship had gotten off to a rocky start after our initial propitious and exciting meeting. Despite the breakup, the relationship was to be rekindled, and this in a remarkable way, a way that neither one of us could have predicted. I was at a popular nightclub, sitting at the bar, drinking a non-alcoholic beer, when she approached. She was there with two friends. Our conversation quickly turned to the finality of our relationship, that it was indeed over, reinforcing the mutual understanding we had established at a previous meeting.

She was walking away when a strong impulse compelled me to tell her that I was Windwagon Smith. "Tell her that you're Windwagon Smith," The Voice urged. While I questioned the wisdom of it, I turned to her, nevertheless, and said, "You know I'm Windwagon Smith, don't you?"

"Who told you to say that?" She asked. "How did you know to say that? Did I tell you about him?"

I assured her that she hadn't, but she knew that herself, but had to inquire anyway, as my referencing of Windwagon Smith was the last thing she would have expected that evening.

She said that a teacher had discussed Windwagon Smith one day when she was in grade school. At the time, she had felt a personal connection to him. Later that day while outdoors and lying on her back, looking up, she saw the image of a white man in the sky. He told her that he was Windwagon Smith, and that one day he would find her and they would marry. Since that first meeting as a small child, she had looked for him everywhere, although in the interim she had married someone else and was the mother of three. Needless to say, after this revelation, this was not the end of our relationship, but the beginning.

"I can't leave you now," she said with decisiveness. "Let me tell my friends that I've changed my mind. We're not breaking up."

She returned a few minutes later to learn more about my previous life identity as Windwagon Smith.

After her sister had moved in with us temporarily, several years after my declaration of having been Windwagon Smith in a previous life, my companion told her about Windwagon Smith, and how he had rescued our relationship when it was on the brink of breaking up. She recounted her childhood story of meeting Windwagon Smith in a supernatural manner, and how he had promised to marry her one day. She told her about the time that I had revealed to her my previous-live identity as Windwagon Smith at a nightclub we often frequented, and how that admission had solidified our relationship.

Later that night, her sister, while on our patio smoking, repeated, for reasons I never learned, the name Windwagon Smith several times. I was asleep at the time but heard her plainly call out my name as though she was standing directly outside our bedroom door, although she had probably said it more mentally than vocally. Thinking that trouble was afoot for her, I immediately ran in the direction of the guest room on the far side of the house, and from there to the door leading to our backyard patio, as the patio light lit up the shades on the door.

I opened the door gently, using it to conceal my semi-clad body, as I poked my head out, and asked, "What's wrong? You keep calling my name."

She looked stunned, as a frown of disbelief distorted her face. "I was calling for Windwagon Smith," she said.

"I know," I told her. "I heard you."

With that, I returned to bed. Later that morning, I heard her call out my name again. Suspecting that she was testing me, and wasn't in trouble, I ignored the call.

A LIFETIME AS A WHITE WOMAN

To confirm that I had lived a life as a woman, I was given an out-of-body episode that showed me rising from bed, not as a man, but as a woman, a white woman, pleading with my male lover not to leave me.

This experience stands out mainly because it's the only out-of-body experience, among hundreds, in which I experienced myself as a woman. I left my body in one of my usual ways, on the astral current. As always, I'm eager to see where my out-of-body experiences will take me, but this time I wasn't prepared for what happened. This time, I found myself in a well-lighted room (I believe that it's a hotel room.), the light coming from a light source fastened to the wall. Although I can't be certain of the time period, the wallpaper is gold, the design reminding me of those associated with Western movies, and that era in U.S. history.

Two people are in the room, and I'm one of them. I'm the one rising out of bed hastily, my heart beating rapidly, my thoughts riveted on the man who was in the bed with me only minutes ago, but is now standing, preparing to leave the room through the door that is on the left side of the head of the bed. I'm in panic; the man has told me that he's leaving, never to return. My hair is blond, my skin white. I'm a beautiful woman, dressed in a warm gown or robe. I'm pleading with the man with the language of my body—with my eyes, arms, and hands—begging him to stay, my heart already breaking, already trying to cope with what is happening, the ominous prospect that I will soon be alone again.

I never learned whether the man stayed or left. One of the persistent themes that run through many of my out-of-body experiences, especially those with reincarnational material, is the theme of being alone, not just lonely, but alone, and it is this aloneness that I have always found unbearable. It's a theme that has beset me in this lifetime (and obviously in lifetimes preceding this one), a theme that I'm only now able to bear with equanimity. This fear of being alone has shaped my existential experiences many times, causing me to do things that may not have been always in my best interest.

The impression that I received from the episode is that I didn't persuade my lover to stay, the experience highlighting another life theme, the theme of *lost love*. This is the only life, to my knowledge, which I spent as a woman, as I wear the male energy more comfortably than the female energy, although it's important to wear both energies equally well in one body, if we're to blend successfully with the energy of the Soul which is androgynous, that is, male and female.

SMALL CHILD, BRIEF LIFE

This out-of-body experience revealed more themes to add to the themes of *aloneness,* and *fear of dolls*. The following experience reinforced two more themes, the themes of *respect for motherhood*, and *loss of parents*. The two themes are related to the heading, "YOU KILLED THEM." As far as I know, the loss of a parent, a mother in particular, in several successive lifetimes, was the extent of the retribution I was required to endure as penance for my wrongdoing, my killing of parents in a previous live. Notwithstanding the punishment, or so it seemed, it exacted the appropriate justice for my crime and sin—my ensuing suffering, a direct consequence of my reckless act of matricide and patricide.

Shortly after leaving my body, riding the astral current that usually sweeps me away as though it's a whitewater rapid, I feel myself come to a soft landing within a dark room. Without warning, I felt myself shrink. This was my first time, as an out-of-body explorer, to experience the sensation of shrinking, and it caught me off guard. I was expecting anything but that. My body actually went from my current height to that of a young boy. Suddenly I was this young boy child, no more than 5 or 6 years old, perhaps less, clothed, but barefoot. Without warning, my little feet began running through a door that my little hands opened upon a dimly-lighted outer room.

It appeared to be a family room. The room was lighted by a lamp. Braced against the wall in front of me was a couch and on the couch sat three black kids, two boys and one girl, not one more than ten or eleven. All three ignored me and looked straight ahead, at what, I couldn't tell. I approached them, and the impression I discerned was that they didn't like me very much. I was a mama's boy. My parents doted on me because I was a sickly child and not as healthy as the others.

I looked behind me and saw a lectern that held a book. I walked to where it stood. It was the Holy Bible. I opened the book with the hope of reading it, but the words kept moving on the page, as though the letters were alive, and were playing a game of hide and seek, all in an attempt to avoid being read. I've heard it said that reading in the astral state is practically impossible. At times it can be, but at other times I've managed to do it, as well as use pen and paper to write.

Believing that the kids wouldn't cooperate with my desire to know who I was in that lifetime, I left the room hoping to find others—perhaps an adult—who could inform me as to who I was, and where I lived. By gathering enough information that I could research, it has always been my goal to confirm my identity when windows were opened upon my past lives. For instant, I ask those I meet at the time, while out-of-body, to tell me my name, or to tell me their name, and our location.

If I'm on a street, I look for names on street signs, all for the purpose of later being able to identify places and names, concrete clues to my identity in that lifetime. With that in mind, I ran down a hallway towards the front of the house. Off to my right was a door. I peered in and saw a woman at a kitchen sink washing dishes. I knew instantly that she was my mother. She knew that I was standing there watching, but ignored me. She was a black woman, perhaps in her early thirties. From her I received a definite sense of love, security, and compassion. I knew that she was the one I should probe, to question, about who I was and who she was.

"Mom," I asked, "what's my name?" She didn't answer me, but looked at me curiously. I asked her again.

"You know your name," she said finally.

I asked again, this time more insistently, "Mom! What's my name?"

She turned and looked at me with a scowl. I knew that the scowl would be the only answer I'd get.

"Well, what is your name, and where do we live?" I persisted not knowing whether the persistence was a trait common to me, or not.

"You know my name, and you know where we live," She said. I could tell that I was overtaxing her vast patience.

"Okay, then, what is my father's name?"

"You know your father's name," She said, looking at me now as though I had finally lost my mind. It was then I heard the door open at the front of the house. From the kitchen door I could see another room, a living room, furnished, but modestly so. A middle-aged black man had used his key to open the door, and was about to enter the house. At that moment, I knew that my father was a minister, that the house was really an apartment. I knew, also, that other families lived in the building, that the building was located in a big city, and that I would be dead soon, my illness claiming me long before I could become a teenager.

Suddenly I was back in my body reviewing what had just transpired. Emotions welled up in me, my mother's love for me in that lifetime still permeated my being. A powerful longing to be with her ached somewhere deep within, the ache hurting so much that I began to cry, the tears becoming a waterfall, the tears falling within because I find it hard to let them fall without. Although no one could see them, the tears fell nevertheless, the loss of my mother growing stronger and more painful with each passing minute. The pain lasted for days afterward. I missed her. I missed her terribly. At the time, I didn't think that I would ever be consoled, not in this lifetime, or a thousand. This painful experience gave birth to my now unflagging respect for motherhood, the value of parents, and an awareness that the death of my mother in this lifetime (She died when I was around two or three.) had left me with a feeling of incompleteness. I tried to overcome the deficiency with the aid of relationships, although I knew the remedy would never be found outside of me. The emptiness only subsided when I reached in and filled the void myself, filled it with the fullness of God. I can now say that I'm complete; the sufficiency was always mine to have, but I had to provide it myself by going within.

USING PAST-LIFE CLUES TO DETERMINE PAST-LIFE TIMEFRAMES

Establishing a chronology for past-lives lived has been a daunting task, made all the more daunting because I have few clues on which to build timelines—the dates on which I was born, or died. From the clues I did receive, it appears that many of my more recent lifetimes were cut short years before I reached middle age. It's easier to account for some lives more than others: For example, it's easier to account for my lifetime as an ape-like creature (my earliest known lifetime, occurring at the dawn of time), my lifetime when I was killed by a runaway wooden wheel, my lifetime when I was contemporary with Jesus, than those lifetimes that followed these lives, notwithstanding my lifetime as a Union officer and prisoner of war.

It's possible that the light display inventor and the mountain man could have lived within the same century, the seventeenth century. Glass windows became common features in English homes during that time. As for the mountain men, French fur traders explored the area later known as Minnesota in 1665. In addition, John Colter (1774-1812), a mountain man extraordinaire, and one of several Army privates, along with several Army sergeants, escorted Captain Meriwether Lewis and Second Lieutenant William Clark on what became known as the Lewis and Clark Expedition which began in May 1804, and ended in September 1806.

I can't place in time my lifetime as a painter of Native Americans. From 1830 to 1850, several Indian nations were forced to resettle onto reservations in Indian Territory, Oklahoma of today, but there's no indication that this was the time period, nor the area in which I had painted. Yet, it's possible that, in the nineteenth century, I could have lived a lifetime as an artist, died, and was reborn in time to fight in the U.S. Civil War.

From the end of the U.S. Civil War, 1865 to 1900, thirty-five years overall, I can squeeze within that timeframe the lifetime when I was a young white woman, and the lifetime of the young man (possibly white) who was beat to death among the metal boxes, both of which would have died relatively young, probably teenagers, seventeen or eighteen, or younger. I recalled these lives, perhaps because they ended tragically and traumatically. From 1900 to 1942, 1942 being the year of my birth in this lifetime, I will have died three times, once as a young man fourteen or fifteen years old, soon after the killing of my parents, a lifetime event to be discussed later, and again at the age of five or six, the circumstances of which I have already discussed. My next death, the last one before my rebirth in 1942, was that of a young Jewish man, twenty or twenty-one years of age or younger, possibly the victim of the Holocaust, the systematic extermination of the Jews, around six million in all, and another five million non-Jews.

Hitler's persecution of the Jews began in earnest with the passing of the Nuremberg Laws. There were only two of them, one, the *Reich Citizenship Law* and the other, the *Law for the Protection of German Blood and Honor*, both passing on September 15, 1935. The Reich Citizenship Law marked the beginning of the establishment of criteria as to who would be granted citizenship rights and who wouldn't.

As for the lifetimes I spent as a prisoner in a ship, or the years spent as Windwagon Smith, or the Asian man, I can't account for. I don't have the necessary clues that will allow me to claim definitively the dates of my birth, or the dates of my death. The Windwagon Smiths whom I did find didn't fit neatly into the timeframes of which I did have clues.

There are those who believe that we live shared lifetimes—although I have no personal evidence to corroborate this—the results of several souls subsumed under One Soul. Each of these several souls would experience, at some level, the lifetimes of the others, and experience them as though they were their own, as indeed they would be, as the One Soul comprises all the disparate souls under its influence despite the number of individu-ated souls the One Soul encompasses.

Not lost on me is the possibility that we have lived, during any one recurring lifetime, lifetimes in parallel worlds and universes. Who we might have been in those parallel worlds and universes is open to con-jecture. It's not uncommon for me to glimpse, in the form of visions and memories, some of the events that my parallel selves have encountered in their worlds, memories so real that I find it extremely difficult at times to separate them from those that are from my supposed real memories in this my current lifetime.

MORE RECURRING PAST-LIFE THEMES

The theme of being detected and the accompanying horror of what detection would mean, a terrible end to my life, first manifested itself with the men among machines episodes. The theme has continued to manifest itself on other occasions during my out-of-body experiences. For example, I'm walking down a long corridor and just ahead of me is a woman, blond, dressed in a nurse's uniform. She doesn't know that I'm there, and I want to keep it that way, but I'm afraid that something, my footsteps perhaps, will alert her to my presence and she'll turn and see me. I'm terrified that she might, but I can't keep myself from following her. Suddenly, up ahead, she stops, and I stop. Slowly, ever so slowly, she turns her head to look at me, and the terror that I feel can't be described, yet I must stay and watch. Sometimes the fear is so great that it causes my astral body to snap back to the physical. The woman in the corridor personifies the theme of being detected, although I can't place her within any particular lifetime.

As with the men in the plant, I'm never discovered, although the fear of discovery is almost too intense to bear. There's a variation on this recurring out-of-body experience. I'm walking down the same corridor. I encounter what appears to be a baby's bassinet. The bassinet has been placed directly against the corridor wall on my right. As I draw closer to it, I see a baby in the bassinet; the baby's head and back are turned from me, and the baby is resting on its side. Like the nurse, the baby turns towards me, slowly, stiffly, mechanically, the whole body turning as one, as though it's a doll rather than a human child. I can't tell the sex of the child, but if I had to guess, I'd say that it's a girl. As with the nurse, also a female, the baby-in-a-bassinet experience is terrifying, the fear so powerful, that many times it has snapped me back to my physical body, well before I could be detected, and before I could learn the nature, or the origin of my fear. What do they have in common, the nurse and a baby in a bassinet, and why do their presence in the long hall fill me with such anguish and dread?

Over time, I have pieced the puzzle together, these two elements from a previous life, thanks to information provided by my Higher Self, but I've vowed to take the reason for my fear to my grave, the depth of my shame so great, and the agony of my remorse so painful.

TWELVE

OFFER GUIDANCE

MY FIRST ENCOUNTER WITH THE VOICE
"WHY ARE YOU DOING THAT?"

And the child Samuel ministered unto the LORD before Eli. And the word
of the LORD was precious in those days; there was no open vision.
And it came to pass at that time, when Eli was laid down in his
place, and his eyes began to wax dim, that he could not see;
And ere the lamp of God went out in the temple of the LORD,
where the ark of God was, and Samuel was laid down to sleep;
That the Lord called Samuel: and he answered, Here am I.[45]

ONE OF THE MOST GRATEFUL AND REWARDING aspects of being able to connect with the *you* in me, has been the accompanying guidance that the connection has provided, a provision associated with The Voice, whose guidance has been ongoing since my first hearing it. Over the years, The Voice has spoken to me often. It's such an integral part of my life now that I'm no longer surprised when it speaks.

---

45 I Sam 3:1-4

During my preteen years, I concealed a feeling that I couldn't share with others, family or friends. I knew that they wouldn't understand, and would merely seek to disabuse me of a persistent thought I was having, and a feeling I was experiencing. The thought, the feeling: I never felt like Earth was my home. As a child, I would stand out under the stars and know that I came from up there. Another thought that haunted me then:

I wasn't born into the world. The world was born into me.

Like many of you, I have always felt close to God and this from an early age. My first experience with The Voice was as a child. One Christmas my father consented to give my brother and me BB guns (air rifles). Given the cost of the guns, and that he was a minister, his consent caught us totally off guard, and not a little surprised. What do you do with a gun? You hunt with it, which is what we did.

That winter red-breasted robins set up temporary lodging in the schoolyard trees, several of which grew on the school grounds across the street from my home. The trees were loaded with a seed-like food for them. They would fill up on the seeds and, because it was very cold, just sit in the trees, seemingly too cold, and too stuffed, to fly away. Even when I approached with my gun, they remained motionless, showing no interest in flying away, although my advancing should have raised alarm.

There were so many of them in the seed-laden trees, I didn't even have to aim. All I had to do was shoot in their direction and a robin would fall to the ground. I must have killed dozens this way, of course, with the intention of roasting and eating them.

I picked up one that I had brought down with my gun, and was amazed how fragile it was in my hand; it was mostly feathers, bone and a little flesh. In flight or sitting on limbs, their feathers gave them the appearance of being plump. However, in my hand, they were delicate and fragile.

Then it happened. I heard it: A man's voice, loud, booming, and unmistakable. "Why are you doing that?" the voice asked. "Don't you know *that* is wrong?" I looked around wondering who was expressing disapproval. I saw that I was the only one standing in this very large schoolyard, under a grey sky, on this very cold day. It would have been unusual for someone to have been there anyway, since it was Christmas break, and school wasn't in session.

Soon after, I began having out-of-body experiences. What's significant about them is that I realized, after emerging from some of them year's later, that I was having conversations with someone who sat behind a white veil, The Voice having a shape, if only a diffused one. The conversations would last for hours it seemed. And most of the time, I couldn't remember what was said, or what was discussed. Even now, when I least expect it, I will get a voice response to a thought I'm thinking, or the answer to a dilemma I'm facing, or reassuring words urging me not to worry about something vexing me at the time.

One such response came while sitting down for dinner, my thoughts reflecting on the various types of prayers, from a prayer of understanding, to that of realization, to that of faith and belief. On behalf of my Inner Wisdom, The Voice broke through to share its take on the various kinds of prayers. It said: "The highest form of prayer is contemplation." Researching prayer as contemplation, I came across a quote attributed to *St. John of the Cross* from his book, *Ascent of Mount Carmel,* who, while drawing a distinction between contemplative and discursive meditation, summed it up brilliantly, at least *my* understanding of contemplative prayer. The following is my take on the meaning of contemplative prayer, perhaps one inspired by The Voice:

Contemplative prayer is a silent, but focused, rejoicing within the God Reality (Infinite Good, Perfection, Life, Love, Mind, Truth), and not an effort to create that reality. It's a subtle difference but one that combines most forms of prayer, whether it's a prayer of understanding, or a prayer of realization.

Moreover, contemplation reaffirms another reality, both human and divine: What you focus on, that is, give your full attention to—whether it's a positive thought or energy or a negative thought or energy—grows and expands exponentially, the extent of which is measured solely by one's attention and devotion.

That evening I selected Love of the several I might have chosen from the attributes of God (Life, Love, Truth, and Mind), and set out to contemplate it, to savor it fully, using the transformative power of focused attention. The results: I experienced Love more profoundly that evening than I had experienced it in years. In addition, the focused contemplation offered other benefits—a stillness of mind, silence, and the cultivation of a valued state of being—including that of Love.

YOU KILLED THEM

The Voice revealed a disturbing past-life event, which, although it tore away at my soul, also allowed me to understand the reason for certain occurrences in my current life. These revelations allowed me to understand what I was experiencing in the here and now, placing those experiences in a larger context, giving me the opportunity to use that understanding to make amends in this lifetime, or to manage these life themes in ways that were more empathetic, and filled with a deeper wisdom.

This experience established a theme that would reappear in future out-of-body episodes. It is by far the most difficult one for me to tell. It deals with parents, siblings, and, for me, the unthinkable. I believe that I heard the music first. It was blaring so loud that it distracted me. I'm in a long hallway. I'm being drawn by the music as well as by a desire to know what awaits me behind a door to my left. The door wins out. I open it and find inside a bunk bed and several cots. Children are resting on the beds, black children, and they all turn and look at me when I walk into the room. I knew instantly that the children are my sisters and brothers. They're all younger than I am, much younger. Each one couldn't have been more than a year apart. And they're all looking at me, and to me, to provide for them. The pressure of it, the crushing responsibility of it, is too much for me to bear. As I hovered over them, they reminded me of a nest of baby birds, mouths opened wide.

Where were our parents? I sat on the bed and peered deeply into their demanding eyes. When I could look no longer, I stood up and left. I was in the hall, again. The music was still extremely loud, distracting me. For a second time, I walked down the hall in the direction of the music, impatient to determine its origin. I could see in my mind's eye a nightclub with dancers stepping high to the beat of the music. I wanted to be one of them. As I walked down the hall, another door, one that I hadn't seen earlier fastened my attention. Once more, I was tempted to follow the music, but my curiosity as to what secrets might hide behind the door tempted me more. I opened the door and walked in. The room was shrouded in darkness. Against the wall in front of me, several feet away, the wall framing two large, curtained windows, I could see, parallel to the wall, the faint outline of a bed, and lying on it the appearance of two sleeping figures. Were these my parents? If not, who were they? From high above me The Voice spoke:

"You killed them."

"What do you mean, I killed them?" I asked The Voice. "I've never killed anyone in my life."

I could hear the music again, and, once more, it beckoned me, distracting me with its loudness. I wanted to lower the volume, or be consumed by it; either way, I would be able to think straight again. Out in the hallway now, I realized that the dark outlines on the bed were indeed my parents, and that I had killed them. I could hardly digest the thought. And I knew why I had killed them. They had deprived their children, had deprived me and my siblings; they had filled their needs at our expense. Even in this lifetime, those who have advantaged themselves at my expense have drawn my ire, creating yet another life theme. We went hungry so that they could eat sumptuously. We were crammed into a small room while they lived in relative splendor. We hardly saw them as I had become both mother and father to a brood who looked to me as their sole parent.

It wasn't fair.

I was a child myself, and I resented their self-indulgence and the burden that they had placed upon my back. For this, I had killed them and felt no regret. That was then; this is now. Now the regret has manifested itself in many ways. In that lifetime, I lost my parents because I killed them. I lost them again when, in another life, I died while still quite young. In this lifetime, I lost my mother to cancer long before I knew her well enough to remember her.

Even after seeing my mother shortly after her death, I didn't learn until I was an adult, after many years had passed, that the lifeless woman I had looked upon was my mother. My oldest sister with whom I was then living had lifted me and my twin brother to a window to look upon a deceased woman who rested in what seemed, at our young age, to be a bed, but was probably a casket. Over her a net had been placed. The room, a bedroom, would have been dark, but for the light from a dresser lamp that cast an eerie glow over her and the room.

As I moved closer and closer to the music—a blues piece—the music grew louder and louder. When I reached the screen door at the end of the hallway, I unlatched it, and looked out onto the night. From where I stood, I could see dark, squatting buildings, and yellow, dull lights streaming from windows that had never been washed. I looked in the direction of the music and yearned deeply to be with those who were closest to it. It was then that I became aware that I was experiencing an out-of-body event and that if I didn't control my emotions, or if I thought too hard about returning involuntarily to my body, I would be snapped back as though I was tethered to a giant rubber band that had stretched beyond its limits. I don't believe that the silver cord is constrained by distance, but usually when I begin thinking about my physical body, it's always a clear indication that I'll soon be returning to it. This time was no exception. I was happy to be free of the loud music, but disappointed that I couldn't investigate its origin

As a result of this out-of-body experience, and the previous one where I would soon die, leaving behind my parents and siblings, I've come to respect motherhood, fully aware that not all mothers are saints, and that some can abuse or abandon their children on a whim. Notwithstanding, I revere motherhood as sacred, and deserving of respect, even when some mothers' deeds dishonor that blessed state. I envy those who knew their mother, and encourage others to cherish their mother whenever possible. The pain I have felt in this lifetime as a result of losing my mother while still a child is incalculable.

In a later out-of-body experience I came upon a young black girl, per-haps no older than two years old, walking in a kitchen all alone. I asked her to tell me her name, and she said that she was my mother. I heard the words in my mind, as her lips didn't move. It was the voice of an adult, and not that of a child. I kneeled down and embraced her, thanking her for having been my mother in this, my current life. In retrospect, I felt her loss once again, and the poignancy of it. But our unexpected meeting in the astral realm made up for some of that loss.

This experience was a reminder that upon death no punishment awaits us, unless we consent to it, or have provoked unpleasant consequences, as a result of cause and effect. Hell, on the other hand, as a place of pun-ishment in the afterlife, presents its own set of problems, and will be dis-cussed later. Whatever we did poorly in one lifetime, we can resolve in future ones: Subsequent lifetimes afford us the opportunity to live out solu-tions to problems posed in a previous life. For instance, the killing of my parents in one lifetime became a problem to be resolved in a second, third, or perhaps a fourth lifetime, the solution of which is worked out through my experiences, reinforcing the understanding that to kill one's parents is exceedingly reckless. It reveals, in addition, a lack of understanding of the purpose of life, and the immense value of relationships.

Through these seemingly negative experiences I gained a greater appreciation for that which I had discounted in a previous life. The ensuing experiences, inclusive of other lifetimes, were not designed to punish, although they appeared to do just that, but allowed me to grow in understanding and wisdom. Further, they were not designed to only exact an "eye for eye."[46] If that were the case, just allowing me to be killed by my children, or by my parents, in succeeding lifetimes, would have satisfied that karma. Instead, the experiences were structured in such a way that I grew in wisdom. Retribution, therefore, was not sought; the death of another— in this case, that of my parents—was not avenged for the sake of justice alone, but that understanding would be advanced. This seems to be one of the purposes of recurring lives and reincarnation: the evolution of the soul, so that it may experience all that it is.

Having killed my parents in a previous life wasn't without consequence, however, despite my belief at the time that it had been justified. The law of cause and effect (the Law of Reciprocity) doesn't take into account the reasons or the justifications that one might invoke at the time to sanction the commission of a particular act, but insists, instead, that the act must now be reciprocated, not for justice entirely, but for the impartation of wisdom.

Justice, then, becomes not merely a human exacting of punishment, for which we have constructed a vast and complex legal system for the sole purpose of meting out retribution, but karmic—as the term is often used in a popular sense, meaning a reaping for what has been sown—a reaping that may extend over several lifetimes, and not necessarily in conjunction with a man-made reckoning, but lasting until the scales of justice have been balanced, or until we have "paid the uttermost farthing."[47]

---

46 Ex 21:24
47 Matt 5:26

What I learned was this: justice isn't about retribution or punishment but about cause and effect, consequences, rather than a mere getting even.

IN RESPONSE TO A FERVENT PRAYER

While yet in my youth, I heard The Voice again, not for doing something as horrific as shooting robins with an air rifle, but while in prayer. When my twin brother and I were six or seven, we often visited my dad's friend, also a minister, and his wife. His friend and his friend's wife were both black. They resided on the same street as my dad, but a good walking distance for someone our age. The wife, a sweet, gentle soul occasioned the visits as much, if not more so, than her husband, who often commissioned us to dig for buried treasure in his back yard, a treasure hunt that turned up more buried potatoes that grew there than treasure.

Thanks to the kindness of his wife, we believed no harm would befall us in their presence. One day, not far from his kitchen, our dad's friend introduced us to a new game. This time, he would test our ability to withstand pain. Where the clavicle meets the sternum on both sides of the rib cage, he used the thumb of his huge right hand to press as hard as he could in the depression, the hollow, or the pit that the juncture of the clavicle and sternum creates at the frontal base of the neck, in the area slightly above the jugular notch, also known as the suprasternal notch. The shock to my system was immediate: I couldn't breathe. I couldn't talk. I couldn't cry out. And on his face was a grin of sick delight in the agony that he was imposing, a face contorted with what can only be described as a maniacal pleasure, a surreal expression that haunts me to this day.

His wife, standing in the bedroom doorway a few feet away, apparently disgusted by the torment that her husband was inflicting on two small boys, finding our agony too much for her refined, maternal sensibilities, yelled out, "Leave them alone!" When she spoke, he released his grip. "If you touch those boys again, I'm going to tell," she threatened.

Her speaking up certainly represented an uncommon moment of courage for her, as I had never, until that moment, witnessed her so much as raise her voice to her husband, but who moved around him with the utmost diffidence and submission. I wouldn't be surprised to know that he abused her as well, although I never witnessed it. My brother doesn't remember the incident, but the impression that the experience left on my young mind was indelible. Outside, walking past the chinaberry trees that bordered the front of his house, we returned home. When we were a safe distance from the threat, I said in earnest to my twin brother, "She doesn't have to worry about us, we ain't ever coming back here again."

And we didn't.

Although we wanted to, we didn't tell our dad about the incident for fear that he wouldn't believe us, but would take the word of his friend over that of his young sons. After all, our tormenter was his friend.

The attack left a deep, emotional scar. The area of my throat where I was assaulted had been so traumatized that it developed a tingling sensation. The persistent habit of using a hissing sound of a sort as a way to stop the tingling in that part of the throat began shortly after the assault, and persisted for years afterward. It was the incessant tingling during the intervening years that eventually prompted me to turn to God and prayer for help. At the time, I was a teenager, but had grown weary of the constant hissing for which I was often told by family members, "Stop that," reminding me that I wasn't the only one who found the hissing irritating. The only time that I didn't hiss to stop the tingling in my throat was when I was absorbed in watching television, or while at the movies.

Having decided to pray about it, I assumed my prayer posture: I kneeled at my bedside, rested my elbows on the bed spread, and clasped my hands into a prayer gesture.

"God, please heal me of this," I said over and over, with the fervency of a drowning man. The Bible states, "The effectual fervent prayer of a righteous man availeth much."[48] I didn't know if that included children, but I would soon find out. I was on my knees for what seemed like hours. My tear-stained face refreshed itself again and again from tearful eyes, as I desperately sought a release from my anguish. The release came in the form of a voice. There was nothing stern in The Voice; it was not as harsh as it was the first time I heard it. The Voice was now tender and mild.

"When you want to do that [stop the tingling in my throat by hissing]," The Voice said, "cough instead."

That was it. Nothing more. Yet that simple advice proved to be the answer to my prayers. Following The Voice's direction, I coughed each time the tingling in my throat occurred, and the subsequent desire to hiss, as a way to soothe or scratch it, overpowered me.

It worked!

Instead of hissing to soothe my throat, and to stop the tingling, I coughed. After a time, even the coughing disappeared, and so did the tingling, and the accompanying hissing, finding at last the peace and the healing I so desperately prayed for, overjoyed that I was no longer a physical victim of the traumatic experience that had occurred years before, although the emotional scars lingered.

As a young man in my twenties, and no longer afraid that my father wouldn't believe me, I recounted the story of my physical abuse at the hands of his friend. I could see that the recounting pained him.

"You know how he died?" he asked, referencing his friend.

I shook my head, and said, "No."

"Two white men killed him along the highway."

He said it in a way that said, his friend had received a measure of punishment for his sins, no doubt one of them the sin of inflicting pain on two young boys for his own sadistic pleasure. I can only pray that the method of his death satisfied the karmic debt that he had built up over a lifetime, but

---

48 James 5:16

that's an outcome that only his Soul knows, as the Soul is the only one who will make that determination, and not he himself alone. Jesus statement comes to mind regarding a child that was brought before him:

And whoso shall receive one such little child in my name receiveth me.

But whoso shall offend one of these little ones which believe in me, it were better for him that a millstone were hanged about his neck, and that he were drowned in the depth of the sea.

Woe unto the world because of offences! for it must needs be that offences come; but woe to that man by whom the offence cometh (Matt 18:5-7).

For some, a single lifetime doesn't allow sufficient time for all karmic debts to be repaid, debts which may be spread over several lifetimes, perhaps offering up one answer to the question: Why do bad things happen to good people?

A MEETING WITH JESUS

Many of us hope to one day meet Jesus, to look upon his holy visage and rejoice in the light of his countenance, the Light of "Our Father which art in heaven." Although most of us feel that we'll meet Jesus when we die, I didn't have to die in this lifetime to meet him, I was privy to such a meeting in a previous lifetime. I was out-of-body at the time, reliving a previous life where men carried swords for weapons and was spartanly dressed. I was dying and I knew it. The figure that approached me I knew instinctively and instantly—it was Jesus. Although I was lying flat on my back, and wounded, I could see him approach. His gait was lively, full of purpose and determination. I knew, too, that although I could see him, others couldn't. I could see him because I was dying and they weren't. I read someplace years later that it wasn't unusual for dying men to encounter Jesus on the battlefield.

He came to where I lay, wounded, mortally wounded. He kneeled next to my head and whispered something to me, words which I have long forgotten. He looked more like the reconstructed face on the Shroud of Turin, bearded and unremarkable, than the Hollywood version that I was all too familiar with, a Jesus with blue eyes, fair skin, and stunningly handsome. This is not to discount the portrait of Jesus by Akiane Kramarik, the child artist who drew a portrait of Jesus titled, "The Prince of Peace," based on visions of Jesus she's experienced from an early age. Jesus can assume any visage he chooses.

I wish that I could remember the words that Jesus whispered in my ear as I lay dying, but I don't. What I do know is that his words carried great import whether they reflected on a previous life, the life I was currently living, or a life to come. The impression that I received from reliving my death was that, in time, in another life, I would live a life that wouldn't be marred by violence, but one in service to God.

A MEETING WITH A LIGHT

On another out-of-body excursion, I was sitting at a long table, talking to a man on my left who sat at the head of the table. Without warning the man disappeared, leaving in his place a bright light and nothing more. The light spoke, not unlike the "flame of fire out of the midst of a bush"[49] from which God called out unto Moses. The light expressed its disappointment with how I was living my current life. I realized from the scolding that the light had great hopes for me in my present life, hopes that I wasn't fulfilling. I felt that I had let it down. Days afterward, the disappointment lingered, casting a dark shadow of regret over my heart and mind, incentivizing my

---

49 Ex 3:2

determination to live in such a way that I might remove the disappointment and restore the esteem of the light.

THEY'RE NOT WHAT THEY SEEM

From time to time, The Voice would alert me to the character and intention of others, especially those I had recently met. They were men as well as women. The warning might be issued at the time of the meeting or later, when I was home, relaxed, and my attention not divided. When The Voice wasn't warning me, I detected that certain people, for no apparent reason, found my company unpleasant, even before we interacted, choosing to keep their distance. I credit this debarring of certain persons into my confidence to my Unseen Guide who sought to protect me even when I didn't know the reason for his protection. Nevertheless, I always heeded his warnings, whether given verbally or as a result of warding off the advances of certain unsavory characters.

A PREDICTION

I had decided to omit this revelation, one received from The Voice, but it kept rising to the surface of my mind like so many submerged flotation devices. Before the turn of the century and before the beginning of the New Age, our current age, the Age of Aquarius, which some believe began in 2012, although there's wide speculation as to the actual date, The Voice spoke these words to me:

You're entering a New Age,

A New Way.

A New Wind shall blow your way

Until the day you die.

The New Age referenced here, might be pointing to the Age of God, as well as to an astrological age. At the time of the revelation, I believed that the "New Wind" would bring more Joy, more Peace, and more Abundance into my life. Indirectly, I suppose it did just that, but not before it rent asunder and shattered all that I then possessed, my marriage, my material goods, and my peace of mind. Most of what I had acquired, or had built over time, was dismantled in short order, block by block, beam by beam, leaving my world in shambles. I would eventually pick myself up and dust myself off, but not without first releasing the Old Age, and starting anew, reconciling my mind to the destruction left by the New Wind, and resolving to build again, and to do so without regrets for what was lost.

Although this New Wind impacted me personally, it would impact the world as well, and impact it in a similar fashion—the destruction of all that is familiar and dear. This Wind of destruction has been blowing upon our world for a time and will continue to blow, destroying social, political, and institutional structures, not to punish us, but to allow us to start anew, to build again, and this time build something that addresses the whole of us, and not just a privileged few. The New Wind will bring a New Way, which can only emerge after the Old Way has been destroyed, and that destruction is the task of the New Wind. The Preacher speaks of these inevitable changes that come to us all as a "season" and as a "time:"

To every thing there is a season, and a time to every purpose under the heaven:

A time to be born, and a time to die; a time to plant, and a time to pluck up that which is planted;

A time to kill, and a time to heal; a time to break down, and a time to build up;

A time to weep, and a time to laugh; a time to mourn, and a time to dance;

A time to cast away stones, and a time to gather stones together; a time to embrace, and a time to refrain from embracing;

A time to get, and a time to lose; a time to keep, and a time to cast away;

A time to rend, and a time to sew; a time to keep silence, and a time to speak;

A time to love, and a time to hate; a time of war, and a time of peace (Eccl. 3:1-8).

THE VOICE PREDICTS A DISASTER

Out-of-body, I found myself at my bedroom window peering into the night sky. Streaking across it was a comet. The Voice said in response to the comet, "When you see the comet again, great destruction will be in its wake." With a little research, I learned that the sighting of a comet portends impending disaster. I didn't know this mythology about comets prior to my research. As a child, perhaps a teenager, I had seen a comet with a long tail make its way across the Texas sky. It was a memorable sight, but one that would pale alongside the one I was now witnessing. At the time of the warning, I believed that the comet would be seen in the external world, but that wouldn't be the case.

A few weeks later, I was out-of-body again, peering out the same window. Across the night sky above me a comet blazed from North to South, signaling, as was foretold, that destruction would soon follow, and follow it did, perhaps a couple of days hence. I was married at the time. My wife and I were awakened by a massive shaking which was only intensified by the passing of a train less than a block from where we lived at the time. It was as though all hell had broken loose. We sought refuge within a doorway, as we had been instructed to do by television and radio during a quake, bracing ourselves there until the shaking had subsided. The 6.5 earthquake on the Richter scale struck at 6:01 a.m. PST on February 9, 1971, and lasted for about twelve seconds—twelve seconds of sheer terror that seemed to last an eternity.

The earthquake that shook a large area of Southern California that morning is known as the Sylmar Earthquake or the San Fernando Earthquake. According to news accounts, the temblor claimed sixty-four lives with most of the deaths occurring at one location, the Veterans Hospital, the quake reducing to rubble two of its main buildings. Damage was wide-spread, and many buildings and structures were compromised. At the passing of the quake, my wife and I readied ourselves for work, grateful that we would live to see another day, and that our small apartment was still standing although the quake threatened for a time to pull it apart.

As with the lore of the comet, many take great delight in dismissing mythological creatures as so many creations of men. Nevertheless, they do exist, not in our external world, but in our internal one. Existing in the internal, or astral realm, are the Unicorn, and the Phoenix, and many others such as the Griffin, the Centaur, and the Minotaur. Within their form they carry a message for those who can decipher them. For example, the Phoenix, which I have seen, represents man as he rises from the ashes of his human selfhood, having destroyed, or reduced to ashes, the mortal aspects of himself. Using the cleansing properties of fire, man can be new born, experience a spiritual rebirth. My vision of the Phoenix came at a time when I was casting off the old for the new, exchanging worldly influences for spiritual realities, the lie for the Truth, and material pursuits for spiritual ones.

Not long after I wrote the previous paragraph, The Voice made this observation: "Out of the ashes, a new you emerged." The reflection came as many have come, shortly after awakening in the morning, and while I meditated and prayed. Although I'm not as perfect as I would like to be, in many ways I am "new," new physically, new mentally, and, most of all, new spiritually. The physical world that I thought I knew, not unlike the shift that occurred during the Sylmar Earthquake, underwent a seismic shift of exponential proportions. I realized over time that the world that I thought was physical was, surprisingly, a mental world, subject to my thoughts, my imagination, and my beliefs.

THE GOD GENE

Over the years, my meditations have brought forth many revelations from a source that I call my Inner Wisdom, also known as The Voice. This time when The Voice spoke, I could see a form, even if I couldn't put a face to it. The form was a figure of a man, that much I could tell, and he was wearing a robe, not unlike those worn in the time of Jesus. He stood in front of me, but it was though he stood in a cloud or a mist that allowed him to be seen, but not too clearly, a diffusive figure, a little more than an outline, but no clearer for it. I could hear him speak from behind the cloud. He said, "There's a truly remarkable gene called the God Gene." At the time of receiving this revelation I didn't recall that I knew of this Gene. After researching it on the Internet, I realized that I had, at some earlier time, read something about the Gene, but had dismissed it then, thinking at the time that it was very unlikely that such a Gene existed, and if so, how was it identified as such. The explanation as to how can be found with a little research, and is as close as your computer.

Despite the explanation of how the Gene was identified, a great deal of controversy still swirls around its meaning, as would be expected, from both sides of the divide, those who believe in God, and those who do not, both using the God Gene to advance their own positions. The God Gene, VMAT2, suggests that spirituality, and, therefore, a belief in a Higher Being, a God, is a foregone conclusion, hardwired, as it were, as part of our human genome. Although I was initially dismissive of the notion of a God Gene, the existence of it doesn't surprise me. We are after all spiritual beings, and as spiritual beings we already possess and express two spiritual qualities, life and mind. Therefore, we project through our physical bodies several God-like attributes—three of which are Spirit, Mind, and Life. The projection of these attributes can be observed to some extent, although they can't be sourced in the physical body. The God Gene, VMAT2, is merely a physical manifestation of that spiritual projection through the physical body, just as certain aspects of our mind might be similarly observed. Our physical body is nothing more than an avatar through which our astral, our non-physical body can project itself, its spirituality, its life, and its mind. It was created perfectly for that purpose and towards that end, including the creation of a gene called the God Gene, VMAT2.

My take is that the existence of the God Gene is Life's way of guaranteeing that man won't become so mired in physicality that he forgets his spiritual origin. The Gene, then, becomes man's escape plan, representing more than an evolutionary assurance that he won't self-destruct, that he will always operate in his best interest, the interest of Life, the interest of survival. What better way to remind Man of his spiritual selfhood than to have at the ready a genetic light switch (an epigenetic marker), which can turn the God Gene "On" when certain environmental factors—internal as well as external factors—such as chemicals, or human affections, are present. What we should take into account is that we can be one of those external, or environmental factors that can turn the switch "On," and that we can do so with our minds, our thoughts, our feelings, or our emotions (love and fear), and that it doesn't turn itself on and neither does it provide the attributes associated with it without external factors first turning on the switch.

These spiritual feelings, then, first emanate from our non-physical body before they become evident in our physical body. It doesn't mean, however, that those who have the switch in the fully-on position can tap the whole of their spirituality, their true nature, but that those with it have a predisposition towards things spiritual, whether that predisposition is activated or not. For me, whether I have the Gene in the "On" position or not, spirituality, an abiding love for God, has marked my life from an early age. I'm told that my mother was a highly spiritual and prayerful person, one who could have passed on to me a genetic predisposition to spirituality.

With a father who was also a minister, a man of the cloth, you'd think that all their kids would have inherited an active VMAT2 devotion to a life of spirituality. Although I can't speak categorically for them all, I can say that some of us appeared to be more spiritual than others in the family.

THIRTEEN

EXPAND OUR VIEW OF REALITY

STRANGE ENCOUNTERS

I F YOU SUCCEED IN CONTACTING THE *YOU* IN YOU, EVERY-thing changes. For one, your sense of reality changes or what you thought was real. What you once thought to be pedestrian is now alive with possibilities, forcing a radical shift in your perspective, altering your perception of a world you thought you knew, for which you must now become reacquainted. Nothing expands your view of reality more than bizarre out-of-body encounters. Unlike some out-of-body explorers, I've never been able to select my out-of-body destinations. God knows, I've tried. Often forced to follow the astral currents wherever they have taken me, I have visited places that defy the rules and logic of this world.

Granted, not all out-of-body explorers are as limited as I am. Some have the enviable ability to select their own out-of-body destinations. Rather than have these destinations selected for them, they can select them themselves, and ahead of time, that is, before they leave their body. As a result, they're at will as to where they will go in the astral realm, a realm that exists parallel to the physical, choosing to visit, in their astral form, family members, friends, or anyone else they wish to visit. Those who happen to see them, often mistake them for apparitions, indicating that not all specters are from the other side, but may reside on our current plane of human existence. It seems we have the ability that some apparitions have, the ability to travel at will on the astral plane. We're compelled, then, to conclude: The supposed division that seems to exist between the dead and those alive is not a real division at all. We all have the ability to venture onto the astral plane, albeit in some people, it's a latent, undeveloped ability.

I can have a destination in mind, but more often than not I will end up someplace I didn't intend. Occasionally I visited a place I wanted to visit, but it was never a planned visit. Usually this happened after spending sometime anticipating a visit to, or becoming emotionally involved in, a certain location. For example, days leading up to a visit to my parents, I was bursting with excitement about my impending visit. One night, out-of-body, I found myself at their house. I didn't go inside on that visit, but have entered on previous occasions. Against the house, I could see a ladder, and on the ground near the house workmen's tools and construction materials. I quickly realized that my parents were having repairs done to the house.

Next, I found myself in the garage, which is detached from the house, but occupies a place near the rear of the house. I walked to the back of the garage's interior and discovered a small room, a room that I didn't remember being there, and hanging on a nail was a pair of my dad's work trousers. I reasoned that my dad had built the room during my absence. Not long after this, I was there again, also out-of-body. This time I was lying in bed in my parent's guest bedroom, thinking about the trip I had just completed, how I managed to get there so quickly, impressed with the shortcut I had taken. Thinking about it later, the short cut had perplexed me. What shortcut? At the time of these out-of-body experiences, I hadn't yet decided how I would travel home. As it turned out, I decided to fly. And indeed this was the shortcut that had perplexed me. It had taken only a few hours to fly from Ontario, California to Houston, Texas, and a short drive from there to my parents' house by car.

When I arrived that evening, the first thing I noticed leaning against the house was the ladder from my previous out-of-body visit, and on the ground, tools and construction material. I used a part of the next day to investigate the room at the back of the garage. I inspected the interior of the entire garage, but found no back room. I was disappointed that this detail of my out-of-body visit had come up short. I then walked to the back of the garage but this time the garage's exterior. And there it was: a room attached to the garage. It was a storage room. Dad's garden tools and other items were stored there. And on the wall, hanging on a nail was my dad's work trousers. Finally, my out-of-body experience substantiated. The storage room had been accessible to my astral body in a way that it hadn't been for my physical body. The barrier of a wall hadn't prevented my astral eyes from seeing the room, nor my astral body from entering it from the back of the garage.

SMALL DOORKNOBS AND A BLUE-GREEN INTERIOR

Not all out-of-body journeys begin with an encounter. Most of the time, the encounters come later. That was true for this out-of-body excursion, as well, which ended with an encounter. It was one of those out-of-body trips that began in darkness and ended in darkness, the darkness of the unknown tinged with the strange. When I arrived at my destination, I opened my eyes, which usually disperses the darkness, sometimes quickly, sometimes in a slow fade, to find myself in a room that looked like a kitchen. The entire room was painted blue green—the walls, the cabinets, the chairs. The cabinet drawers and doors were fitted with small, blue-green knobs. As interesting as that was, the color of the kitchen wasn't what made the room stand out. It stood out because the kitchen and everything in it was made for someone who was diminutive. It could have easily been built for one of J. R. R. Tolkien's *Hobbits*. I felt like a giant in the midst of it. I thought to open the cabinets and to look through the drawers, but I wanted to see more of this world. I knew that at any moment I might be snapped back, involuntarily, to my body.

When on an out-of-body jaunt, the prospect of returning to my physical body without warning is always uppermost in my mind, if not always consciously considered, a return trip which can't be prevented once the astral body is in the return mode, that is, when the physical body begins to tug on the astral, signaling an end to the out-of-body excursion. I knew that if I allowed my curiosity free rein, and didn't discipline it with a hierarchy of interests, I might miss something that I *truly* intended to see and didn't.

Because of this possibility, I have often passed up a smaller curiosity for a larger one. It didn't take long for me to reach the small door that led outside. It had one of those little green knobs. I pulled on it and the door opened on a world much like ours, except that I could tell that the house was in an isolated area. For miles around, it was the only structure I could see. I was standing on a landing from which stairs, from a second floor, descended to the ground below. From my vantage point, I could see trees and mountains in the distance. The kitchen and living quarters were upstairs. Was this a duplex, or a house that used its bottom half for non-living purposes?

Below a woman was preparing to ascend the stairs, and when she saw me, she was startled but unafraid. I surmised that she lived in the house, and I didn't want to wait around and explain how it was that I was just inside her home and was now leaving. I bounded down the stairs, rushing past the woman who watched me descend. Her diminutive physique made the room at the top of the stairs an accommodating place for her.

PONDEROUS, CORPULENT CREATURES

The strangest of all my strange encounters in the astral realm were the ponderous, corpulent creatures that danced out on stage to entertain spectators. I've had hundreds of out-of-body experiences over the years. Many of them have taken me to weird and wonderful places I never knew existed. There I've encountered creatures and beings that were equally weird and wonderful. Of all my experiences in the astral realm this one stands out as the most bizarre. I entered a massive building that looked the world like a theater, the one where live performances take place. Inside, rows of seats sloped toward a large stage. I'm the only one present. If there are others, I don't see them, but I have the distinct feeling that I'm not alone.

I took a seat near the front, perhaps no more than five rows from the stage. Lights illuminated the stage from an unknown source. The rest of the theater was enveloped in a gloom, yet many things could be discerned, as the seats, the walls and the fixtures reflected the light from the stage. I'm in an expectant mood, wondering what will transpire on stage. Will it be a play? A concert? A comedy routine? While my mind was entertaining such thoughts, from the right side of the stage, I spied a movement.

And then I saw them: They lumbered out on stage, large corpulent beings, their flesh hanging over their bodies in layers—over their stomach, their arms, and their legs. Even their huge heads were massive folds of flesh. They must have stood nine-feet tall. In awkward, heavy movements they danced across the stage, one behind the other, to a strange rhythm, and it all seemed to work with a grace and ease that belied their ponderous bodies. If I were to describe them as ugly, I would mislead. Another word would have to be invented to describe the whole of their appearance. These beings were both repugnant and fascinating at the same time. I couldn't distinguish their sex, as their clothes didn't reveal their gender, but the impression I received was that their energy was more masculine than feminine.

Were they from another world, dimension, or time? I had no idea. What I did know was that I wanted to find the exit as fast as I could, their size alone threatening my composure. There was something unsettling about the experience. I'm sure that it had a message for me, even if I couldn't quite decipher it. These creatures with large flat feet resonated with me somehow. They had an import that I couldn't exactly put my finger on. They didn't seem all that bright, these beings. And although they were too large to dance with the same grace and beauty of smaller, lither beings, they nevertheless danced to the best of their ability, to the best of their skills, and to the best of their knowledge. And I admired them for the effort.

FEAR OBJECTIFIED AS A DEMON-LIKE CREATURE

There is no fear in love; but perfect love casteth out fear: because fear hath torment. He that feareth is not made perfect in love.[50]

This was one out-of-body encounter I would have gladly passed up, but that wasn't to be. Despite the unpleasantness of the encounter, it taught me much about the power of fear, and fear's antidote, love. For all the help I often received now and again from the other side, it seemed that, more often than not, I'm all alone, and on my own—all alone to confront my fears, all alone in how to interpret my out-of-body experiences, and all alone in finding ways to cope with the aftermath of those experiences.

Perhaps it was possible to ask for and receive help, but help was rarely offered, further adding to the alienation I often felt when I ventured into unknown mental and astral realms. These ventures left me with one inescapable conclusion, consciousness is far more complex than we've ever imagined. With the use of our corporeal senses, we're allowed to perceive what we can of our physical world, to evaluate our place within it, as well as imagine how we might shape and form our external environment to suit our needs. I speak of an external environment, as though it's separate from our internal environment, but our consciousness can and does form and

---

50 I John 4:18

shape both environments, our internal and external environments—one is as malleable as the other.

Our consciousness has other functions, too. In addition to forming and shaping our internal and external environments, it creates them as well, along with creating what resides within them. In our external environment this creation is not as obvious as it is within our internal environment. Fear, for example, creates one kind of experience, love, another. Fear brings darkness, ugliness, pain and suffering, while love brings light, beauty, health, and joy. You may not be accustomed to thinking of pain and darkness, or health and light as forms, but they are nevertheless. Because of the creative nature of our individual consciousness, these objects often have unique formations, formations that may be perceived with our physical and non-physical senses alike.

For months I lived with a fear so great, that it gripped me, heart and soul. I couldn't define the nature of it. It had no name. It had no identity. In other words, I couldn't point to a single thing in my world—a situation or a person—and say that this was the source of my fear. The fear was so extreme that it consumed all the moments of my waking existence. It was a palpable presence, a controlling presence.

When the fear became so intense that it was unbearable, I confronted it. At the time that wasn't my purpose. It just happened. One night I found myself out of my body, and in a room. The room had an attic, accessible through a door in the ceiling. In this attic resided a gnome-like creature; it was abnormally black, with an Uncle Remus tar baby-like appearance, a viciously ugly creature, with sharp, long claws. The creature's energy felt more male than female. Before I could react, this hideous creature, arms and legs outstretched, leaped from its perch in the loft, and landed squarely on my chest, its sharp claws digging deep into my shoulders and torso, and where the claws dug in, a sharp pain riveted my attention, and underscored my predicament.

Without thinking, I grabbed its bulbous body with both hands and tried with all my might to pull it off. The more I pulled, the tighter it gripped and the deeper it dug, making my pain all the more excruciating.

Because the creature had grown more persistent in its effort to cling to me, I pulled all the harder. In desperation I yanked as hard as I could. With that, it released its grip, and the force with which I pulled sent him flying through the room. I believe at that point he gave up, vanquished, as he didn't return, but ran away on stubby legs. My fear had become objectified through this creature. The pain of his sharp claws was the pain I had endured daily for several months. I can't say which came first, the fear or the impish demon. It could be that the demon brought the fear or the fear created the demon. If it's the latter, then we'll create now, or hereafter, our personal heaven or hell, predicated on the thoughts we entertain, whether they are thoughts of love or thoughts of fear.

This battle with the demon, culminating in its defeat, ended my daily bouts with my ever-present irrational fear, marking the beginning of mostly fearless days, or days where my fears were at least identifiable ones.

OTHER DIMENSIONS, ANOTHER TIME
I SAW MY HOUSE AS IT WAS BEING CONSTRUCTED

In the astral realm it's possible to visit many places. It's also possible to explore many time periods. The past and the future are just as accessible as the here and now. Reliving the past or peering into the future, as implausible as that may sound, is within the grasp of the out-of-body explorer. You may not always determine the direction of your out-of-body travels, or which lifetime you're permitted to review, yet the possibility of traveling backward and forward in time is definitely within your reach. Whenever I've had these time-traveling experiences, I have always brought back knowledge to ponder, or vital information to take note of. For this reason, I believe that my many journeys into the past or the future were directed by my Soul, my Higher Self, for the purpose of advancing it. By allowing me to relive moments from the past, or to live moments from the future—moments that don't yet exist in my physical reality—I'm given the opportunity to redirect, and re-create the present using the surety born of hindsight and foresight.

The colonial house I lived in for a time was built just after the Second World War. It was a white, wood-siding dwelling that had a guest house and a detached garage close by. I loved the house, but it was on a street that was heavily used by JPL (Jet Propulsion Laboratory) employees as a route to and from work, and by the local bus company as a turn-around point. The last run for the bus was sometime after midnight, and the first run before six in the morning. The result: We live on a street that was busy and noisy, with a sleep time that was frequently interrupted by the noise. Although we liked the house, we sold it in due course in our search for a street that was quieter and not so well traveled. After searching for a while, we found our perfect home, a house situated on land running the full length of the wider, circular end of a large and quiet cul-de-sac.

One night, before I moved to my new residence, I found myself walking through the colonial in my out-of-body state, finding it under construction. I could see studs, planks on the floor, saw horses, and the like. What I was seeing was a house under construction, but without workers present. If the time there coincided with the current time, late night, there would be no workers on site. I think it was my love for the house that sparked this out-of-body experience, transporting me into the house's past. Having been astral projected into a house that was half-built was a little unsettling, but it allowed me to know the house in ways which only the builders got to know it.

I WAS RICH IN ONE DIMENSION, BUT LIVING IN THE SAME HOUSE

When the encounters aren't with other beings, or creatures, but multi-dimensional locations, you find yourself questioning the nature of time, as well as the fixity of the reality that takes place within that time. If you think that it would be amazing to go back in time to see your house being constructed, think what it would feel like to find yourself in the same house but have it exist in another dimension, a parallel world.

It was the same colonial, but different. Everywhere I looked, the house looked every bit the house of a rich man—the furniture, the paintings on the wall, the ornate trimming, the plush carpet. This was not the house of my here and now existence, but the house of my dreams. For all its grandeur, and opulence, there was no reason to believe that the house didn't exist, but belonged, instead, to a parallel self in a parallel existence. Possibly, without his knowledge, I had become him for a while, living within his body and within his home for a time. Unlike me, this parallel self was rich. Unlike me, he enjoyed a lifestyle I could only imagine.

I wondered at times if it were possible for him to be me, if only for a moment. If I could be him, perhaps he could be me, exist in my world for a time, provided certain propitious conditions aligned themselves. Perhaps while we slept. Perhaps while we were lost in reverie. Perhaps while we were consumed by our desires, or by our fears. Are doppelgangers, then, a physical manifestation of this phenomenon? How often do our parallel selves from other dimensions cross over into our reality without our knowledge, and how often do we cross over into theirs?

NOT QUITE BACK YET

I lived in an apartment once with a front and back entrance. To reach the back entrance I had to walk up a flight of stairs. Once on the landing it was difficult to recognize one renter's entrance from another. This was especially true at night. After climbing the stairs one night, and finding what I believed was my door, I inserted my backdoor key in the lock, and turned it. I opened the door, and walked into my kitchen (or so I thought). I went into the adjoining dining room, and that's when I realized that things didn't feel quite right. It was like trying on a pair of trousers that weren't my own, although I thought they were, and finding the fit uncomfortable.

The room was dark, and the light switch was still a few feet away. With my unease growing, I stood motionless, listening. And then I heard it—a woman's voice—ask, "What are you doing in here? You'd better get out of here!" I stammered my apologies and retreated, grateful that the woman hadn't shot me or hit me with a frying pan or a rolling pin, thinking I was a burglar, or worse. Unknown to me at the time, my backdoor key fitted my lock, and my neighbor's lock as well. Finally, in my own apartment, I breathed a sigh of relief, although hours later I still smarted with embarrassment.

I told you about this event because something similar happened after an out-of-body flight. Upon returning to my body, I opened my eyes and looked around. Nothing was out of place. When the astral current swept me away, I was in my bedroom, in my bed, with my wife sleeping next to me. She was still asleep. I woke her to tell her about my out-of-body journey. She wasn't happy that I had awakened her, and didn't wish, at the time, to talk about my out-of-body excursion. In fact, she was angry, and chided me for having left my body. I turned over in bed, disappointed that she hadn't listened. I looked about the room knowing that in a few hours I would have to rise and prepare for work.

And then it happened. Again, I was swept away by the astral current, only to find that I hadn't, as I believed, returned to my room, my bed, or my wife. I only thought I had. I was fully back now, realizing to my dismay that I had taken a detour, had opened a door that looked like my door, had entered a room that looked like my room, but which in fact belonged to another, an alternate me, in an alternate reality. Although the first room to which I returned looked like the room I had left, it didn't fit as comfortably as it now did. I knew that I was back. I woke my wife but she had no recollection of our earlier discussion. The room that I had first entered looked the same as the room I was now in—including my bed, and my sleeping wife—but it was not my room.

Taking this and similar experiences into account, I hypothesized the existence of parallel universes, worlds identical to our world, peopled with humans just like us, but not really us, merely alternate versions of us. While traveling outside the body, it was possible to stumble upon these other worlds, and these other selves, and to think that they are us. I believe that we're connected in some way to them, but live most of our life discretely, unaware of the existence of the others. I wondered if my parallel selves during their out-of-body journeys in parallel universes, stumbled upon me occasionally, and for a time became me, only to learn later that they'd taken a detour and landed short of their mark. I'd like to think that I'm on to something here, that these other selves and universes will integrate some day and I will be aware of all the many selves that I may be. I can hope can't I? I have the key (the out-of-body experience); all I need now is to turn the key in the lock.

FOURTEEN

REVEAL THE PAST, PRESENT, AND FUTURE

VISIONS AND FUTURE TRAVELING

And it shall come to pass afterward, that I will pour out my spirit upon all flesh; and your sons and your daughters shall prophesy, your old men shall dream dreams, your young men shall see visions.[51]

GUIDANCE CAN COME IN MANY FORMS, AND THE *YOU* in you have no shortage of means to inform specifically and generally about our lives and the lives of others, expanding on the English proverb, "to be forewarned is to be forearmed." Having the ability to leave my body is only one of several abilities I possess of supposed supernatural origin. I won't enumerate them all, but I would like to remark on my ability to discover things that others may be hiding, and my ability to see the future. I call them visions. They may be related to my out-of-body ability, and remote viewing, even though they have a different feel. These visions come when I lie down to relax, or meditate. I distinguish them from dreams by their clarity, revelatory nature, and sense of immediacy (you feel

---

51 Joel 2:28

that you are actually there when certain things are occurring). As always, the visions revealed that of which I had no prior knowledge.

SLAUGHTER KILLING SOMEONE

For several years I worked at a juvenile detention center. As part of their various duties, the inmates were required to work and attend school. Many of them worked inside the school proper, and I had several working for me. One in particular, I'll call him Slaughter, took a liking to me. And I liked him; he was a hard worker and personable. All the center inmates respected him, or, should I say, feared him: He was known as someone you didn't want to cross. Knowing his reputation, I hired him anyway. When I met Slaughter, I hadn't been working at the center for very long. He quickly reassured me: "You ain't got nothing to worry about. I ain't gonna let anybody hurt you." And I believed him. He had a way about him that said, "If I like you, I'll go to hell and back for you."

One evening after work, I reclined on my bed to meditate before dinner, as was my custom. After about ten minutes, I was inside a barbershop. It was dark and the only light I could see streamed in from small windows near the ceiling. In the middle of the room was a barber's chair. And in the chair a man sat. I assumed that the man in the chair was the barber, resting there between customers. Behind the man stood Slaughter. In one quick movement, he wrapped something around the man's neck, and used it to choke the life from him. He had approached the man from behind, out of the shadows. Either the man didn't know he was there, or he was unsuspecting. That's when I knew that Slaughter, as likeable as he was, and as protective as he was, was also a murderer. I didn't know if the event I had just witnessed was in Slaughter's past or in his future. Nevertheless, I kept the vision to myself, as I didn't want him to know what I knew of his past or possibly his future. I don't think he would have continued to like me.

INSTRUCTOR AT THE SCHOOL WITH A BLIND EYE

Immediately after the first vision, I had another; this time it involved an instructor at the very same juvenile detention center. It was as though the film in my mind had fast forward, shifting my location in the process, as I was no longer with Slaughter in the barbershop, but was now at the center. The instructor was a teacher in the school. Attending class and completing high school was an essential part of the inmates' rehabilitation, as it prepared them to reenter society on a par with their peers. As I stood facing him, standing outside the entrance to my work location, the teacher, a white male, positioned himself in the doorway, just in front of me, and over his right eye was a black patch. Although he never wore one, the patch over his eye in my vision revealed that he was blind in that eye. Anyone looking at him wouldn't have known, because there was nothing to give it away. One of the prerequisites for working at the center or remaining employed was that you, as an employee, had to have a certain level of visual acuity. If the teacher was blind in one eye, this would have been reason enough to force him into an early retirement.

The next day, as fate would have it, or my vision, he came to my work location. He was a man of considerable bulk and easily filled the space of my door. I asked, as he stood in the doorway, as in my vision, "Hey, is there something wrong with your right eye?" His response was physical before it was verbal. The startled expression on his face instantly turned to anger, informing me that I had touched a nerve. "Who told you that? Who told you that?" he demanded. For a second, I thought he would hit me. His voice was filled with rage, and he glowered at me with both eyes, the good eye and the bad eye. Realizing my predicament, I hastened to put him at ease, explaining that I had seen him squint his right eye from time to time. My explanation seemed to calm him, as the conversation quickly switched to a more pleasant and innocuous subject.

Because the two visions—Slaughter killing someone, and the instructor with a blind eye—occurred sequentially, during the same meditation session, I never doubted the accuracy of the first vision, although I thought it best not to reveal what I knew to Slaughter for corroboration. It just seemed ill-advised, especially in light of the fact that the killing of the barber might have been in his past, and something he'd not want known, not by me or the authorities. Given how the center instructor had responded to my inquiry regarding his eyesight, I never regretted confronting Slaughter with my knowledge, as it might not have been well received.

MY DAUGHTER AS A GROWN WOMAN WHILE YET A LITTLE GIRL

My daughter couldn't have been more than nine or ten when I caught a glimpse of both our futures. More than a vision, this was an out-of-body experience that offered a preview of a time yet to come. She was married. Her husband was white and he reminded me a great deal of the actor, Richard Boone, who played Paladin on television. I could see the groom sitting in what appeared to be a restaurant, surrounded by people seated in chairs at tables throughout the room. I had the feeling that my daughter had only recently married. I was standing outside with her now, realizing that our then strained relationship would remain strained. I knew, too, that we would never be close, not even after she had reached adulthood. It had always been my hope that once she became a grown woman the ice between us would thaw, and we could be friends, even if a father-daughter relationship wasn't possible. Knowing the disquieting future of our relationship brought tears to my eyes, then, and years later.

My daughter did indeed marry. The groom was white, as my out-of-body experience had shown me many years prior. Before the wedding, I hadn't met her fiancé, so I didn't know his race. The wedding took place within an enclosed garden. Everywhere I looked, an assortment of flowers could be seen growing. Large goldfish swam in a pond beneath a crossing, a small pedestrian bridge. It was a beautiful setting for a wedding, and those in attendance spoke approvingly of the couple's choice. The bride was escorted down a long shady path by her uncle. The minister directed them through their vows, and when it was over, guests retired to the reception site, which seemed to double as a restaurant. Apparently, they had secured the garden and the restaurant as much for their proximity, as for their convenience. True to my out-of-body vision of things to come, people were seated at tables throughout the reception site, while my companion and I, and several others, sat at booths arranged along a wall with wide windows. Also true to my vision of more than a dozen years earlier, my relationship with my daughter was still strained. Alas, I had not been her choice to give her away, nor was I the first to meet her new husband among the guests in attendance. Feeling a little down, my escort consoled me, and encouraged me to do what most fathers do at weddings, dance with their daughters. She consented to dance with me. While we danced, I told her how proud I was of her and wished her much happiness.

I don't blame my daughter for our strained relationship in this lifetime, only myself. Were it not that I killed my parents in a previous life, precipitating events in this lifetime for the purpose of engendering a greater understanding of the parent-child relationship, we would be closer. During all our lifetimes, our Souls collaborate to bring us just the right experiences to effect change, the result of a shifting of our perspective. If there's a moral here, it's this: Our actions in any lifetime, whether for the good or for the bad, are returned to us in kind, if not in our current lifetime, surely in lifetimes to follow.

NEW HIRE

When a position in my office became vacant, it became my responsibility, as manager, to hire a replacement. Desiring to hire the very best of those who I'd soon be interviewing on the morrow for the vacancy, I prayed, asking God to direct me to the most promising candidate. While praying in this manner, I saw her, clearly, a woman with a round face, standing outside my office. As a candidate, she would be one of several hoping to fill our vacancy.

The next day, I recognized her instantly, although I had only seen her once and that once in a vision. I did hire her. Her work was above-average, and she fitted in perfectly. By hiring her, however, I did have to face the ire of those who believed that they had more experience and was better qualified. Despite their anger, I knew I had made the right decision, as I hadn't made it alone, but with the help of one who is as omnipotent as He is omniscient. My new hire was married, and in time my wife I became rather close to the couple, and considered them friends.

After a time, she moved on. I don't recall the circumstance of her leaving, but it had nothing to do with her job performance. I never regretted my decision to hire her over supposedly more qualified candidates. She had been God qualified, and that was good enough for me.

FUTURE VISIONS: CHRISTMAS

When I first met her, I'll call her Christmas, she wasn't born yet and she hadn't been given a name. Still I knew many things about her. While yet in the womb, Christmas had been diagnosed with a life-threatening condition known as holoprosencephaly. Medical specialists weren't sanguine about her chances, and didn't believe that she would live for very long following her birth, the mortality rate for her condition being so high. I wrote to the child's mother, telling her about another mother with a child like hers, the prognosis of which was equally grave, but who remained optimistic, and never gave up. The woman's child, although expected to die, beat the odds and lived. I told her that her baby, like the woman's baby, didn't have a death sentence. Like the child whom the medical establishment believed would die, but didn't, no one knew for certain how long her child would live. Over time, our assurances were tested by the dire predictions of her doctors.

One night while meditating, I found myself out-of-body, living out a scene that even now has not been fully realized, but did give me the hope I would need to see myself through what would be trying times for me and the child's family. In the scene, I was with Christmas's maternal grandmother in a small grocery store—perhaps a country store. The store had only one grocery checker, a detail that only reinforced the country store ambiance. Christmas had been really active during our shopping trip. She had run through the aisles, and played with the vegetables. She was now in the front of the store with me and her grandmother. Her grandmother was paying for the groceries we had just selected. Hoping to corral her, I said sternly, "You had better be good. I don't have to babysit you." Immediately she ran to a wall not far away, and hopped up on something I didn't recognize, and sat there as still as she could.

She was a beautiful child, with shoulder-length golden hair about her face, a short neck, and torso, with arms and legs that seemed too long for her short torso. After her mother had delivered her, I recounted this vision to her as a way to reassure her that Christmas wouldn't die, as her doctor feared might happen, that one day she would walk, run and jump like other children. She took some solace in my vision, but I don't think that she believed me.

I'm happy to say that Christmas did live, and is now a teenager, although my vision of her walking, and running, and jumping has yet to be realized. Over the years, Christmas grew into the girl I first envisioned, and well beyond the age of her initial visional appearance, the Golden Child of our first meeting. She's now maturing into a beautiful young woman. Upon reflection, I realized that Christmas resembled her paternal grandmother. She still has shoulder-length golden hair and a short torso, to which are attached long arms and legs.

AN OLD MAN

On at least two occasions I have experienced myself as a much older person than I am today. While meditating, I was suddenly someone else. Although this someone else was me, it was an *older me*. I felt ancient. And for a moment, I thought what this older me thought, I remembered what this older me remembered. I was this older me. And then I realized, just as suddenly, that I wasn't this older me, this older man. Yes, by certain metrics, I'm a senior citizen. But the *me* that I was in my meditations was a much older me. I had the feeling that he was in his eighties, or nineties, or older.

On an earlier occasion I saw myself standing in front of this older man. It was like seeing him in a mirror. I didn't recognize him. He was very old, with gray hair, and wrinkled skin. He looked familiar, but for the life of me, I couldn't place him. I wondered, too, why I was there with him. Then, in a twinkle of an eye, I was inside the old man. I was looking out from his eyes. And Oh My God, I felt so very old. And the realization struck me: I *was* the old man. Now I understood why I was there. The experience assured me that I wouldn't die soon, but that I would live to become the old man that I was then envisioning.

AN OUT-OF-BODY VISION OF GOD

Oh that my words were now written! oh that they were printed in a book!

That they were graven with an iron pen and lead in the rock for ever!

For I know that my redeemer liveth, and that he shall stand at the latter day upon the earth:

And though after my skin worms destroy this body, yet in my flesh shall I see God:

THE YOU IN YOU   185

Whom I shall see for myself, and mine eyes shall behold, and not another; though my reins be consumed within me (Job 19:23-27).

God wasn't there at the beginning of my vision. I was standing in the living quarters of some Greek or Roman dignitary. I heard a commotion out on the balcony, and walked in that direction. You could tell that the people were there to welcome a war hero: Celebratory noise originated from above and below. In the midst of this din, I hear this said of their conquering hero, now returned: "He must be a god."

When those words were spoken, I was back inside the house, which appeared to be an upper level of the structure. Out of the corner of my eye, I had seen a male figure enter the room from above, actually drift down as though he had wings, and slowly light on the floor. He, too, was amused by all the commotion, but when he heard the utterance from the crowd, "He must be a god," referencing the leader of the army now marching through the streets of the city, his face noticeably, visibly changed, displaying disappointment.

Although he had the youthful figure of a young man, dressed in a robe of some sort, he also had age grooves cut deep within every inch of his face. I knew that this young man was God, or a representation of Him, eternally young and eternally old, all at the same time. He didn't look in my direction, but looked upward as he spoke:

"I will make my Truth, and I will send Him forth into the world. And I will call Him Christ. And I will send Him also unto the latter-day saints."

REMOTE VIEWING AND HEARING

Again, the kingdom of heaven is like unto treasure hid in a field; the which when a man hath found, he hideth, and for joy thereof goeth and selleth all that he hath, and buyeth that field.[52]

---

52 Matt 13:44

I suspect that the technique I'm about to reveal works in real time, the here and now, and may be used to transport one's self into the future, or the past, although I never used it for that purpose. I'm including a discussion of this extrasensory ability, because of its apparent connection to the out-of-body experience. Rather than traveling to a variety of places by using the astral body, one may use this technique to transport one's self with the use of one's consciousness only. The technique may be used to transport consciousness to any physical location, including locations in the past, the future, or to other dimensions, as well.

Although many methods have been developed to help one learn remote viewing, or to enhance one's current ability, I will provide here the method that I have successfully used. The method is straightforward, requiring no mental exercises (no relaxation drills, no meditations, and no complicated procedures) to acquire the skill. All that's required are the traits that are essential to acquiring any new skill—patience, focus, and a willingness to practice until the new skill is fully learned.

I learned the technique from a book I read when a teen, the name of which I have long forgotten. The person who wrote the book had too much time on his hands, literally. He didn't wish to have all that time on his hands, but it couldn't be helped, he was recuperating from a serious illness. During his convalescence, he entertained himself by observing what was going on inside the only person who was available to him: himself. As he reclined, flat on his back with his eyes shut, peering into the darkness, he discovered something startling and baffling: He could make out a tiny light.

The light had surfaced after he had spent long hours surveying the darkness within his mind. Intrigued, he focused all his attention on the light, hoping to make it grow, hoping to see what he could see within it. As he stared at the light, it soon grew brighter and larger. And as he had hoped, he did see things within the light, frightening things, monstrous things, images that were twisted, bizarre, and all too real. This is where the author's story ended. With the telling, he invited readers to follow him, to venture, as did he, into the mysterious realm of the mind. Yet, for all his daring, and initial curiosity, he stopped just short of discovering the real treasure hidden there.

At the time, I didn't need much encouragement. I was in my first year of high school, hadn't seen much of the world, and was eager to join the author's meanderings along the pathways of the mind. Finding a straight-back chair, I sat down, upright, and closed my eyes. As instructed, I peered hopefully into the darkness behind my eyelids in search of the elusive light. The author had recommended no other preparation, such as relaxation techniques, chants, or meditation. He believed that these amazing grotesque images could be found by anyone willing to locate and enhance the light that was waiting to be discovered. It didn't happen right away. It took several days and as many attempts, before I could make out a silvery, at times bluish, light that played hide-and-seek with my interior vision. At first, the light would appear briefly, and then wink off, like some firefly.

I leveled my gaze at the light as best I could, and was rewarded at times with a steady light, and in that light I could make out the image of things that tantalized my mind with their strangeness. At first the images swam into my mind, and then quickly swam away, as if they were elusive fish. They weren't always as clear as I would have liked, but as the light grew brighter, and larger, the images took on an eerie sharpness. What I was now seeing was grotesque, and monstrous, faces with twisted and misshapen features. I made no attempt to affect the images I was seeing; at this point, I was just satisfied to finally see them, albeit images that shapeshifted without warning.

Years later, I concluded that these grotesque images were so many scarecrows, erected by the Soul to discourage those who might happen upon the light from venturing farther. It appeared that the Soul didn't want us to have this level of access to the light, and its powers—at least not while in the physical realm—as it would destroy the carefully-constructed illusions that govern our world, and our perception of reality.

With additional practice, I was soon spending most of my nights—wakeful nights that should have been spent sleeping—visiting weird and wonderful places. For many my age, Saturday afternoon matinees became the magic carpet that transported young moviegoers to exotic locations and introduced them to a wealth of sights beyond their ken, and beyond their access. My newfound skill promised to do what the movies did, but do it better. Unlike the movies that others produced and directed, cinematic thrillers that held me captivated for a few hours, I could, by evoking the light, direct what I wanted to see on my mind's screen. I could tell the light to take me to all those exotic places that the movie screen had taken me before, but with an added bonus: I was now the producer, and the director of my own movies, and the leading man in every scene.

Of the places I visited, I frequented museums the most. Living in a small town, with a small town's cultural limitations, faraway museums held a special attraction for me. It was a rare night that I didn't ask the light to take me to one of the world's great museum. I never knew which one. It didn't matter. What mattered was that I was treated, nightly, to sights I had never before seen. My recollection is that I feasted on a smorgasbord of visual treats, and that I did so while walking from one display to another, often reaching out to touch one fascinating object after the other.

With persistence, I had ventured farther into the light than the person from whom I had gained knowledge of it. He had stopped at the point where the grotesque images appeared. In time, I learned that I had opened the third eye, and had entered the inner sanctum of the Soul (the Garden of Eden), and from that vantage point, could travel the dust-laden passageways of the past, or leapfrog into a future yet to be discovered, or meander along shores of now-occurring events, taking in the various vistas stretching before me, experiencing them in real time.

Because these nocturnal escapades deprived me of sleep, which I needed if I was to stay awake during class the next day, I abandoned them. Had these ventures into the light been mere dreams, I would have awakened refreshed. I didn't. Only recently have I ventured to open my third eye again, concerned that the skill had been lost with the passage of time. Assurance that I could came in this manner:

A night of sleep may bring anything, vivid dreams that have answers to the questions I've posed during the day, or answers to questions that I'm not aware that I have posed. This morning was one of those mornings. Upon waking, The Voice, my Inner Wisdom, informed me, "There's no place like the heart," which reminded me of another Bible verse, this time from Proverbs: "Keep thy heart with all diligence; for out of it *are* the issues of life."[53] Soon after The Voice spoke, I was greeted with another experience: Against the darkness behind my eyelids, a screen appeared that was not unlike a large-screen television, or a rectangular movie screen. Filling the screen was green foliage of some kind. I tried to identify the foliage, but couldn't. The foliage wasn't projected on the screen, rather the screen moved over the foliage, as though I was looking out of a plane's window. The green foliage, and the boundary of the screen, were the only things visible. After a while, the screen stopped moving and disappeared. What I had seen on the screen was remindful of the scenes I had seen years ago as a teenager, when I accidentally activated (opened) my third eye.

A few days after the experience, which left me quite puzzle as to what I had seen on my mind's screen, I was directed to know the identity of the green foliage, and its location, as well, probably because I wanted to satisfy my curiosity, and my Soul had complied. There was a street not far from my home which entered a neighborhood that I hadn't explored. While passing the street one day, the impulse to explore where the street led overwhelmed me to such an extent that I quickly surrendered, not knowing where that decision would lead me.

---

53 Prov 4:23

I left the main thoroughfare onto the street that entered the unexplored neighborhood. Without any real goal except to explore, I drove aimlessly along streets lined with homes that couldn't have been more than a dozen years old. After several turns, I came to a dead end marked by a wire fence that my car could have easily breached had I a mind to do so. And there it was, a portion of the scene that I had seen on my mind's screen. Beyond the fence a watermelon field tilted to the left, and inclined, the field giving the appearance of being suspended in the air. Were it not for this vantage point, I wouldn't have recognized the scene. It was the same field of foliage shown on my mind's screen, the same scene that I had seen days before, but from above. The field of watermelons was the foliage that I had seen previously on my mind's screen, the only difference, I was seeing it with my physical eyes rather than my astral ones.

Using my third eye, I had seen similar scenes from my youth. This event stressed the importance of the heart and its many uses: There's no place we cannot go, and nothing we cannot see; these things are only a heartbeat away, a location within us that knows no boundaries, and is as infinite as the God whose image and likeness we bear.

It's likely that Leonardo da Vinci used a similar method—the opening of his third eye—to see the future. The History Channel in one of its "Ancient Aliens" segments unwittingly suggested that possibility. In the show titled, "The Da Vinci Conspiracy," it explored, among other topics, Leonardo da Vinci's lost years, years he possibly spent in a cave. The cave is the only clue we have as to how and where da Vinci may have spent his missing years, two years in all, from 1476 to 1478.

Upon returning to society after his self-imposed absence, da Vinci enjoyed a surge of creativity unlike any prior to his baffling absence. The show reflected upon da Vinci's obsession with twisted, bizarre, monstrous, misshapen images of people, speculating that perhaps these images may have been inspired by alien beings. That's when I experienced an *aha moment*, a moment of enlightenment; the dark cave and the grotesque images resonated. The narrator believed the cave to be real (and that's likely), but the *real* cave existed, not without, but within. If the cave was a physical one, it's possible that he sought seclusion there to explore the cave within. Da Vinci may have used the cave and its pitch-black darkness to enter another cave, the one accessible through the portals of his mind. Before entering the mind's inner sanctum (the Shekinah, the holiest of holies), he would first have to bypass the cave's sentries—frightful images, grotesque, twisted, misshapen faces—stationed there presumably to scare away the weak-hearted, and the casual traveler. Interestingly, one of da Vinci's early works was of a serpent-headed Medusa.

> *So he drove out the man; and he placed at the east of the garden of Eden Cherubims, and a flaming sword which turned every way, to keep the way of the tree of life* (Gen 3:24).

If the keepers of the cave do their job well, the average seeker of knowledge will be too intimidated to venture beyond the cave's opening. I have always been perplexed by da Vinci's grotesqueries, but I think I know now the reason for his preoccupation. For the strong of heart, and the intrepid adventurer, the light that first beckons, in which the monstrous images are brought to life, has the power to transport those stalwarts who enter the light to any location that they choose, regardless of time or place, into other dimensions, other worlds, the past or the future, as well as to locales within the here and now. The time da Vinci spent in the cave proved to be fruitful. He returned with ideas that wouldn't exist practically for hundreds of years. It's more than likely that he used the cave to travel into the future. From da Vinci's fertile mind, his contemporaries saw the invention of futuristic objects that defied the technological expectation of his times: a mechanical lion which moved on its own, a submarine, a tank, and flying machines.

Because the technology of da Vinci's time was so limited, he couldn't have possibly created precisely what he had seen in the future, although he did a superb job of emulating them with the tools and knowhow that were accessible to him at the time, apprehending, as he did, the underlying principle upon which they operated.

If a cave actually existed, its inky interior—a goodly distance from its entrance—would have served well da Vinci's journey within, his melding with the light that awaits those who successfully enter the vast and illimitable cave of their mind. More than once, I have found myself in a physical enclosure that allowed no light. It wasn't long after, that I would see images take form in the darkness. Some might call them hallucinations, accepting as real only those objects that appear tangibly in their day-to-day existence, finding it a simple task to dismiss all others as illusions.

VIEWING

After bin Laden evaded capture by our U.S. military, jokes about his possible location surfaced overtime in the news media and from some in our government. It was commonplace to hear speculations about his whereabouts—one conjecture in particular—that he was probably holed up in a cave along the Afghanistan-Pakistan border. But I knew better. I knew better because I was shown his whereabouts, not sufficiently to reveal his mailing address, but sufficiently to reveal that he wasn't living in a cave, but in a modest home, not unlike those we live in here in this country.

Using remote viewing, I saw what appeared to be our equivalence of a living room, a room appointed inelegantly, a surprising twist for a man purported to be so wealthy. From my perspective, I seemed to be standing in his living room, looking out over a scene that was awash with brilliant colors, saturated with a bright, sharply-defining light, as is often the case with visions, the room belonging unmistakably to a house and not a cave.

After visiting the lair of the head of Al-Qaeda, I always chuckled about the jokes that circulated at the time regarding his location, but not for the reason that others laughed; I knew that this much-sought-after fugitive wasn't playing house in a cave, but was living large, albeit modestly, in a house that would go unnoticed, but for its occupant, were people aware of who owned the house.

Further, I remote viewed the location of Steve Fossett's remains, months before the wreckage of his plane was spotted from the air in a rather remote area, and before a hiker found Fossett's pilot's license and several hundred dollar bills. I was listening to one of my favorite radio programs, Coast to Coast AM, with host, George Noory, when his guest, a *remote viewer,* explained how he and his remote-viewing team were using their abilities to find Fossett, but with mixed results.

Many news accounts of Fossett's tragic end describe him as a sixty-three-year-old millionaire adventurer, who, on that fateful day, Sept. 3, 2007, took flight in a single-engine Bellanca, and soon after disappeared. Meditating at bed time, I asked the Source within where Fossett could be found. Immediately, three lakes appeared within my mind's eye. I *Fast Blast* the Coast to Coast AM radio show to reveal to the host where Fossett might be found. Of course, nothing came of that. I learned later that the lakes were in the Mammoth Lakes region. My psychic information may not have been specific enough to find Fossett, but it would have narrowed the search area considerably.

HEARING

This ability surfaces from time to time, sometimes at my behest, and sometimes as a result of my having established intent, either because of curiosity or because of something I may have learned from the news. Regardless of which, I was told the location of Saddam Hussein before he was found. Wanting to do my part in the search, I attempted to alert the Defense Department, the White House, and other government officials, but without success.

Revealing Saddam Hussein's location did give me a severe attack of conscience, as I'm reluctant to use my abilities when they may cause harm to another. In addition to the government, I sent an email to a well-known psychic investigator. It was sent August 5, 2003 at 9:10:35 AM Pacific Daylight Time, with the subject: *Location of Saddam Hussein, August 05, 2003, Circa 7:35 a.m. Pacific Time.*

Content of the email:

I received the following impressions regarding the location of Saddam Hussein. I thought that I would share them with you. It's practically impossible to reach anyone in the government who may be able to operate on psychic tips.

As of Tuesday, August 05, 2003, 7:35 a.m. Pacific Time, Saddam Hussein may be found in the City of Tikrit. It's my belief that he is near water, possibly the Tigris River, or a water treatment plant.

Because he moves around periodically, this information is only accurate for the above given time.

I wasn't shown where Saddam Hussein was hiding, but was given his location audibly: "Saddam Hussein may be found in the City of Tikrit, near water," The Voice had said. I reasoned, therefore, that he was hiding near the Tigris River, or perhaps in, or near, a water treatment plant. When Saddam was eventually found near his hometown of Tikrit in a spider hole, one news account observed how close he had been to the Tigris River, and, ironically, not far from the opulent palaces that he had constructed with the use of money stolen from the Iraqi people.

When Saddam was found, I reminded the psychic investigator of my previous email in which I had revealed his whereabouts. Saddam was found on December 13, 2003, a little over four months after I psychically received his location and sent emails to the psychic investigator and the government. After receiving my follow-up email, reminding him of the earlier email, the psychic investigator emailed back and asked me questions regarding my psychic ability. Here's my response:

I believe that my answer is going to disappoint you. When it comes to something as unpredictable as the mind, it's difficult to shine the light of scientific inquiry upon such a mercurial process as psychic ventures. I can't say that my results will always be 100 per cent accurate. This is because we as humans are constantly changing our minds about what it is we want. For example, we may program ourselves to fail if the results or outcomes are something that frightens us, or in some way prove undesirable.

Let's say, if I know that by giving what I know about the location of Saddam Hussein may result in his injury or death, I may unwittingly sabotage the accuracy of my efforts to locate him. This is because of my natural aversion to hurting another. It's as though the soul gives you the answer you're seeking, a correctness that is totally subjective. Before it gives the answer it seems to ask: "Do you want the answer that is ostensibly correct, or the one that you can live with?"

However, if I put aside these concerns and ask many times and the answer is always the same, then I can say with some measure of reliability that the answer is correct.Can I tap this ability consistently? The answer is yes. But I can't rush it. Like a water pump that must be primed before the water flows freely, I find that I must prime my mind sufficiently to bring forth an answer. It's almost as though I must convince the power within that I'm earnestly seeking an answer before it will respond.

The scientific community thrives on experiments that can be replicated. And I believe that you're seeking a level of certitude or performance that will satisfy that community's strict requirements when it comes to proof. I'm not sure if I'm that guy.

How I came to know this psychic investigator is a story in itself. As an occasional guest on Coast to Coast AM, he used one of his guest appearances to announce that he was conducting an experiment, and asked for volunteers. Using a series of questions, he would test our psychic ability. I, and several others, signed up and, soon after, started receiving emails with symbols on them, asking that we choose the symbol among several that had been preselected as correct—a multiple-choice challenge, having only one answer.

All went well for a time. While in meditation, I would ask my Inner Wisdom to select the symbol that represented the correct answer, and without fail I was shown a symbol in my mind's eye that later proved to be the preselected one. For several weeks, I received additional emails, with new multiple-choice symbols, all of which I answered correctly, that is, I correctly chose the preselected symbol.

It all came apart on the last question. For the last question, we were presented with a picture of a man, a white male. We were assured that he resided in a particular state within the United States. We were told further that the man's location couldn't be determined by his appearance or the background against which he stood. We were then asked to give the location of this man, the state in which he currently resided.

This final question, for a couple of reasons, threw me for a loop. First, because it was a departure from previous questions, which had asked participants to choose the preselected answer from just a few—four or five possibilities—and not a few dozen. And second, unlike the others, the final question was essentially an open-ended question, requiring that I choose not from several potential answers, but from fifty.

Not willing to accept defeat, I asked my Inner Wisdom for the man's location, clearly questioning my ability to divine the correct answer. When the answer came, "Texas," I dismissed it, believing that I had forced the answer, mainly because Texas seemed too predictable: It was my state of birth, and the place of my upbringing. Not satisfied with Texas as the answer, I continued to press for the correct answer. After a time, I was given another answer. I don't recall the name of the state I finally submitted as the answer, but when the location of the man was later revealed, it was the wrong answer. I don't believe that any of the participants correctly answered all the questions, as the number dwindled with each succeeding question until there were none.

After conducting a post mortem, I concluded that my Inner Wisdom, after initially giving me the correct answer, provided an answer that would satisfy my queries, even if it wasn't the right one. When I rejected the first answer, it gave another, albeit incorrect, eager to please and satisfy my persistent imploring. This experience stressed the importance of being clear about what I wanted, as Life doesn't always deliver that for which we ask— whether it's an answer to a specific question, or any other desire—but that which we expect to receive, despite the asking.

MISCELLANY

Over a lifetime, I have received many predictions about the future, most of which were accurate, and were later realized. I've brought together several more visions, and predictions, some of which are no longer visions, but have become starkly real, visions with which we're currently coping, and not too well. I could have easily expanded on the ones I've chosen to include here. It's almost impossible to convince others of the accuracy of these visions, while they're still in their nascent stage, especially those with unhappy outcomes. It's just as impossible to convince them to take proactive steps to mitigate the threat, or to evade it altogether. Nevertheless, the visions and the predictions did give me the opportunity to send up prayers as a way to lessen the severity of the soon-to-be physical manifestations of these visions, as they move from the mental realm to the physical realm.

1

THE ULTIMATE WEAPON

The first vision began innocently enough. I was standing at the front of a church, not far from the pulpit. To my left, perhaps three or four pews back, sat a casually dressed black man. He stood and walked to the front of the church and faced me. He lifted what he had in his hands on a level with my eyes. It appeared to be a tablet of some unknown material, about three or four inches thick, and twice the size of a loose-leaf notebook. Upon the surface things were written.

He said, "These things are in your future."

I looked at the tablet and read the first entry, "The ultimate weapon."

I knew that the ultimate weapon was another name for the nuclear bomb. After reading the first line, I shrank from reading the others, the fear engendered from reading the first line was just too great. This vision came a few months before a magnitude 9.0 earthquake struck off the coast of Japan, on Friday, March 11, 2011 at 2.46:24 p.m. and led to a tsunami that resulted in the meltdown of three Fukushima Daiichi nuclear power plant reactors. The nuclear accident displaced at least 300,000 people. Best estimates say a complete cleanup will take decades rather than years. As destructive as this accident has been, and may yet become, it's my prayer that this was the "the ultimate weapon" that was in my vision, and not some future, more deadly, version that could descend the world into a nuclear winter, notwithstanding the controversy around the theory.

2

DAYS OF WORRY

Years before global warming, or climate change, became a dinner-table topic, The Voice warned me with the following information: "Someday you'll have to worry about this." While The Voice was yet speaking, I saw large chunks of ice break away from a glacier and fall into the water below. I knew that this falling, this breakup of the glacier was the result of global warming. Although The Voice didn't attribute the glacier destruction to manmade activity, I strongly felt that man, despite denials from certain quarters in our nation, had a hand in it. Only recently have satellite images revealed a troubling scene: Possibly the largest chunk of ice, perhaps five square miles, has broken from a Greenland glacier, an ice loss known as a calving. The cause for worry here is the concomitant problems that will ensue if the calving continues—a rise in the sea level that the glacier loss will certainly produce, the presence of more icebergs in shipping lanes, and the ongoing threat to freshwater.

3
SURREAL MOUNTAIN RANGE

The flight to Raleigh, North Carolina from Los Angeles would require several hours non-stop on a wide-body jetliner. My wife and I flew there overnight to visit her family—her siblings and her parents. The weather in Raleigh was cold that time of year. My father-in-law compensated by setting the temperature controls at an uncomfortably high temperature. During our stay, I had one out-of-body experience, and that was the night before we were scheduled to leave for home. During this nocturnal excursion many miles from home, I found myself flying high over a mountain range. It was still night, and below I could see the jagged edges of the mountain extending well into the distance beneath me. The sight was bizarre. At the time, I didn't believe that it could be a part of my physical world. It had to be a scene from another world, perhaps an exoplanet.

That morning after breakfast, I mentally revisited the scene I had witnessed while out-of-body, dismissing it once more as too fantastical to exist on planet Earth. On the flight back, I happened to look out the plane's window, either at the request of the pilot, or simply out of curiosity at what lay below. And there it was: the mountain range, jagged edges and all. It was a surreal sight, made more surreal by the nighttime darkness. It was as I had seen it in my out-of-body journey only a day before, and at the same height as the plane, the moonlight eerily accentuating the mountain's jagged edges. "Seeing is believing," goes the idiom. Had I not seen it with my own eyes, I wouldn't have believed the existence of such an unlikely sight in our world. More than likely, the mountain range over which we flew to return to Los Angeles, and LAX, was the Sierra Nevada Mountain range. Since we were traveling from East to West, using the pilot's pre-established flight path, one I wasn't privy to, I can't rule out the Rocky Mountains as the mountains over which we might have flown as well.

4
BATTLEGROUND STATES

On the morning of November 6, 2012, I did what I usually do upon waking, spend a little time in bed meditating. It was a special day for the nation; it would be the day that the people of the United States would elect their next president. For months leading up to the day, we the people were treated to a series of debates featuring the incumbent president, Barack Obama, and his worthy challenger, Mitt Romney. During that time, we had heard from political pundits, statisticians sifting through poll numbers, and even from a few prognosticators who claimed to know what the outcome of the race would be, and who would emerge victorious. Many of the claims came down to who would win the battleground states, the swing states. Nine swing states, or battleground states, had been identified, nine that could swing either Left or Right, Democrat or Republican, the result of poll averages. The states were Colorado, Florida, Iowa, Nevada, New Haven, North Carolina, Ohio, Virginia, and Wisconsin for a total of 110 electoral votes.

With the election buzzing around in my head, that night I lay me down to sleep, knowing that my vote had long been submitted by mail, and I could spend the day listening to the various news channels give their last-minute thoughts on voter participation, the implications of poll findings, the results of exit poll interviews, and a tallying of votes cast in election districts or voting precincts, as they came in from the East Coast and the Midwest.

As I meditated that morning, The Voice, as it often does, provided pertinent information about who would win the battle for the battleground states, the information predicting who would win the White House, hours before even one poll closed in the country. The Voice predicted, quite accurately, as it turns out, "President Obama will win the battleground states." With that prediction, the race for the White House had been decided. Whoever won the battleground states would be our next president.

5
METAPHYSICAL HEALERS AND PSYCHICS

It's hard to find a Facebook page that doesn't have at least one statement purporting to speak the truth about some aspect of human life—about human interactions, or the human condition, or human relationships. I read one such statement not long ago. In chiding prose, it dismissed the notion that humans can be healed by prayer alone by pointing to hospitals bursting at the seams with sick people, and the notion that people can predict the future, by pointing to the paucity of lottery winners who have won by this method. Despite statements like the abovementioned, I have used prayer to heal myself on many occasions. In addition, metaphysical healers have successfully healed many patients as part of their healing practice, and psychics have predicted winning lottery numbers. When California joined other states by establishing its own state lottery in 1984, I set out, a few months after the first tickets were sold in 1985, to use my psychic abilities to learn the upcoming lottery numbers for a given date.

One evening while watching television in the family room, lying flat on my stomach with my head resting on my arms, I chanted, "I know the lottery numbers," clearly expecting to receive the numbers for the next lottery drawing only a few days away. As I lay there, three numbers on the screen glowed bright enough to set them apart from the others. I wrote them down. I then asked, "Where are the others. I need six numbers." The Voice answered, "Keep watching." I would like to say that I kept watching, but not long after seeing and writing down the three numbers that glowed on the television screen, I fell asleep. And I would have forgotten the whole matter, had I not been watching television when the winning numbers were announced. That's when it hit me, that's when it all came flooding back, that I had been given three of the winning numbers, but had fallen asleep before receiving the other three. I wrote down the winning numbers as they were announced and compared them to the ones I had received earlier from The Voice. All three numbers matched. Had I played them, I would have won perhaps seventy-five to a hundred dollars, a respectable amount, but a far cry from the millions I might have won had I received and played all six numbers.

6

THE WISE ONES

All the questions about the future of the planet and of humans come down to one question, the question of survival. A world in turmoil, convulsed by one tragic event after another, I asked God from the depths of my despair, "What will become of us?"

His answer: "The Wise Ones shall prevail."

For a time, I interpreted God's answer to mean only the Wise Ones would prevail, when in fact, I soon divined, the Wise Ones would not only prevail personally, but because they were wise, they would apply their wisdom in ways that would permit us all to prevail. The nightly news provided more than enough reasons to bring the world to an end, but not in the way that most envision when they hear the words, "the end of the world." They often interpret them to mean the end of our physical world, the ultimate destruction of all life on the planet, rather than the ultimate destruction of the evil, and the fear that beset us at every turn, presenting themselves as personal challenges—sin, sickness, and death—as well as collective challenges, challenges that embroils most of the world when it comes to meeting them, challenges of famine, of droughts, of displaced populations escaping the ravages of another challenge, that of war. I pray that I'm one of the Wise Ones who will, along with an unknown number of others who work in the Light, but hidden from the world, help the world to overcome, to prevail.

On December 3, 2015, one day after the mass shooting that occurred in San Bernardino, California, which resulted in the deaths of at least 14 and the wounding of 21, my self-appointed commission to work as one of the *Wise Ones* for the world became a formal one. The Voice instructed, "Go into all the world and preach the Gospel," the *Good News*, which I understand to be the primacy and supremacy of the Kingdom of God, the Kingdom of Love. As with God's commission to "Feed my Family," this commission was not to be taken literally, but spiritually. Although similar to the previous one, this time it seemed to ask that I step up my efforts to bring the Kingdom of God, the Kingdom of Love to the entire world, which I'm now doing, using my understanding that *Love is all there is*. Presently, I'm unseeing the world as it now appears, and seeing it as existing in the Kingdom of Love, and Love only. We're told that when the "kingdom of God is come nigh unto [us]"[54] good things follow, as in the ensuing passage:

And as ye go, preach, saying, The kingdom of heaven is at hand.

---

54 Luke 10:9

Heal the sick, cleanse the lepers, raise the dead, cast out devils: freely ye have received, freely give (Matt 10:7-8).

The sermon I choose to "preach," then, is one of action rather than oratory—a sermon of understanding, a sermon of realization that the Kingdom of God, of Love, is the only Kingdom that exists, not just within my own country, but within the whole world, not just within the whole world, but the entire universe. On the same date, while meditating, I was given a vision, but was told not to reveal it. As much as I'd like to, I will honor the request of the one who made it, one who I could see plainly, one wearing regalia fit for a king. Suffice to say, the vision has great import for the world.

7
SUPER BLOOD MOON

If we're in the "time of the end,"[55] or the "last days,"[56] as many believe, referencing the recent Super Blood Moon as their evidence, then the end of the world might be nearer than many expect. Not long ago, it seemed the whole world was watching, anticipating a rare sight, a Super Blood Moon, a full eclipse of a Super Moon not seen since 1982, the next one not due until 2033. Some believe that biblical prophecy predicted the last Blood Moon. They point to the Blood Moon's consecutive appearances, four in all, a Tetrad, including the more recent one, a Super Blood Moon, during an unusually brief period, one spanning almost a year and a half. They also noted that the dates of these Blood Moons coincided with several Jewish Holidays. Some turned to biblical prophecy for an explanation, believing that the last Blood Moon signaled the end of the world:

---

55 Dan 12:9
56 II Pet 3:3

And I will shew wonders in the heavens and in the earth, blood, and fire, and pillars of smoke.

The sun shall be turned into darkness, and the moon into blood, before the great and the terrible day of the Lord come (Joel 2:30-31).

Leading up to this rare event, I remained skeptical, knowing that any such revelation would be shown or given from a place within, and not a place without. This understanding, however, was later modified after I recalled Jesus' statement:

These things have I spoken unto you in proverbs: but the time cometh, when I shall no more speak unto you in proverbs, but I shall shew you plainly of the Father.

(John 16:25)

What could be more plainly stated than a Blood Moon, but not just any Blood Moon, but a Super Blood Moon, Super because of its nearness to Earth, making it appear larger in the eastern sky, appearing earlier than I had expected, and not long after sundown. I watched it for some time, and later, after the full eclipse had taken place. I hadn't expected anything unusual to happen, as a result of the Blood Moon, and neither was I looking for anything.

The morning after the eclipse, I retired for the night at my customary time. Again as usual, I began to pray and meditate. That's when I experienced something new, something different. As I prayed, I felt the firmness of my prayers. It was impossible, or so it seemed, to express doubt of any kind; my mind was clearly blocked from that occurring. And, too, there was no fear. It was as though fear had been wiped from my mind. When I tried to entertain fear, I couldn't. It was as though a partition, a wall, had been erected between fear and my mind. It couldn't penetrate the barrier and I couldn't break it down.

I realized later that if the world is to end, it would end with the removal of fear from our world; it would mean the destruction of fear, and not the destruction of our physical Earth. In short, we could end the world—the shadowy doubt, fear, and our preoccupation with sin and darkness—and still keep the Earth intact. If doubt and fear can be blocked from our minds, then any other negative thoughts or feelings could also be blocked, that is, not allowed to manifest themselves. It's my firm belief that the Super Blood Moon marked the beginning of the eradication of fear, and therefore evil, in the world, that this was just our first installment, that the full eclipse of the moon eclipsed more than just the surface of the moon, but the presence of fear in our world. With the Super Blood Moon came a lessening of fear in the world, and I was allowed to feel what that eventuality would feel like, a preview of things to come, so to speak. I have often wondered how we humans could dwell in a Heavenly State at some future time, and still be susceptible to all the human thoughts, and beliefs, we have accumulated over multiple lifetimes, although we have rejected them for the heart's sake, that it might be kept with all diligence.

I now had my answer.

The afterglow of this experience was such that I found myself laughing out loud from time to time, almost involuntarily. The feeling that lingered was powerful and profound, lasting for most of the day. This rarest of events, a Super Blood Moon, created another event, not a rare event, but an improbable one, one that seemed impossible before it occurred, my inability to feel, or to invoke fear, or doubt, blocked, as they were, from even being consciously entertained. When I tried, my mind refused to cooperate, stymieing my efforts to consider these two negative states of mind, asserting, instead, a mental state that was devoid of both doubt and fear.

Prompted to add the dates on which the Blood Moons occurred, the Tetrad, I came up with the sum of 55. I was a little surprised that the sum of the dates constituted a double number, and wondered if 55 had any numerological significances. Returning to the bedroom at the time, I received another surprise, the time on the clock read 5:55, that is, 555. This was too much of a coincidence, so I looked up both 55 and 555, and learned the following: The number 55 has many meanings, some associated with Christianity, including prayer, Jesus Christ, and the Virgin Mary, to name a few. The number 555 was identified as an Angel Number, one of several. The number, if seen sequentially, predicts a watershed in our life, a message from our angel or a guide, signaling that an unprecedented change in our life is imminent, or that it has already begun. It's my prayer that this book will be that watershed, and that its timely, urgent, message will be promulgated worldwide.

PART THREE:

WHO'S THE OPPOSITION?

FIFTEEN

INVISIBLE ENEMIES OF HUMANITY

Put on the whole armour of God, that ye may be able to stand against
the wiles of the devil. For we wrestle not against flesh and blood, but
against principalities, against powers, against the rulers of the darkness
of this world, against spiritual wickedness in high places. Wherefore take
unto you the whole armour of God, that ye may be able to withstand in the
evil day, and having done all, to stand. Stand therefore, having your loins
girt about with truth, and having on the breastplate of righteousness.[57]

HUMANITY HAS ENEMIES. THESE ENEMIES DON'T always plot and scheme in the daylight, or in the open, but use darkness and shadows to carry out their assault against the human race, namely, their hidden pursuits to promote their own nefarious objectives. Not all of us are in the dark about the directed malevolence taking place throughout our world daily, activities which impact us individually, and collectively, which, if they were exposed and discussed openly, might cast doubt on the revelators' credibility, if not their sanity. To make this assertion carries with

---

57 Eph 6:11-14

it a certain amount of risk, a risk which will preclude a full disclosure of the matter, forcing me to yield the floor, for now, to conspiracy theorists.

Much has been said about Satan, hell, demons, and ghosts, either to support their existence or to debunk, and dismiss them. With varying degrees of regret, I've encountered all these things, either directly, or in visions, or as a result of my many out-of-body excursions. In the interest of full disclosure, I'm obligated to share most, but not all, of my experiences as they pertain to them, well aware that the discussion will resonate with some more than others.

The Bible has referred to Satan, the devil, as the "god of this world,"[58] establishing the world as his exclusive kingdom for now, which gives expansive meaning to Jesus' petition to God: "Thy kingdom come. Thy will be done in earth as *it is* in heaven."[59] I had thought to exclude this topic altogether, but relented, believing that to omit a full exposition of the out-of-body phenomena would obstruct the message around the experience, rather than illuminate it.

Undeniably, the next several topics will be the hardest for me to write. My equivocation around these several topics was so heightened that on several occasions, I had convinced myself to set aside these fear-based accounts of several of my less-appealing experiences. To set them aside, however, would have rendered my account of the out-of-body experience incomplete and, for that reason, not a full representation of the totality of that experience, nor a full unveiling of the *you* in me. I demurred further because I couldn't definitively catalogue these experiences, so that the reader could make sense of them without being unduly troubled by their own preconceptions.

---

58 II Cor 4:4
59 Matt 6:10

SATAN

Satan, the personification of evil, is perhaps the greatest enemy of humanity: He oversees much of the growth and expansion of wickedness in our world, promoting the reach of darkness as it climbs to new heights, heights that seek to block the salutary rays of love, and the beneficial influence of the divine.

Nothing inspires more fear than a discussion of Satan and hell. As a young man, having reached a point in my life where I was reconnecting with my spirituality, I was shown a vision that revealed how Satan might be defeated. The vision came after a day of directing and redirecting my thinking to align with my highest spiritual ideal—the purification of my thoughts. In the heavens, I saw two cherubs, both appearing as males, unclothed, at first a goodly distance from the other, fly swiftly toward the other, slamming their cherubic bodies into the other with a great force.

This they did several times before one of the cherubs fell hard to the ground, and, upon landing, turned into a bearded man who slithered upon his belly the way that a serpent might, standing finally and walking away from what had been the scene of a great angelic battle.

A voice above me said, "He lost much skin today."

It's very likely that the cherub that I saw, and who I had recruited to battle Satan, was Michael, the archangel who wages war against Satan. On other occasions, Satan, each time assuming a different form, was shown to me again, not as a chubby cherub, but a serpent of mountainous height and width, and again as a monster reminiscent of the one from the movie *Alien*. It was while I was being shown this *Alien*-like monster that I heard these words from The Voice: "He is a god, but there is one greater." After The Voice spoke, the following Bible passage resonated stronger:

> But if our gospel be hid, it is hid to them that are lost: In whom the
> god of this world hath blinded the minds of them which believe not,

lest the light of the glorious gospel of Christ, who is the image of God,
should shine unto them (II Cor 4:3-4).

HELL

Hell may be thought of as an enemy of humanity, as so many humans have restricted their freedom, perhaps excessively, for fear of being banished there upon being judged for their sins, and wrongdoing. If we follow the Ten Commandments, and do unto others as we have them do unto us, we needn't circumscribe our life to such an extent that it's not a life, but a preparation to live after death. Recently I read a description of hell purportedly shown in a vision by an apparition of the Blessed Virgin to a young Portuguese girl by the name of Lucia Santos. How a peasant girl was chosen to receive these heavenly visitations and the messages she was given—the Three *Secrets of Fatima*—have been the subject of speculation for years.

One of the messages (the first secret), we're told, of the several received, spoke of hell, complete with a fairly alarming description of this nadir region. When I read this description of hell, I was stunned. In many ways, I could have written it myself. The description reads, accordingly:

"Our Lady showed us a great sea of fire which seemed to be under the
earth. Plunged in this fire were demons and souls in human form,
like transparent burning embers, all blackened or burnished bronze,
floating about in the conflagration, now raised into the air by the
flames that issued from within themselves together with great clouds
of smoke, now falling back on every side like sparks in a huge fire,
without weight or equilibrium, and amid shrieks and groans of pain
and despair, which horrified us and made us tremble with fear. The
demons could be distinguished by their terrifying and repulsive like-
ness to frightful and unknown animals, all black and transparent.
This vision lasted but an instant. How can we ever be grateful enough

to our kind heavenly Mother, who had already prepared us by prom-
ising, in the first Apparition, to take us to heaven. Otherwise, I think
we would have died of fear and terror."

While in my twenties, after a day of struggling with my own inner
conflicts, I, too, was shown a vision of hell. In every particular, except for
two details, Lucia's vision was identical to mine. Whereas she saw demons
torturing the hapless souls condemned to this region, I didn't. But, unlike
me, she didn't see the devil himself. We both saw souls, as black embers,
with an occasional fiery red springing from their depth, lifted aloft by the
intense heat below, only to fall again into the merciless flames below.

Despite similarities, her vision differed from mine in one vital particular: In my vision, I saw the serpent, the devil that resided in that place
of unimagined horror and torment, a serpent as high as a mountain and
as wide. When it turned its massive form, the movement alone sent souls
nearest it flying, as sparks might rise from the center of a fiery furnace.

Whether such a place actually exists, only Satan knows. A prominent
New Age book accounts for hell as an experience that we create for ourselves, while others, some outside of traditional religious beliefs, dismiss
hell altogether. For my part, I believe hell exists, as it serves a purpose,
despite its restrictions on how some live their lives, constraints that it often
imposes on those who believe that they might be sent there to be eternally
punished for the sins that they have committed during their lifetime. When
criminals are sentenced after being found guilty of a particular crime, for
a specified number of years behind bars, with or without the possibility of
parole, it's done for three reasons: 1) to remove the felon from society; 2) to
rehabilitate, if possible; and 3) to serve as a deterrent. For some, a stint in
prison may mold more responsible citizens, those who're willing to uphold
the law, work within its framework, and contribute constructively to a society whose trust they have violated.

For others, not even the threat of capital punishment for a capital crime is sufficient to deter them from performing certain acts of criminality. To tell them that manmade laws and penalties provide only one type of justice, that another justice exists, intractable, unseen, and unrelenting, a justice that requires that the "uttermost farthing" be paid before the scales of justice can return to its once-balanced state, would require a proof that only the testament of experience can provide.

What usually goes unnoticed is that life has a built-in deterrent, omnipresent and implacable, having the authority of law, divine law. The Bible states the law this way, "Be not deceived; God is not mocked: for whatsoever a man soweth, that shall he also reap."[60] This rule may be found in several iterations, including various religious teachings, philosophy, ethics, and psychology.

In another biblical passage the rule is stated this way: "And as ye would that men should do to you, do ye also to them likewise."[61] The popular form of this caveat is called the Golden Rule, and is expressed this way: "Do unto others as you would have others do unto you." This law implies that if we sow good then good will be returned to us. If we sow evil, then evil will be returned to us. In Ecclesiastes we read: "Cast thy bread upon the waters: for thou shalt find it after many days."[62]

As with human laws, generally, ignorance of the divine law is no excuse, as it's written indelibly on the surface of the soul. Fortunately, we're never ignorant of this divine Law of Reciprocity, even if, on occasion, we ignore it, or act in spite of its warnings, the reproach of our conscience. If we don't wish others to steal from us, we shouldn't steal from them. If we don't want others to hurt us, we shouldn't hurt them, and so on.

Although it's normal to oppose bad things happening to us, our aversion to bad things happening to us hasn't always deterred us from doing

---

60 Gal 6:7
61 Luke 6:31
62 Eccl 11:1

bad things to others. We're quick to sow seeds of pain, hurt, and malice, forgetting that once those seeds germinate and grow sufficiently to be reaped, we, too, will also have to consume what we have sown. With the passage of time, we may have forgotten when the seeds were sown, only that now we're facing a table laden with all types of fare that we wish we didn't have to eat, but eat we must.

All too often, the time between my sowing and my reaping has been almost instantaneous, allowing me to connect the former to the latter. It might have been a sowing of fear, or a sowing of a negative emotion, or a sowing of an unkind thought. While watching television over a decade ago, a comment by one of the speakers produced such outrage that my anger erupted unexpectedly and violently, shattering the light bulb above me, sending glass shards throughout the room. This outcome is one of the reasons I work ceaselessly to keep my temper in check—for the protection of others and myself.

In like manner, those who have sown bitter seeds towards me have found that, sooner than later, they have had to eat the fruit of their own bitter thoughts, words, or actions. Are they aware of this? Probably not. Yet, the Law of Reciprocity is still in full effect with or without our knowledge.

This was a long build-up to a larger observation: What if in this lifetime, or any lifetime, we sow more than we can reap? What then? How do we repay the karmic debt we've incurred? Is it possible, then, that we created hell just for that purpose, so that those who're indebted beyond their ability to pay in the usual, incremental way, over several lifetimes, may expedite the balancing of Justice's Scales, accelerating the day of their redemption?

Having seen hell, and the suffering of the souls that have been remanded there, it's not that farfetched to believe that it was intended for just such a purpose, where souls voluntarily consign themselves for a specific period of unimaginable pain and agony until their karmic debt has been paid.

Hitler and a few others of his ilk may have availed themselves of such a fate, not able to balance the Scales of Justice in any other way.

For others, who can't use the traditional means of paying off a karmic debt, and whose sins (or transgressions) don't rise to the egregiousness that would send them to hell to expiate them, reaping in several alternate realties simultaneously might do the trick, resulting in the full payment of debts accumulated over a lifetime. Forgiveness, as well, can play an important role in the cancellation of karmic debt, allowing us to short circuit the connection that exists between cause and effect. Instead of collecting on a debt owed, we can choose to not seek recompense for a wrong that occurred in this life, or a previous one, thus ending the cycle of retribution for a previous wrong. If we connect with the Christ within, we, too, can forgive sin in this world sufficiently to do the works of God, to cancel the debt of sin that manifest itself as illness and physical impairment. Consider the following:

And, behold, they brought to him a man sick of the palsy, lying on a bed: and Jesus seeing their faith said unto the sick of the palsy; Son, be of good cheer; thy sins be forgiven thee.

And, behold, certain of the scribes said within themselves, This man blasphemeth.

And Jesus knowing their thoughts said, Wherefore think ye evil in your hearts?

For whether is easier, to say, Thy sins be forgiven thee; or to say, Arise, and walk?

But that ye may know that the Son of man hath power on earth to forgive sins, (then saith he to the sick of the palsy,) Arise, take up thy bed, and go unto thine house.

And he arose, and departed to his house (Matt 9:2-7).

How much of a deterrent would it be, then, if it was common knowledge and a well-accepted fact, that if you sow evil, evil will be returned to you, and if you sow good, then good will be returned to you, in full "measure, pressed down, and shaken together, and running over, shall men give into your bosom?" Would it matter to the potential evil doer to know: "For with the same measure that ye mete withal it shall be measured to you again?"[63]

DEMONS

Demons are enemies of humanity, as they're used as agents to inflict pain and punishment, or they operate on behalf of themselves, using those of a fragile mind, or those predisposed to evil, to bring hardship, pain, and suffering upon those who become their host for an indeterminate time, or upon the whole human family.

If Satan and hell are enough to send shivers up the spine, then demons represent a close third. Two demons that come to mind immediately are the succubus and the incubus, both entities showing up in the literature on the subject of demons, usually as folkloric creatures. As demons, they mainly use subterfuge to entice their victims to engage in sexual fantasies. When their victims are sexually aroused, these demons use that manufactured arousal to extract the sexual energies that these fantasies induce.

At least twice, a succubus has attached itself to my astral (nonphysical) body, while I remained entranced in my physical body, constructing sexual scenes and images to arouse sexual energies for the purpose of experiencing what it can't experience in its state of incorporeality. Each time, after I recognized that the thoughts (images I was seeing) didn't belong to me, but were induced by something external to me, I ended them. For my audacity, I was always attacked. The attacks were vicious and sustained. Claws, sharp, and long sank deep into my flesh, seemingly as punishment for my discovery of it, and my unwillingness to participate in its efforts to generate sexual energy.

---

63 Luke 6:38

There is nothing in the physical realm to compare with this demon-induced pain, not a toothache, a deep cut, or a smashed finger. Had I been outside the body, rather than inside, I don't think I would have felt the pain. This doesn't mean that the incorporeal body cannot experience pain—the torment associated with hell belies that—but that I have never experienced it while in my astral form, and separated from my physical body. Instinctively I seized the demon with my astral hands with the hope of dislodging it. The harder I pulled, the deeper it sank its claws. The more I struggled to remove it, the more it seemed to be a part of me. It was as though I was attempting to remove a leg or a foot from my physical body, so complete was the attachment.

It reminded me of the wood ticks that I removed as a small child after wandering into the woods that surrounded our small clapboard house. As this wood tick, a tiny parasite, fed on my blood, this demon tick, an astral parasite, fed on my sexual energy. Although I could remove the tick gorging itself on my blood, by repeatedly, but gently, squeezing and applying pressure on its small body, until it released its grip on my flesh, and I was able to extract it, head and all, this sex-crazed demon was not so easily dislodged. While to leave the tick's head under the skin after extraction could create problems, so would leaving a succubus in place.

While under the thrall of these entities, I always tried first to break the spell, the trance that I was in, but usually to no avail. With a tremendous force they would hold me under, as they sought to take me (while I resisted) to a depth where escape seemed impossible, and struggling useless. On both occasions, I gave up the struggle and called out to God to intercede on my behalf. When that didn't work, I denied the demon's power over me. This approach never failed.

GHOSTS

Ghosts, or apparitions, are enemies of humanity because they're more often purveyors of mischief than blessings. Hearing a great deal about ghosts on radio, and television, and reading about them in print, I thought it would be a great idea to use my out-of-body ability to connect with them. I remember my first attempt vividly. I was lying in bed under the influence of one of my pre-out-of-the-body trances when I ask innocently, "I want to see a ghost."

My request didn't result in my seeing a ghost, but it did result in my sensing, on all sides of me, the unsettling presence of others in the room. They didn't speak, but they did communicate in a fashion, and not too politely. Something or someone pierced my leg with a sharp object. It felt like the point of a pitchfork or a Trident. The sharp tip penetrated the side of my left knee, at the point where the upper and lower part of my leg are connected near the kneecap, or patella. The pain that ensued was so intense that I would have wailed in unspeakable agony had I the power to use my vocal cords to do so. The pain was so severe that I resolved in that moment to never use my out-of-body abilities in a reckless manner again.

On another night, this time on my way to work, traveling on a dark road which took me past a graveyard, I watched this ungainly male apparition, suddenly caught in my headlights, run from the cemetery on my right, across the road, to an embankment on my left, its feet touching nothing but air. Thinking it had seen me, I slowed down, hoping to be treated to an up-close view. Thanks to my car's bright headlights, I was given a clear view of both sides of the road, including the left side where the high embankment would have challenged the agility of Olympic broad jumpers, or spry animals, if they had chosen to scale it. When I approached the place where I last saw him, there was nothing there; there were no men, no animals, and no ghosts.

In my twenties, I experienced yet another sighting. Through serendipitous means I found myself dating a young woman that I had previously attempted to woo, but unsuccessfully. She lived in an apartment that she claimed was haunted, not by just any ghost, but a poltergeist, as he (I learned later that the presence was a man.) was fond of moving things around. I didn't think much of her revelation, believing instead that she was mistaken. And I would have dismissed her claim out of hand, but for the fact that I, too, only recently, had experienced a ghostly encounter of my own.

Her apartment, with space aplenty for a modest kitchen, a large dining area, a smaller family room, and a bedroom, were all connected by a hallway. Her apartment was on the second floor of a quadruplex, which appeared to have been built many years earlier, perhaps pre-World War II. She lived there alone with her two kids, and rarely had guests, but that was soon to be remedied. While she sat on a loveseat to my right, and I on the couch, which rested against a wall, just below a window, facing a television set, we watched television in silence. As I watched, I noticed a pair of men's trousers to the left of the set, but on my right. My first thoughts were: I didn't notice anyone coming in and standing there. There's no way I would have missed someone, no matter how engrossed I might have been in the television.

Perplexed, I moved my gaze slowly up the person's pant legs to a coat and finally to the face of a man who wore a brimmed hat. He was a middle-aged white male, wearing a long overcoat over a suit coat, the material of which appeared to be tweed, and from under the hat's brim he stared menacingly at me.

Suddenly realizing what it all implied, I leaned forward, pointed at the man, and yelled, "A ghost!" After my outburst, the man quickly disappeared. Although I had seen him quite clearly, my friend hadn't. But that would soon change. On another evening, as we both sat together on the couch watching television, she went to the set to adjust the picture, tweaking it with the vertical or horizontal hold control knobs. She had knelt in front of it only briefly when she said hurriedly, "I feel fear in the hall."

Slowly, we tilted our head in the direction of the hall, terrified as to what we might see there. Standing in the hall, midway the dining room and the family room, was the outline of a black figure, a silhouette, shrouded in darkness, with no definable features, except that where the heart may have been, a bright, white light glowed, the light seemingly more translucent than opaque.

For all the world, the dark figure met the description of what is now referred to as a "shadow person." Without warning, and before we had time to gather our senses or collect ourselves—mentally, emotionally or physically—the dark figure in the hallway sped towards us, gliding, not walking, as though it was suspended on a line that transported it in our direction.

In her eagerness to escape a potential threat, my companion bounded suddenly in my direction, landing on top of me, which sent the couch, which rested just below the second-story window, backward with such force that I wasn't able to see the advancing terror, the window, nevertheless, holding firm, although it had to support the weight of the couch and its two occupants now pressed hard against it.

Afterward, I purposely held back my account of what had happened so as not to color her experience. I was not surprised to learn that her version mirrored my own. For hours, the presence of the entity could be felt—palpably, unmistakably—as though it had become an integral part of the enclosed surroundings. And although the apartment was kept uncomfortably warm in the winter, the air in the room was now icy cold. Along with the unmistakable presence of the apparition permeating the room, a smarting frigidity hovered in the air.

If you wish to continue sleeping peaceably at night, you may not want to read about my final encounter with the bellicose presence, what turned out to be a very jealous male apparition. My companion had stepped out for the night. Her leaving angered me. Now alone, I reclined on the bed in the adjoining bedroom, instead of my customary place on the couch, and quickly found myself in a trance, and in the trance's accompanying paralytic state. But this trance would be different: My whole body, every inch of it, front to back, head to toe, side to side, suffered the crushing press of an invisible force. My whole body felt as though it was in the clench of a giant vise. The pain was excruciating.

I knew that the pain emanated from the apparition, from the male ghost that I had now seen on two previous occasions. I knew, too, that he was angry. He was angrier with me than I was with my companion. And I knew why: It was because I was angry with her, and he didn't like it. For that anger, he was now punishing me. And punish me he did. Not until I had assured him that I wouldn't be angry with her again that he relented, that the crush from the vise ended, and the awful pain stopped.

EXTRATERRESTRIALS

I classify extraterrestrials as the opposition and enemies of humanity for the reason that they haven't explicitly and definitively revealed either who they are or their intentions. Until they do, wisdom would dictate that we proceed with utmost caution and circumspection.

Like many Americans, I read Whitley Strieber's very popular book, *Communion*. For many, the extraterrestrial Grey on the book cover proved too much an enticement to pass up. I'm not sure how long after reading it that I had my first close encounter of the third kind, sort of. When it happened, I don't believe I was thinking about the book or the Grey featured on the cover. I had only recently rented the apartment in which I was now living. I rented it shortly after separating from my then wife, with a divorce pending. For some reason, I had walked into the living room which was still sparsely furnished, the room having nothing more than a rented couch against the most expansive wall, and my own twenty-inch-screen television resting a short distance in front of it.

I happened to look up. Just a few inches in front of the couch, but on the ceiling, dark, oval-shaped eyes within an almond-shaped head looked down upon me, appearing more insect-like than animal, the image of Whitley's Strieber's Grey. It made no sound, but it was a ringer for the Grey on Strieber's book, *Communion.* The image wasn't vague and diffused, but sharp and clear, as though it was alive rather than an image emblazoned on my ceiling.

In disbelief, I said out loud to no one in particular, "Nah, you can't be there."

Wanting to see if it would still be there if I walked out of the room and returned, I immediately walked all the way to my bedroom, well on the other side of the wall that divided the living room from the bedroom, waited for 60 seconds, and walked back.

It was still there, in the same place, looking down on me. The hair on my head, and neck stood up, as shivers convulsed my entire body. I didn't know what to make of it, and rather than ask it any questions, like, "Who or what are you, and what do you want?" I just stood there, dumbfounded.

Slowly, the image faded until I couldn't see it any longer. After this experience, I read that extraterrestrials were using Strieber's book as a portal of a sort, as a way to enter our world, and to make themselves known. The writer didn't give the source of his revelation, how he had obtained it, and neither did he authenticate the accuracy of his account. I only know this: Before reading the book I had never to my knowledge seen anything remotely resembling an extraterrestrial. Since that first sighting, I haven't seen Greys again, yet who knows what tomorrow may bring. I have had, however, other extraterrestrial encounters.

From this experience, I realized that we don't have to be in our astral state, as in the account to follow, to see extraterrestrials, but that they can reveal themselves in our physical world, making themselves visible to our physical eyes, further expanding on their interdimensional capabilities and extraordinary range.

More than a decade ago, extraterrestrials revealed themselves again to several humans, all men, and all white, but for one, me. We weren't physically-taken abductees but out-of-body abductees, seized and transported to their ship, presumably docked above our planet, but in a space that existed in an astral dimension, one beyond our physical realm. When we became aware of our plight, we were lying down on what appeared to be gurneys. I lifted myself using my left elbow as leverage, positioning my upper body to take in the entire room as well as others who might be present. And there were others. Like me, they were looking around as well, startled, with wide-eyed disbelief at their predicament. Not one of us attempted to get up and leave our gurneys.

The ship seemed circular, the hull concaved, the way that flying saucers have been described by a number of witnesses over the years. In front of our gurneys stood the only other person in the room, beside us men. She was a white woman and wore what resembled a white nurse's uniform and white shoes. In her left hand, she held a pointer, and with it she pointed at a lighted screen attached to a wall in front of her. As she pointed, she spoke out loud, and not telepathically, but slowly and deliberately, punctuating her words with pauses, as though she was thinking and making calculations as she spoke.

I don't recall the strange symbols that were on the screen, but, as she pointed at them, bringing the pointer into contact with the screen, she said, "On this date (She provided an actual date, which I have now forgotten.), and at 5:30 a.m., there will be an earthquake." As soon as she had provided this prediction, I was back in my body. I then jotted down the day and the time. Not for a moment did I doubt the accuracy of the prediction; that's how certain I was that it would occur. Did the ETs also implant this certainty in the impartation of the information? So convinced was I of the earthquake prediction that I was willing, after arriving at work that day, to go out on a limb and tell co-workers of the impending quake.

Because the earthquake wouldn't occur for a few months, I don't believe that my co-workers took me seriously, but since I was the manager, I was given the benefit of the doubt, and wasn't challenged on the likeli-hood that I could actually predict an earthquake, and do so several months in advance. When the fateful day was a mere several hours away and while I was still at work, I reminded the staff again of the impending earthquake.

"Do you remember that I told you a few months ago that there would be an earthquake tomorrow morning at 5:30?"

"Yes," was their reply.

"Well, tomorrow morning is that day."

I didn't think for a minute that they believed me. That night I went to bed with the earthquake on my mind, and my bedside clock in clear view. At the time, I lived in an upstairs unit of a two-story apartment. On cue, at 5:30 a.m., the Earth shook, and the apartment unit swayed with the Earth's movement, waking me from my slumber. Using an abundance of caution, I exited the building by the stairway and took cover in my car until the shaking stopped.

It was my turn to work the night shift that day, so I didn't arrive at work until noon. As I walked to my office, one of my co-workers stopped me.

"Mr. Hunt," she exclaimed, "you were right. There was an earthquake this morning."

I smiled and nodded my assent.

"Will you tell us when the Big One (meaning an earthquake along the San Andreas Fault) is going to happen?"

I assured her that I would. Other co-workers who knew about the prediction looked at me as though I had two heads, not sure how a mere mortal was able to predict an earthquake, and foretell it months in advance. I felt like a magician who had pulled off the world's cleverest trick, and did so without revealing a single clue as to how the trick was done, or how to duplicate it. Damage to our facility was minor, although the shaking left behind sure signs that something powerful had struck and that the building had suffered a mild attack—books had been thrown from the shelves in sundry places.

Throughout my section of the country, several men, myself included, had been chosen to testify about the existence of extraterrestrials, and their astonishing ability to predict earthquakes, leaving us humans wondering about what other marvels they may have up their galactic sleeves, and just how vast their intelligence and technology.

Those co-workers who witnessed this display of pre-knowledge are still alive and can attest to, and corroborate, my story, at least the part where I predicted an earthquake. I thought it wise, at the time, to keep to myself the source of my prediction, and how I came to know months in advance the precise day and time of the earthquake. Predicting an earthquake was one thing, having that prediction come from an extraterrestrial was another. Such a revelation would have further strained credulity, and perhaps damaged my unblemished reputation as well.

I'm convinced that these extraterrestrials used us, a dozen men or so, to spread the word of their existence, this after demonstrating compelling proof of their presence among us, and their superior capabilities. With the publishing of my book, perhaps these men will come forward and confirm their experience on the alien ship, that contact was indeed made with extraterrestrials, and done in such a way that it left convincing evidence of their existence—the evidence that the woman in white had established by doing what we humans weren't yet able to do, predict the exact day and time of an earthquake, and to do it months beforehand.

Despite my discussion of ghosts, demons, and humanity's negative conditions, the Greatest Truth is that nothing really exists, but God—good and perfection—and that which He has created, a creation that reflects Him and nothing else. No form of human reality has the permanence, the certainty, or the eternality of ultimate reality. To be sure, I've written about these things as though they are *real*, but, happily, they're not, they're mere illusions, or they'd be as real and as eternal as God, Himself, competing with Him for primacy.

Only God, and what God creates is real. That which we create, individually and collectively, is short-lived and impermanent. Were it not that way, our creations, existing concurrently with the creations of God, would assume a reality of their own, and compete with the creations of the divine, introducing discord and darkness into eternal harmony and light. All things real come forth from the absolute, the real and eternal: "All things were made by him; and without him was not anything made that was made."[64]

Although man has an adversary in Satan, God has no adversary, no opposites, and no opposition. Because He has no equal, we know Him as God Almighty, His Great Power exceeding that of the enemy. In Revelations we read: The "four and twenty elders" worshipped Him, "Saying, We give thee thanks, O Lord God Almighty, which art, and wast, and art to come; because thou hast taken to thee thy great power, and hast reigned."[65] "Perfect and an upright," even Job was beyond the destructive reach of Satan, eliciting the following complaint from him:

> Hast not thou made an hedge about him,
>
> and about his house, and about all that he hath on every side? thou hast blessed the work of his hands, and his substance is increased in the land.
>
> But put forth thine hand now, and touch all that he hath, and he will curse thee to thy face (Job 1:10-11).

For Satan to test Job's fidelity, he first had to appeal to God to remove Job's Protection, the "hedge about him." Before God assented to Satan's request, He restricted his power over Job:

> Behold, all that he hath is in thy power; only upon himself put not forth thine hand (Job 1: 12).

---

64 John 1:3
65 Rev 11:17

From God's perspective, all is like Him, Perfect, Holy and Good. In Habakkuk 1:13, we're told this about God: "*Thou art* of purer eyes than to behold evil, and canst not look on iniquity." The dubious honor of beholding evil belongs to us and us alone, if we decide to eat from the tree of knowledge of good and evil. Now, we, too, can choose to be so pure of heart, that all we see is God, good. Satan's power, we're told, is a *liar's* power, a *deceiver's* power, a power subject to the almighty power of God:

> *And I saw an angel come down from heaven having the key of the bottomless pit and a great chain in his hand.*
>
> *And he laid hold on the dragon, that old serpent, which is the Devil, and Satan, and bound him a thousand years,*
>
> *And cast him into the bottomless pit, and shut him up, and set a seal upon him, that he should deceive the nations no more, till the thousand years should be fulfilled: and after that he must be loosed a little season* (Rev 20:1-3).

To be free, we must turn our back on Satan, the tempter, liar, and deceiver, and state, as did Jesus, "Get thee behind me, Satan: for it is written, Thou shalt worship the Lord thy God, and him only shalt thou serve."[66] We turn our back on Satan when we refuse to acknowledge that he has power equal to that of God; refuse to give him attention, or recognition; refuse to fall for his lies, and his deceptions. When we're tempted, we must remember Jesus' declaration: "The first of all the commandments is, Hear, O Israel; The Lord our God is one Lord."[67] What kind of opposition could a liar and deceiver mount, if we refuse to believe the lie, and realize the truth in all situations? What does it say about an adversary who uses—as his weapons—illusions and deceptions with which to attack the Children of God? As an adversary, Satan is a failure. The following biblical passage underscores that failure: "He was a murderer from the beginning,

---

66 Luke 4:8
67 Mark 12:29-30

and abode not in the truth, because there is no truth in him. When he speaketh a lie, he speaketh of his own: for he is a liar, and the father of it."[68]

Remember: without the "lie," and without the deception that the lie sponsors, Satan, the "liar," and the deceiver, is impotent—powerless to do us any harm. He can only harm us when we believe the lie and fall for his deceptions.

There is another verse in Isaiah that seems to contradict the purity of God's eyes:

That they may know from the rising of the sun, and from the west, that there is none beside me. I am the Lord, and there is none else.

I form the light, and create darkness: I make peace, and create evil: I the Lord do all these things (Isa 45:6-7).

Upon examination, another conclusion might be reached. Here God announces His Allness ("there is none beside me"), and how that Allness gives seeming existence to that which He's not. Were it not that He "formed the light," the supposition of a "darkness" couldn't exist. Were it not that He "make peace," the supposition of the absence of peace, "evil," couldn't be "created." The only sinless and non-evil place is inside God, Love, Light and Peace. Outside of Love (our true reality) nothing is real, nothing exists, only illusions (darkness and evil), counterfeits of reality.

Notwithstanding the Allness of God—good—there appear to be two parallel realities: one good and one evil. Yet, a tree of knowledge of good and evil can't really exist in truth, for it would usurp God's reality, which is the only reality that exists. The acknowledgement of any other existence, by way of experience, or thought, is patently false, as there can be only one God, not two, if God is recognized to be infinite and omnipotent. Either God is real or He's not. My experience tells me that the truth resides in the former and not the latter.

---

68 John 8:44

PART FOUR:

HOW TO CONNECT TO THE *YOU* IN YOU, AND THE GOD IN *YOU*

SIXTEEN

STAYING CONNECTED

IN REALITY, YOU'RE ALWAYS CONNECTED TO THE *YOU* IN you that is your astral body. It is the *you* that surrounds the physical body, the *you* that shrewdly comports itself as a physical being, when in fact the physical being that you believe you are, isn't really you at all. Be assured, you never stop for a moment being an astral self, a spiritual being. You may not believe that you are. You may not believe that a spiritual being even exists. But that doesn't change the truth: You're not your physical body; stated another way: Your physical body is not *you*. Although there appear to be three of you, a physical you, an astral (or spiritual) *you*, and a Soul You, in truth, there's only one of you, (the Soul You) and that *You* is *one* with the whole of YOU, with all that exists, with what is known as the All-in-all.

Hundreds of books have been written promising their readers and out-of-body experience if only they followed their techniques. Some believe that lucid dreaming—that is, dreaming while you're aware that you're dreaming—is tantamount to an out-of-body experience.

It's not.

Some swear that sleep paralysis, a condition that has affected many at one time or another, is the same as an out-of-body experience.

It's not.

Yet, a lucid dream may be used as a launching pad for and out body experience. Many times I have literally stopped my dreams and lifted myself from my body, as it lay in repose upon my bed, to find myself standing in my bedroom.

And, too, sleep paralysis, when the body is asleep while the mind is awake, may also be used as a prelude to an out-of-body experience. Those in the throes of sleep paralysis have already reached the prerequisite stage from which to leave their body. The next step, which may be the hardest, requires only that they exit the physical body, a task that's understandably hard when you realize that the astral body and the physical body are mutually attracted, and only disconnect under the most challenging of circumstances.

One writer recommends visualizing a place with which you're familiar—such as a room in your house—and will yourself there, invoking a command, if necessary, such as, "Take me to my living room." Because I experienced vibrations over the third eye—that is, the middle of my forehead—and over my heart, as a usual prelude to an out-of-body excursion, I was often swept away by a force identified in the literature as the "astral current," riding as though I was atop a magic or flying carpet. It wouldn't surprise me to learn that this was how the magic-carpet mythology, and folklore, had its beginning.

THE ASTRAL YOU
WAYS OF LEAVING THE BODY
THE ASTRAL CURRENT

For many years, I had no name for the *astral current*. At some point during my reading of the literature on astral projection (another name for the out-of-body experience), the term was used and defined. Immediately, I knew what was being discussed because of my experience with the current. The description of it told me that I wasn't the only one who left the body in this way. Many out-of-body explorers, I learned, at one time or another, had traveled on the current, were lifted out of their bodies, and transported in a manner similar to mine. Numerous times over the years, this current has carried me to various places and has introduced me to sundry experiences, some of which took place during previous lives, the yet unlived future, and while exploring uncharted worlds, worlds that can only be described as existing in other dimensions.

Shortly after my physical body was transfixed by an astral trance and paralysis, the current would sweep me away, totally disconnect my astral body from the physical. Once disconnected, I was compelled to ride the current to its destination, a destination to which I never had foreknowledge. Once in the current I couldn't stop it, and neither could I direct it. Perhaps on an unconscious level, or on a Soul level, my destination had been predetermined, but, on the conscious level, I had to wait until I reached my destination to know what was in store. It's very likely that riding the current was a journey initiated by the Soul, my Higher Self, for the purpose of imparting information, or to allow for the recall of a previous-life experience.

During the ride, I have opened my eyes, and when I did, all I could see most of the time was blinding lights flashing by, and at incredible speed. When I did see things while traveling, it was people's lofts, treetops, and strange landscapes. This way of traveling was amazing. It required no other vehicle, but my astral body, to travel from point A to point B. In time I learned other methods for leaving the body, but this method was the first, and because it was first, it remains my sentimental favorite. Had it not been for the current, it might have taken me years to consider the feasibility of leaving the body, and even more years to discover the means to do so.

RISING

Once the condition for leaving my body had been achieved, it was still necessary to find a way to separate the astral body from the physical. It's only automatic when the astral current, not unlike a flying carpet, slips underneath my astral body and whisks me away. If this didn't happen, I had to find another way to separate. The method I have often used to initiate a separation from the physical body was the one I have used to lift my physical body from its reclining position. I merely sat up in bed, threw my legs over the side, and stood. This is what most of us would do to rise from bed, as it's quick and it's simple. And this is where we'd be mistaken. It's not as quick nor as simple as it might sound at first blush. In fact, this very simple act comes with a mighty effort. Most out-of-body explorers have had to master some technique to facilitate their leaving of the body once in the trance, or paralysis state. One in particular, Robert Monroe, used what he called the "rotation technique," which served him well.

What makes leaving the body a difficult task, for me and other explorers, is the state of paralysis that ensues once we're in the grip of a trance. To move even a finger becomes a mighty struggle. Try as I might, the body does not cooperate. And if the body is weighed down with heavy covers, or blankets, it makes the task that much more difficult. It's not impossible for me to move my astral body, or to separate from the physical at this crucial time, and under the aforementioned conditions, but it will require all my strength, determination, and focus.

Let me clear up a possible misconception. Throughout this discussion, I've referred to my two bodies—one astral and one physical—as though they're separate and apart. Actually, the distinction between the two often becomes blurred, given that I'm never quite aware of having two bodies, only one. When my astral body leaves my physical body, it still feels as though I'm taking my physical body with me, that it's my physical body in motion. Additionally, when I'm out-of-body, it's hard to tell the difference between sleepwalking in my physical body, or walking while in my astral body. I won't know for sure one way or the other until other elements come together. My surroundings may appear different and I may find that I can fly or float. There are other clues that may give it away. What I'm doing, then, in this attempt to move my body, is to move my astral body, but the sensation will be that I'm moving my physical body, as the experience is the same.

LUCID DREAMS AS A LAUNCH PAD

Not all out-of-body experiences begin with a trance and paralysis; some may be launched from within a dream. The key here is to *know* that you're dreaming while you're dreaming. Books have been written on the subject of lucid dreaming, and how to use these dreams of heightened awareness to initiate an out of body experience, some of them advising readers to use certain methods or techniques before falling asleep that will alert them while sleeping that they are sleeping, giving them the opportunity to use the dream state as a vehicle for leaving the body. The books are useful to the extent that their instructions require the reader to focus on the sleep to follow, and on the desire to awaken during sleep; this focus is usually enough to direct the mind to awaken (to become aware) during sleep. It is becoming conscious (aware) during sleep and knowing that you *are* sleep that make lucid dreams lucid. Without this awareness, our dreams continue to be what they have always been: our acting out a role, usually without the knowledge that we're in the dream state, and that the dream world is not the one in which we usually live. In short, while in the dream state, we accept our dream reality as the only reality, and our dream world as our everyday world, notwithstanding the bizarre nature of many of our dreams.

Just before falling off to sleep, I have programmed myself, with the use of autosuggestion alone, to awaken while sleeping. Intention is usually enough to direct my mind to do so. While dreaming, almost anything in the dream may remind me that I'm sleeping. Once I'm aware, I merely stop the dream—actually will it to stop—and proceed, using the *rising* method, to leave my body. Once out of the body, as I've already specified, I may raise my arms over my head and command myself to fly, a superhero ability that is every child's dream, or leave my house by some other means, one less exhilarating.

Aware of being awake while sleeping, my consciousness shifts from the sleeper-dreamer to the sleeper who's awake and can now change the dream story at will, whereas before I was just a sleeper, and a helpless participant in the dream, as well, rather than its creator. Another advantage of this dream-state awareness is the ability to remember these lucid dreams and out-of-body experiences in ways that ordinary dreams do not afford. Within the scope of fifty to sixty years, I have had many of out-of-body experiences, and I can still remember them with a great deal more detail and clarity than I have ever recalled a dream, unless that dream reached the intensity of a nightmare. Some critics have likened these out-of-body experiences to a mental state associated with ordinary dreams. If that were the case, why then would these out-of-body dreams be retained in memory longer and more vividly than any others? Could it be that lucid dreaming, and out-of-body excursions represent a phase of consciousness dissimilar to those states associated with sleep, or being awake, or hypnotized?

HOW TO LEAVE YOUR BODY

You've read at length about what the astral body can do, what it's capable of. You've followed my exploits in the astral realm, learned about the various lives that I have lived and my various astral encounters, encounters that have altered my view of reality. Having read this far, you'd probably like to know how you, too, may avail yourself of the potentiality of the astral body and its many abilities. I can't promise that I can make you an out-of-body traveler—either a first-time traveler or a frequent traveler—but I can promise you that I will give you my best advice for doing so, techniques and methods that I have used successfully over the years.

Of all the methods available, your best hope for achieving an out-of-body experience is autosuggestion. I recommend that you wait until bedtime to use this method. While you're falling off to sleep, give yourself the suggestion that you will leave your body. Create a mantra similar to this one, using the elements included here, or use this one in its entirety: "Tonight, my astral body will travel outside my physical body." If possible wear something light to bed. Cover your body with something light, as well. Wearing something heavy, or placing something heavy over the body may impede the astral body's ability to leave the physical. Remember, the physical body acts as a magnet. For that reason, the astral body will need as much help as possible to disconnect from, and to leave, the physical once that connection is compromised—that is, once the astral body finds that it can leave the physical body despite the onset of the trance state.

If you succeed in inducing a trance state, where the physical body is asleep and the mind is awake, don't be surprise if you find that you can't move your body. As I've stated before, this condition is called sleep paralysis, and is one of the conditions that might precede your ability to leave your body. Sleep paralysis is not that uncommon, but few know that it can be used to achieve an out-of-body experience. In the trance state, your consciousness will be situated atop your body as though it's a pyramidal capstone, and your body the base of the pyramid. The pyramid on the back of the U.S. one-dollar bill captures it perfectly and precisely. In the trance state, consciousness is centered in the third eye (which is also the all-seeing eye, or the Eye of Providence), the eye seen within the pyramid's capstone. The third eye, or the all-seeing eye within the capstone, is seemingly separated from the base of the pyramid, just as your lower physical body in the trance state is seemingly separated from your consciousness and awareness, no longer within the embrace of it.

Since we're unique, and individual, this, as well as other phenomena might attend an out-of-body episode. If you're not whisked away on the astral current in this state, don't be discouraged, it only signals that you'll have to do the heavy lifting yourself. If fear manifests itself at this point, do your best to remain as calm as possible. To experience fear at this time is not uncommon, as you're in new territory, an unknown realm to your conscious and more awake mind, although the new territory is the playground of our sleeping self and our astral self. Frank Herbert, the author of Dune, sums it up nicely, how best to defeat fear in what is called the *litany against fear,* as chanted by the Bene Gesserit. I recommend it.

I've composed my own *litany against fear,* one that I use when misfortune strikes, when trouble arouses more fear than determination, when determination is the right frame of mind for meeting a difficult situation with courage and the assurance that I will emerge victorious. The litany (recitation) uses each letter of the word, *FEAR,* transforming it in the process, using it to transform the situation from an intimidating one into one I know I can meet head-on and conquer. The word, FEAR, then becomes an acronym for: *Face Every Adversity Resolutely.* To see an outcome of my choosing, a positive or constructive one, rather than the one that fear chooses, requires resolve. This litany provides that resolve.

Assuming that you have managed to moderate the onset of fear—fear of your new environment or the seemingly helpless state of paralysis that has beset you—the greatest task is still ahead, that of separating the astral from the physical. As I stated previously, Robert Monroe used a "rotation technique" to leave his body, which I modified substantially to actually roll out of my physical body onto the floor. I have used this method successfully and can attest to its effectiveness. In addition, I have exited the physical body simply by sitting up and throwing my legs over the side of the bed and standing, the very same act I have used in the physical to rise from bed in order to leave my bedroom. Don't be disappointed if on the first departure out of the physical body, or on several, you don't see the silver cord, or catch a glimpse of your physical body. Only after several years had passed was I even aware of the cord, or believed that I had left a physical body behind. Because of the juxtaposition of the physical and the astral, you may experience being in two places at once, or alternating between the physical body and the astral body. Once out of the body, and standing, you can walk to the nearest exit, or you might try lifting off by using the flying technique that I identified before. Raise your arms over your head, pointing hem towards the ceiling and issue the command: "Go mind!"

Once in flight, you can enjoy the view from that vantage point, what's above and what's below, or you can attempt to direct your flight to a predetermined destination, although I've never had much luck in choosing where I'll end up. If you don't achieve *lift off*, there's always the nearest window or door from which to leave your domicile for the greater outdoors, and what awaits you there. You may be tempted to knock on the doors of neighbors, or to walk the streets, or to attempt to fly again now that there's nothing over you such as a ceiling and a roof to stop you. If you decide to fly, you'll find that you can flap your arms, your astral wings, to accelerate and to direct the astral body in flight. Although you're in familiar territory at the beginning, be prepared to have the familiar become the strange and the bizarre, as you'll find as did Dorothy in *The Wizard of OZ*, you're not in Kansas anymore.

Fortunately, you won't have to worry about returning to your body. If anything, you'll have to worry about returning too soon, that is, before you're ready. Sometimes, the very thought of your physical body while in the astral is enough to snap you back to it. Other times, without giving it any thought, you'll return automatically, involuntarily. You won't always know in advance of it happening that you're returning to your physical body; one minute you'll be in your astral body at some astral location, and the next minute, you'll be back in your physical body, perhaps still entranced and paralyzed, or fully awake and in control. Returning to the physical, therefore, is a great deal simpler than leaving it in the first place. There's no ritual to follow, no procedural requirement, no methodology to adhere to. Your physical body, for better or for worse, is merely a thought away.

Frankly, I don't think it matters what method you use to leave the body—whether one that you provide yourself, or one that is provided for you—only that you use it, and use it often, until the desire to leave the body reaches critical mass, reaches such a burning intensity that the desire can't be denied. If you're looking for a compilation of techniques and methods to assist in the inducement of an out-of-body experience, look no further than the techniques and methods compiled in the well-researched book, *Leaving The Body—A Complete Guide To Astral Projection,* by D. Scott Rogo, who, after researching the subject and experimenting with various methods, succeeded after a time in leaving his body.

Once critical mass has been achieved your mind will create the out-of-body experience for you, hence the necessity of persistence, and a fidelity to one method or another. In the end, it won't be the method you use that will allow you to leave your body, but the degree of focus that you bring to the process. In this, as in all things, what you focus on in this world brings you closer to the thing desired, as the whole universe will conspire to give you what you desire, if you desire it long enough, and intensely enough. If you desire a specific house on the block rather than a house with similar attributes, you may find that your desire will go unfulfilled. If you desire a particular person of your acquaintance, rather than one who has that person's qualities or personality, you may find that your desire will go wanting, or that it will be realized, but only for a short time. That's because your Soul, or your Higher Self, has Plans of Its own, and It won't allow your human plans to conflict with Its Plans for you and for others, as they, too, have desires.

THE GOD IN YOU

You've learned that there's another You in *you*, other than your astral body (the astral *you*), known as your Soul, or your Higher Self, or your God Self. Connecting with the Soul in *you* is a far more important use of your time than connecting with the astral *you*. By connecting with the Soul, you open up a universe of possibilities, and the effort shouldn't be dismissed simply because, at first, the lure of leaving the body appears more appealing. I wrote this book to remind those who read it that we're more than humans living in physical bodies and subject to all the limitations that seeming reality suggests, including a vulnerability to illness, growing old, and dying. Know this: We're veritable gods. Since our advent in the flesh, we have mostly permitted our physical senses to define us, the nature of reality, and the world in which we live. As a result, we have lost sight of a sense that could transform us, and not just us, but the world in which we live, as well.

I'm convinced that had humans spent as much time developing their spiritual sense as was spent developing our modern-day wonders, and hadn't relied so heavily on the various sciences to unravel the mysteries of the universe as a way to enhance human existence, many of the concerns that now vex the human race, shortages of everything from good health, to ample food, to potable water would have been as short-lived as is our human life in physical bodies.

By choosing to manipulate our physical world to bring about what we could have effortlessly achieved by using spiritual sense—electing to focus on effect, that which is manifested, and that which is visible, rather than *cause* itself, the invisible, spiritual Source of all that is—is tantamount to choosing to walk across the Mojave Desert when we have access to cars, busses, or some other modern-day conveyance. Better yet, we could have saved both time and discomfort by jetting across it, rather than walking, or riding. With spiritual sense, we can access a transportation system that's truly not of this world, which, if employed, could transport us clear across the world, the galaxy, or the expanse of the universe, not on physical wings, but wings of thought, and wings of Spirit.

THE VIRGIN BIRTH

Because of his spiritual birth, Jesus was able to manifest Spirit to a larger degree than those who preceded Him, or those who came after Him, possessing, from the time of awareness, a spiritual sense of existence. Mary,

Jesus' mother, "was found with child of the Holy Ghost,"[69] suggesting that before and doing the birth of her son, she dwelled in Spirit, surrendered fully to the *Love of God* within herself, resulting in Jesus's spiritual birth and His ensuing appellation, "Son of God,"[70] or Son of Spirit, or Son of Love, giving him a spiritual head-start that suppressed the human tendencies that would have reinforced the testimony of physical sense as the whole of reality.

Similarly, it behooves all parents—fathers, as well as mothers—to remain as spiritual as is possible during the gestation of a new physical life, to surrender to the *Love of God* within us from morning to night, during the full nine months of pregnancy, and thereafter. Were we to, children would enter the world spiritually primed to live out their physical lives in their native milieu, Spirit. This alone would usher in a New Age of Spirit, God, an age that would transform the world, as human nature falls to spiritual nature, and spiritual sense becomes the primary sense with which newborns, soon to be children, and then adults, view their world and themselves.

For those who weren't born with a spiritual edge, practicing the presence of Love as often as is practical throughout the day will develop a spiritual sense. Going within will reinforce the spiritual sense attained, and open doors to non-physical realms, portals to other dimensions, including parallel worlds and parallel lives. As we develop spiritual sense, we'll find that it gives us access to many places—to other worlds, and dimensions, as well as the past, and the future.

The quickest way to develop a spiritual sense is to follow Jesus' directions. When asked, "Master, which *is* the great commandment in the law":

"Jesus said unto him, Thou shalt love the Lord thy God with all thy heart, and with all thy soul, and with all thy mind. This is the first

69 Matt 1:18
70 Matt 16:16

and great commandment. And the second is like unto it, Thou shalt love thy neighbour as thyself" (Matt 22:37-39).

It matters not who you are, where you live, or the religion you prefer, if any at all, or the culture that reared you, if you're expanding your heart with the potency of love, spiritual sense is yours for the taking. All can know God without the benefit of formal education, or religious intervention. Paul offers insight into this love, expounding on its nature, when he speaks of "charity," which I understand to mean, a love that's given without expectations of receiving love in return, that is, universal and impersonal ("For if ye love them which love you, what reward have ye?").[71]

Charity [love] suffereth long, and is kind; charity [love] envieth not; charity [love] vaunteth not itself, is not puffed up, Doth not behave itself unseemly, seeketh not her own, is not easily provoked, thinketh no evil; Rejoiceth not in iniquity, but rejoiceth in the truth; Beareth all things, believeth all things, hopeth all things, endureth all things (I Cor 13:4-7).

They who love, with or without the benefit of formal religious instructions, who have made love their home, will express God, Love, and also manifest Love's exquisite virtues as outlined above. By inference, they will gain insight into Love, God, and His divine nature, simply by dwelling in the "secret place." There's an infallible way to learn of God, to know Him. I got up in the middle of the night. On my way back to bed, The Voice said, "Be still and know that I am God [divine Love]."[72]

---

71 Matt 5:46
72 Ps 46:10

THE SABBATH

My Inner Wisdom assured me: All things which were created on a certain day of the seven days of creation all share the same characteristics. Man is no exception, created, as he was, on the sixth day, the day on which the "beast of the earth"[73] were created. It's not surprising, then, that Cain's mark, and the mark of the beast are 666, or as stated in Revelation, "Six hundred threescore and six,"[74] representing his three-part nature, his soul, his body, and his mind, the number corresponding with the sixth day of creation, one day short of the wholeness that comes with the seventh day, the day of the Sabbath, completing what is lacking, and rendering 666 as 777, transforming beast-man into God-man, reforming his three-part nature—his soul, body, and mind—as he remembers the Sabbath (the seventh day), that he was made in the image and likeness of God, and not the beast. I found only one reference in the Bible identifying a person as having the number 777, or seven hundred, seventy and seven, the number of years he had lived, and that was Lamech:

> And Lamech lived an hundred eighty and two years, and begat a son:
>
> And he called his name Noah, saying, This same shall comfort us concerning our work and toil of our hands, because of the ground which the Lord hath cursed.
>
> And Lamech lived after he begat Noah five hundred ninety and five years, and begat sons and daughters:
>
> And all the days of Lamech were seven hundred seventy and seven years: and he died (Gen 5:28-31).

---

73 Gen 1:24
74 Rev 13:18

The Christ, or the Image and Likeness of God, is the Sabbath. Cain slew Abel. As the offspring of Adam and Eve, Cain bears the *mark*, or the image of the beast,[75] while Abel bears the image and likeness of God, by virtue of his righteousness.[76] From the beginning these two brothers existed in contradistinction, for only *one* could please God, as only one came from God, and that one Abel. Cain was of the Earth, earthy, hence a "tiller of the ground,"[77] taking after his father Adam (Red Clay or Red Earth) while Abel, taking after his mother Eve ("the mother of all living"[78]) was a Shepherd, one who reserved for God the best that he had to offer of that which he shepherd—the best of his life, of his thoughts, of his words, of his actions—the "firstlings of his flock and of the fat thereof."[79] Cain gave of his best, the fruit of the Earth, the ground, which had already been cursed by Lord God, but God (Spirit) is not of the Earth, the ground, and such a gift, no matter how humbly given, will always fail to please God (Spirit): "Then shall the dust return to the earth as it was: and the spirit shall return unto God who gave it."[80]

> *Come unto me [the Christ], all ye that labour [work] and are heavy laden, and I will give you rest. Take my yoke upon you, and learn of me; for I am meek and lowly in heart: and ye shall find rest unto your souls. For my yoke is easy, and my burden is light.*[81]

As the Sabbath, the Christ fulfills the promise of a *rest* for the "heavy laden," first seen in this passage from Genesis:

---

75 Gen 4:15
76 Heb 11:4
77 Gen 4:2
78 Gen 3:20
79 Gen 4:4
80 Eccl 12:7
81 Matt 11:28

And on the seventh day God ended his work which he had made; and he rested on the seventh day from all his work which he had made (Gen 2:2).

We have yet to enter into this *rest*, this *Sabbath of God*, but continue to "labour," even after being told that God has "ended his work." The *Age of the Beast* will end when the *Sabbath* begins, but no man knows the day or the time of this momentous event, only God. The two sons—Cain and Abel—represent the condition present at the creation of man, as each assumed the potentiality of the "beast of the earth" as well as the *image and likeness of God*. It's the nature of the beast to kill the image and likeness of God, if the beast or carnal nature is indulged. It becomes our task, then, to keep the beast at bay, to adhere to the truth of our being, our likeness to God, and to keep that likeness holy or whole—to shepherd our life, thoughts, words, actions, so that they please God, and obey the first and most important commandment of the ten:

Thou shalt have no other gods before me.[82]

The name, Abel, has several meanings. The one meaning that warrants the "respect" afforded Abel by God (Lord God) is that of "breath," or "breathing spirit." We see this reference to "breath," at the creation of Adam: "And the Lord God formed man *of* the dust of the ground, and breathed into his nostrils the breath of life; and man became a living soul."[83]

Once Abel, our truer self, the self that pleases God with his offerings, has been slain by the Cain of our being, it becomes our duty to slay the slayer. A mark was placed upon Cain, the *mark of the beast*, "lest any finding him should kill him."[84] Carrying the beast's mark, we forfeit our truer nature, the nature of Abel, a nature that's a step closer to our one true

---

82 Ex 20:3
83 Gen 2:7
84 Gen 4:15

nature, the Image and Likeness of God, and we live out our lives as Cain. This distinction between the spiritual man and the "natural" man, the man more beast than Godlike, is carefully and precisely drawn in this passages from First Corinthians, Chapter 15 of the King James Version of the Bible:

> It is sown a natural body; it is raised a spiritual body. There is a natural body, and there is a spiritual body. And so it is written, The first man Adam was made a living soul; the last Adam [Jesus the Christ] was made a quickening spirit. Howbeit that was not first which is spiritual, but that which is natural; and afterward that which is spiritual. The first man is of the earth, earthy; the second man is the Lord from heaven [the image and likeness of God, spiritual] (1Cor 15:44-47).

As the Christ, or as the Image and Likeness of God, his true identity, Jesus represented the nature of Abel more than he did Adam or Cain in the Creation allegory. Just as Adam was created first, and not Eve, Cain was born before his brother, Abel. This order of creation and birth is important, which the preceding passage acknowledges by stating: "It is sown a natural body; it is raised a spiritual body." When some from the crowd asked Jesus how they "might work the works of God," they were told: "This is the work of God that ye believe on him whom he hath sent."[85]

Wanting to take it a step further, I asked God, How can I do the works of God? The answer: "You must be born again," that is, after the Spirit, and not the flesh, after the Son of God, the Son of Love, our real nature, and not the beast. Also implicit in the answer of Jesus to a question from the crowd was the need to be born again, by accepting the Christ nature, the Son of God nature, as your own true nature, *to believe on him*, which allows you, too, to enter the Kingdom, and, thereby, wield the power of God.

---

85 John 6:29

"And whatsoever ye shall ask in my name [in the nature of the Son of God]," said Jesus, "that will I do, that the Father may be glorified in the Son" (John 14:13).

Also, speaking of the Christ whom he exemplified, Jesus said this:

Abide in me, and I in you. As the branch cannot bear fruit of itself, except it abide in the vine; no more can ye, except ye abide in me. I am the vine, ye are the branches: He that abideth in me, and I in him, the same bringeth forth much fruit: for without me ye can do nothing (John 15:4-5).

The beast may at times appear to imitate God-man, the Son of God, the Mosaic might, as did the magicians in Pharaoh's court on a few occasions, but they'll never surpass God-man, simply because the power of the beast, human power, flesh and bone power, carnal mind power, is not real power and not equal to the power of God, the power of Spirit, the power of Love. Because we seem to have been made in the image of the beast, and the image of God, we must choose which of the two we wish to express (press out), but we can't express them both without dire consequences. We're admonished, "No man can serve two masters: for either he will hate the one, and love the other; or else he will hold to the one, and despise the other. Ye cannot serve God [Spirit] and mammon [worldly wealth, worldly power]."[86] If we choose to serve God, then we must slay Cain, who bears the mark of the beast. "For whosoever will save his life shall lose it: and whosoever will lose his life for my sake shall find it."[87]

We're living in the *Age of Cain.* We're living in the lair of the beast. If we don't slay the beast, the beast will slay us. And if it slays us, it will take us that much longer to *save our life,* to recognize our true nature as *Sons*

---

86 Matt 6:24
87 Matt 16:25

of God.[88] This was Jesus' mission, to remind us of who we are, to help us remember our divine nature, a nature that had eluded us until Jesus' advent in the flesh, the result of having the image of the beast and its nature always before us, always in our sight.

> *And the LORD said unto him, Therefore whosoever slayeth Cain, vengeance shall be taken on him sevenfold. And the LORD set a mark upon Cain, lest any finding him should kill him* (Gen 4:15).

To *kill* Cain is not an easy task. To do so will bring down the "vengeance" of all the worldly beliefs that we have previously trusted to sustain us, from our beliefs about our body, about our life, and about those with whom we interact. Because of the severity of this *vengeance*, the agonizing inner struggle within—the denial, and the forsaking of the natural, material, physical self—that precedes the killing of Cain and afterward, so that Cain doesn't rise again will seem "sevenfold" in its magnitude as we seek to follow the Christ, our ideal nature. Jesus, in his beatitudes characterizes the struggle against Cain (the carnal mind), and the anguish that it invokes, as a state of *mourning* for that which will be lost (our carnal life), "Blessed *are* they that mourn: for they shall be comforted,"[89] and as a *persecution.* "Blessed are they which are persecuted for righteousness' sake: for theirs is the kingdom of heaven."[90]

We see the *seven* again in the "sevenfold" vengeance that will be visited upon us when we endeavor to kill Cain, suggesting the severity and the fullness of the "vengeance," until the work is done (the total destruction of Cain and the beast he represents), and not before. In short, we must overthrow ourselves, our human self, our "flesh and blood"[91] self, the beast, the "carnal mind," if we're to see ourselves as we truly are, the Sons of God, the

---

88 I John 3:1-2
89 Matt 5:4
90 Matt 5:10
91 I Cor 15:50

Sons of Spirit, the inheritors of the Kingdom of God. We have this assurance from Jesus:

> *And when he had called the people unto him with his disciples also, he said unto them, Whosoever will come after me, let him deny himself, and take up his cross, and follow me.*
>
> *For whosoever will save his life shall lose it; but whosoever shall lose his life for my sake and the gospel's, the same shall save it.*
>
> *For what shall it profit a man, if he shall gain the whole world, and lose his own soul?* (Mark 8:34-36)

Aware of the warfare between Adam, including Adam's offspring, Cain (the carnal mind) and the Christ, the Image and Likeness of God, Paul, in the Book of Romans, reveals the nature of the battle, and how it may be won, with these words:

> *For they that are after the flesh do mind the things of the flesh; but they that are after the Spirit the things of the Spirit.*
>
> *For to be carnally minded is death; but to be spiritually minded is life and peace.*
>
> *Because the carnal mind is enmity against God: for it is not subject to the law of God, neither indeed can be.*
>
> *So then they that are in the flesh cannot please God* [in the same way that Cain couldn't please God with his offering].
>
> *But ye are not in the flesh, but in the Spirit, if so be that the Spirit of God dwell in you. Now if any man have not the Spirit of Christ, he is none of his.*
>
> *And if Christ be in you, the body is dead because of sin; but the Spirit is life because of righteousness.*

But if the Spirit of him that raised up Jesus from the dead dwell in you, he that raised up Christ from the dead shall also quicken your mortal bodies by his Spirit that dwelleth in you (Rom 8:5–11).

As long as we're *minding* the things of the flesh, we can't please God (Spirit), and the Spirit of God cannot dwell in us. If man is to continue as Earth inhabitants, it's imperative that he observes the Sabbath Day, "Remember the sabbath day to keep it holy [whole]."[92] We keep it whole, by remaining in the Sabbath, the 777, and resisting the beast, 666, the influence that seems to holds sway in this world of materiality, and *flesh and blood*. "Love not the world, neither the things that are in the world. If any man love the world, the love of the Father is not in him."[93]

We remember the Sabbath, 777, when we remember God, our spiritual nature, and develop our spiritual sense, our true sense, and, dwelling therein, repudiate the *beast* that would *mark* everyone born into the world, as our human birth inclines us more towards the beast than the divine, that is, unless our birth had the benefit of Jesus' birth, a virgin birth, whereby the Holy Spirit fathers the child. We, too, may experience this virgin birth, "Ye must be born again,"[94] when we're born of Spirit, of God, and of Love. As for the beast, its end will come with our salvation, as foretold in the following verse from Isaiah: "No lion shall be there, nor *any* ravenous beast shall go up thereon, it shall not be found there; but the redeemed shall walk *there*."[95]

THE LITTLE CHILD

And Jesus called a little child unto him, and set him in the midst of them,

---

92 Ex 20:8
93 I John 2:15
94 John 3:7
95 Isa 35:9

And said, Verily I say unto you, Except ye be converted, and become as little children, ye shall not enter into the kingdom of heaven.

Whosoever therefore shall humble himself as this little child, the same is greatest in the kingdom of heaven (Matt 18:2-4).

The qualities often associated with children and childhood are often described as that of "innocence" and "receptivity." There's another quality, one which rarely comes to mind, the quality of *dependency*. Children are, for better or for worse, dependent upon parents for everything—all that supports life and maintains it—whether those parents are their biological parents, or their parents of necessity. For us to have God as a Parent again, our Sole Provider, we must become as *little children*. Regrettably, many of God the Father's prospective children can't enter the Kingdom of Heaven because they're either too rich, or too proud, or too grown, that is, too old in the ways of the world. As long as they're adults in heart and mind, providing for themselves those things which they believe they desire, or need, or want, they can't enter their Father's House, the Kingdom of Heaven, for that Kingdom is reserved for the *poor*. "Blessed *are* the poor in spirit: for theirs is the kingdom of heaven."[96]

In the preceding scripture, as well as other scriptures, Jesus speaks highly of the state of being referred to as *humbleness*. In another passage, Jesus says this:

Come unto me, all ye that labour and are heavy laden, and I will give you rest.

Take my yoke upon you, and learn of me; for I am meek and lowly in heart: and ye shall find rest unto your souls. For my yoke is easy, and my burden is light (Matt 11:28-30).

---

96 Matt 5:3

Jesus is often described as the meekest man to have walked the globe, and if we're to follow him as he commanded, we would do well to emulate that meekness. "Take my yoke upon you, and learn of me; for I am meek and lowly in heart: and ye shall find rest unto your souls." Before the advent of Jesus, Moses was said to be the meekest: "Now the man Moses *was* very meek, above all the men which *were* upon the face of the earth."[97] In the statement that follows, Jesus acknowledges without equivocation who is the one actually responsible for performing the works of God:

Believest thou not that I am in the Father, and the Father in me? the words that I speak unto you I speak not of myself: but the Father that dwelleth in me, he doeth the works. Believe me that I am in the Father, and the Father in me: or else believe me for the very works' sake (John 14:10-11).

As long as we see ourselves as the source of our life, our mind, our health, or what have you, rather than God, to that extent do we stand proud and rich before God, and not meek and humble, and, to that extent do we run the risk of losing it all. It is said of pride, "Pride *goeth* before destruction, and an haughty spirit before a fall. Better *it is to be* of an humble spirit with the lowly, than to divide the spoil with the proud."[98]

To be prideful, then, is to source ourself as the source of all that we possess, including our mind, our life, our wealth, supply, abundance, our livelihood, and so on. This prideful state of mind is as one who is rich unto himself, since it is this *prideful* mind that is the source of his good. To be meek, on the other hand, is to be poor unto one's self, and to be poor in spirit is to be rich towards God, for to be poor is a blessed state, a state that appoints the poor as the possessors of the Kingdom of Heaven. And since the poor are meek, as well, they are sure to inherit the Kingdom (the source of all good), and the Earth, as well, that which is expressed or manifested before God, His "footstool."[99]

---

97 Num 12:3
98 Prov 16:18-19
99 Isa 66:1

The admonition, therefore, is this, that we don't claim ourselves as the source of anything, not the source of our jobs, our homes, our companions, not the source of our earthly assets, nor our heavenly treasures, Mind, Life, Love, Truth, but recognize God as the Source of both earthly and heavenly treasures: "seek ye first the kingdom of God, and his righteousness; and all these things ['What shall we eat? or, What shall we drink? or, Wherewithal shall we be clothed?'] shall be added unto you."[100]

Another way is suggested in this biblical passage, "let your communication be, Yea, yea [affirmation]; Nay, nay [denial]: for whatsoever is more than these cometh of evil."[101] In keeping with this declaration, we can say, God's Life is my life ("For with thee [God] *is* the fountain of life."[102]). God's Mind is my mind ("Let this mind be in you, which was also in Christ Jesus."[103]). God's Love is my love ("God is love; and he that dwelleth in love dwelleth in God, and God in him."[104]). God is my business ("wist ye not that I must be about my Father's business?"[105]). God is my sustenance ("I have meat to eat that ye know not of."[106]). God is my water ("whosoever drinketh of the water that I shall give him shall never thirst; but the water that I shall give him shall be in him a well of water springing up into everlasting life."[107]).

Or we can use denial: I have no life but God's Life. I have no mind but God's Mind. I have no love but God's Love. I have no business but God's Business. I have no sustenance but God's Sustenance. These affirmations and denials can be adapted to include almost anything—any state or condition—anything for which we can reasonably establish God as the Source, thereby placing these conditions and states beyond the reach of chance,

---

100 Matt 6:31-33
101 Matt 5:37
102 Ps 36:9
103 Phil 2:5
104 I John 4:16
105 Luke 2:49
106 John 4:32
107 John 4:14

and the vagaries of life, as they're sourced in God, the eternal, inexhaustible Fount from which all things flow.

We *can* source ourselves, but only when we understand, as did Jesus, that we're *one* with God, and that to source ourselves *is* to source the Father ("I and *my* Father are one."[108]). Because Jesus was able to unite with the Christ, and to know his oneness with God, he was able to source himself as the Way, the Truth and the Life: "I am the way, the truth, and the life: no man cometh unto the Father, but by me."[109] His was the ultimate act of meekness, a willing and complete submission to God the Father, providing support for another of His sayings, which, as with the previous one, reinforces his oneness with the Father: "Verily, verily, I say unto you, The Son can do nothing of himself, but what he seeth the Father do: for what things soever he doeth, these also doeth the Son likewise."[110]

Again, what distinguishes children from adults? It's children's utter dependency on parents, and not for a few things, but for all things—the roof over their heads, the food they eat, and the clothes they wear—all their human needs. Likewise, we should *humble* ourselves, as do children, and acknowledge God, as children acknowledge their parents, as the source of all that they are, and all that they need—and in the case of God as Parent, the Source of all that they need materially and spiritually.

If we're to manifest more of God in our lives, it's crucial then that we allow God to be the Source of all that we desire, all that we wish for, and all that we need, no matter how small, or how large; no matter how concrete or how abstract; no matter how tangible or intangible. "Son, thou art ever with me, and all that I have is thine,"[111] said the father to his stay-at-home, elder son, in Jesus' parable of the prodigal son.

Trust is yet another attribute or quality of childhood, one which most children have in abundance out of necessity, as they're forced to, because

---

108 John 10:30
109 John 14:6
110 John 5:19
111 Luke 15:31

of their age, to look to, to depend on, and therefore trust, their parents to provide for *their living* even as the Prodigal Son had allowed his Father, prior to his striking out on his own to "journey into a far country, and there wasted his substance with riotous living."[112] When we leave Our Heavenly Parent, God the Father, the Source of our Living, we subject ourselves to a life of want, a life of deprivation, and a life of misery: "And when he [the Prodigal Son] had spent all, there arose a mighty famine in that land; and he began to be in want."[113] To avoid famines in our lives—of health, peace and joy, food, shelter, or what have you—it behooves us to remain as close to Home, divine Love, as is possible, and to manifest childlike qualities as we turn to God, "Our Father which art in Heaven" to "give us this day our daily bread," to meet our spiritual as well as our material needs.

Then were there brought unto him little children, that he should put his hands on them, and pray: and the disciples rebuked them.

But Jesus said, Suffer little children, and forbid them not, to come unto me: for of such is the kingdom of heaven (Matt 19:13-14).

Jesus, once again, in the following passage stresses the importance of childhood, and childlike qualities (humbleness, for one) in reference to obtaining the Kingdom of Heaven:

At the same time came the disciples unto Jesus, saying, Who is the greatest in the kingdom of heaven?

And Jesus called a little child unto him, and set him in the midst of them,

And said, Verily I say unto you, Except ye be converted, and become as little children, ye shall not enter into the kingdom of heaven.

112 Luke 15:13
113 Luke 15:14

Whosoever therefore shall humble himself as this little child, the same is greatest in the kingdom of heaven.

And whoso shall receive one such little child in my name receiveth me (Matt 18:1-5).

Jesus said, "Except ye be converted, and become as little children, ye shall not enter into the kingdom of heaven."[114] In another place, Jesus reassures, "The kingdom of God cometh not with observation: Neither shall they say, Lo here! or, lo there! for, behold, the kingdom of God is within you."[115] For us to find and enter that Kingdom within, we must acquire childlike qualities, childlike traits, the trait of Innocence (Suckling newborns are the embodiment of innocence as they haven't as yet been corrupted by the carnal mind.); the trait of Purity "Blessed are the pure in heart: for they shall see God" (Love is the Great Purifier);[116] the trait of Dependency, where God becomes the possessor and the Source of all that we desire, "Son, thou art ever with me, and all that I have is thine";[117] and the trait of Trust, Humbleness or Meekness, "Blessed are the meek: for they shall inherit the earth."[118]

One of the most profound statements about Trust or Meekness may be found in this statement of Jesus:

All things are delivered unto me of my Father: and no man knoweth the Son, but the Father; neither knoweth any man the Father, save the Son, and he to whomsoever the Son will reveal him.

Come unto me, all ye that labour and are heavy laden, and I will give you rest.

Take my yoke upon you, and learn of me; for I am meek and lowly in heart: and ye shall find rest unto your souls.

---

114 Matt 8:3
115 Luke 17:20-21
116 Matt 5:8
117 Luke 15:31
118 Matt 5:5

For my yoke is easy, and my burden is light.[119]

We need, therefore, "Father, I thank thee that thou hast heard me."[120] *Trust*, "And I knew that thou hearest me always"[121] *Trust*. We need, too, "Son, thou art ever with me, and all that I have is thine" *Trust*. I can think of no greater demonstration of faith than *trust*. When we trust God, we surrender everything to Him—the method, the process, the timing, as well as the particulars, of how He will answer our prayers. We set aside, at that point, all worry and concern, all fear and trepidation about that for which we have prayed, knowing that God's Omnipotence and Omnipresence can't be challenged, and that His Will cannot and will not be thwarted by an earthly show of power and authority, knowing, too, that the "Lord our God is One Lord,"[122] having neither an adversary to oppose Him, nor one to mount a resistance to His Almighty Will.

---

119 Matt 11:27-30
120 John 11:41
121 John 11:42
122 Mark 12:29

EPILOGUE

T HIS SECTION OF THE BOOK IS ARGUABLY THE MOST important, as it's the place where I'm allowed to offer my final reflections, allowed to recapitulate salient concepts, and summarize conclusions—all the thoughts, information, and insights that I wish for you to take with you now that my book is winding down, and soon to be set aside. My prayer is that once you have completed this book, you will continue the writing of it—between the covers of your life, within the chapters of your soul, and upon the pages of your daily communion with God.

Beloved, now are we the sons of God, and it doth not yet appear what we shall be: but we know that, when he shall appear, we shall be like him; for we shall see him as he is (I John 3:2).

I don't believe in accidents. The details of my birth and how it came to be that I acquired the ability to leave my body didn't happen by chance. My Soul played a major role, a pivotal part, in directing this outcome, a role with which I wasn't always conversant, but one with which I agreed. On one level, I gave my consent, evidenced by my willingness to participate in, and assent to, an extension of consciousness.

I

Using the limitlessness of consciousness, we can communicate with the living and the dead, the living with or without the benefit of modern-day devices such as phones, and the Internet, but telepathically, and the dead with the same ease as with the living, also telepathically. At some point, those who die move out of range; they no longer respond directly to our inquiries, nor our desires to be with them. It's not impossible to reconnect, but it does require an enormous effort, or a persistent desire. Ghosts, on the other hand, for perhaps a number of reasons, remain in locations with which they're familiar. It may be they're refusing to believe that they're dead, that they're no longer living in a physical body, despite possessing a new body and a new reality, a reality in which the restrictions of the old reality can be altered or suspended.

Although I've written at length about the *you* in you, I must confess that such a you, as represented by your physical body, doesn't exist. There is no physical you. That you is an illusion. There's only the astral *you*, and its many permutations, also called the spiritual *you*. And, then, there's the Higher Self, the You in *you*. Beyond the astral, or spiritual *you*, you're nothing more than a speck of light in a heaven of infinite possibilities. The illusion of the two yous, a physical you and an astral *you*, is so convincing, we're certain, beyond cavil, that our physical you is us, when in fact the astral, the spiritual *you*, is the only *you* that exists. What the space suit is to the astronaut, and a diving suit to a deep-sea diver, the physical body is to the astral *you*; it allows you to operate and function within an otherwise hostile environment, the material, physical world.

Perhaps the most important thing I've learned from having lived so many lives in our physical world is the importance of living life by doing as little harm as is humanly possible, and, to use the resources at my command, to do as much good as is feasible. As physicians are asked to observe the virtues of the Hippocratic Oath, we, too, are asked to follow a similar Oath, a guidance beyond the statutes codified in our civil and criminal codes, or the social rules of conduct that direct the behavior of all members of society, doctors and laymen alike. My Oath, the one to which I adhere, which I call the *Perfection Oath*, is from that section of the Bible referred to as the Beatitudes, and is the one that Jesus, Himself, established. I quote it here in its entirety:

> *Ye have heard that it hath been said, Thou shalt love thy neighbour, and hate thine enemy.*
>
> *But I say unto you, Love your enemies, bless them that curse you, do good to them that hate you, and pray for them which despitefully use you, and persecute you;*
>
> *That ye may be the children of your Father which is in heaven: for he maketh his sun to rise on the evil and on the good, and sendeth rain on the just and on the unjust.*
>
> *For if ye love them which love you, what reward have ye? do not even the publicans the same?*
>
> *And if ye salute your brethren only, what do ye more than others? do not even the publicans so?*
>
> *Be ye therefore perfect, even as your Father which is in heaven is perfect* (Matt 5:43-48).

On this journey, we get to see life from many perspectives, including that of many races, different genders, and diverse life conditions, sick, healthy, wise, foolish, poor, rich, important, and insignificant. In addition, we get to redeem previous-life debts, "forgive us our debts as we forgive our debtors"[123] in a manner that the Soul dictates, usually by having us experience what others experienced at our hand, or experienced because of us, whose debt we're in, or whose debt we incurred as a result.

---

123 Matt 6:12

If only we'd realize this one maxim, "What we do to others, we do to ourselves," and function out this great truth in our day-to-day reality, we would end the karmic cycle—the cycle of cause and effect, of action and consequence—the cycle attributed to negative debt, and began to create a new world, one built on our oneness, rather than on the appearance of separation. This karmic indebtedness is individual and collective; it's a debt that's borne by each of us individually, and by us collectively, entire nation-states.

Individually, we may reenter life, that is, reincarnate under many human circumstances for the sole (soul) purpose of settling a karmic debt. We may reenter as the sworn enemy of the one we held as the enemy; as the victim of those we victimized; as the exploited of those we exploited; and as a slave of those we enslaved. When Europeans brought Sub-Saharan Africans to the New World to be enslaved, that ill-advised act led to their own enslavement. When they sought to "pacify" Native Americans, it was they who were pacified. In subsequent lives, it was they who reincarnated as blacks, and as slaves. It was they who became the overpowered indigenous people. The bottom line: What we did in previous lives is impacting, and will continue to impact, our current life, whether we're aware of that impact or not. There's no escaping it, the things that we sowed in previous lives (if the debt wasn't paid then), we will reap in subsequent lives, until the scales of justice are balanced and our debt satisfied.

Oftentimes, the Truth is not socially or politically digestible, and may lead occasionally to a heartburn of conscience, or a souring of the disposition, or a pushing away from the table of reality, refusing to eat what has been tasted, finding the fare too inedible for its bitterness, or its saltiness. Yet, this is the very time to make the unpalatable palatable, to introduce the necessary condiments of Truth and Love to reclaim The Feast that welcomes all as The Family they are, and not just friends or neighbors.

Then said he also to him that bade him, When thou makest a dinner or a supper, call not thy friends, nor thy brethren, neither thy kinsmen, nor thy rich neighbours; lest they also bid thee again, and a recompence be made thee.

But when thou makest a feast, call the poor, the maimed, the lame, the blind:

And thou shalt be blessed; for they cannot recompense thee: for thou shalt be recompensed at the resurrection of the just (Luke 14:12-14).

* * *

Purge out therefore the old leaven, that ye may be a new lump, as ye are unleavened. For even Christ our passover is sacrificed for us:

Therefore let us keep the feast, not with old leaven, neither with the leaven of malice and wickedness; but with the unleavened bread of sincerity and truth (I Cor 5:7-8).

II

Verily, verily, I say unto you, He that believeth on me, the works that I do shall he do also; and greater works *than these shall he do; because I go unto my Father.*[124]

I look wistfully to the day when Christians will emulate Jesus' works to the same degree that He's revered. He made it abundantly clear that we could, and He fully expected that we would, leaving behind for his disciples in all times and in all climes, precise instructions on how to achieve that Christly objective. As the first fruit of what is possible, many living today are denying themselves and are following the Christ, if not fully, then in part. As more humans enter the Christly "rest" of their potential, they'll

---

124 John 14:12

find their burdens lighter—that they're not as heavily laden—and that their labors are few.

They'll also find that their *labors* are not restricted to just this world: We live out our lives in this physical realm, and simultaneously in parallel worlds. Bleed through, when these parallel-world activities seep into our current existence, is not unusual, although it can be confusing for those so afflicted. Memories from parallel lives often come to the fore when I'm meditating or just before falling off to sleep. When it has happened to me, these parallel-world memories from alternate realities, have seemed so real that I couldn't immediately separate them from my current physical reality, believing them to be, if only for a short time, memories from my supposed real-world reality. Each time, the truth shocks me back to reality, the reality that the experience was indeed my experience, but one that took place, not in my present reality, but in a parallel one.

As I stated in an earlier chapter, and will restate here for its significance: While still quite young, I was the recipient of an Inner Wisdom, a Voice that guided, reassured, and protected, a Voice of Wisdom that continues to this day. It may be The Voice of my Soul, my Higher Self, or of an unknown guide. I've never asked, and I've never been told. But if I had to guess, I'd say that The Voice emanates from my Soul, my Higher Self, as I've sensed His presence many times while traveling out-of-body, or in dreams, regularly appearing as my twin brother, a person with whom I'm comfortable, and don't fear. I believe that those who put forth the effort can connect with this Inner Wisdom, provided they open themselves to The Voice by shutting out the chatter, the incessant internal talk that consumes our thinking, and replacing those thoughts with silence, with the stillness that comes when we plumb our inner depths, and reside there in the quietness.

Clearly there's more to us than meets the eye. It's almost a cliché that we're using a mere fraction of our overall potential, often said about the extent of our mental capabilities. Having spent time in my astral body, experiencing its many abilities, I'm convinced that there's more below the surface, infinitely more, than even I have discovered. Only God knows our limits, if, indeed, limits exist at all. As extraordinary as the astral body is, its environment is equally extraordinary, one which includes the astral realm, untold dimensions, worlds, and alternate realities, extending from the infinitesimal to the infinite, the whole of God limitless existence.

This is not a complete account of my various ventures into the astral realm, not a full account of my many previous lives, not a complete revelation of things to come, nor things that are occurring; not a comprehensive account of my hundreds, if not thousands, of out-of-body excursions. The experiences presented here are nothing more than a representation of thousands of experiences over a lifetime.

In this lifetime, and in others, we group reincarnate. Because very few of us are aware of it, very little attention is given to our spiritual lineage. The physical body, which becomes our host during a given lifetime, may be used to discover those who came before us, those with similar physical DNA, our progenitors. But it's our spiritual lineage, our spiritual DNA, that's the most important. For sure, those who died before us, our physical ancestors, may reappear in the same physical lineage, but that's determined by the Soul in collaboration with other Souls, once more reinforcing the truth: We're not our bodies; we're immeasurably greater than our physical vessels.

During each lifetime, we are drawn to be with certain people, if only for a short time. Our Souls make this happen, usually without our knowledge, ruling out the possibility of chance meetings, and chance relationships. If we find that we're alone, that, too, is planned. At times, it appears that many who are drawn together would have been better off keeping their distance, or that their relationship was anything but orchestrated, including those who are considered "unequally yoked,"[125] or coming from disparate backgrounds, or different racial groups or cultures, or belief systems, or finding themselves star-crossed lovers, a Romeo-Juliet attraction.

---

125 II Cor 6:14

When we meet for the first time those persons to whom our Souls have guided us, the usual feeling, besides one of attraction, or at first repulsion, is that we know the other persons to whom we're attracted, that the other persons are familiar, evoking a sense of familiarity that says, "I know you. I have always known you." It's a familiarity that says we've arrived *home* after a long absence, even if these persons decide at some point to move on. We choose in conjunction with our Soul to be with others, even as they choose to be with us, as friends, family members, wives and husbands, just as we choose at the Soul level to part company soon or late, or to stay together for an entire lifetime.

III

Draw nigh to God, and he will draw nigh to you.[126]

As we "draw nigh to God," we'll find the opposition less threatening and powerful. In a state of oneness with God, Jesus' reassurance will become out reality:

And Jesus answered him, The first of all the commandments is, Hear, O Israel; The Lord our God is one Lord: And thou shalt love the Lord thy God with all thy heart, and with all thy soul, and with all thy mind, and with all thy strength: this is the first commandment.

And the second is like, namely this, Thou shalt love thy neighbour as thyself. There is none other commandment greater than these.[127]

Here is true "meekness," that we love God supremely, love Him without reservation, without concern for, or pursuit of, or focus on, any human or heavenly aspirations other than Love, that we love God with all our heart, with all our soul, and with all our mind, and with all our strength, love Him

---

126 James 4:8
127 Mark 12:29-31

more than we love our own life, our own creature comfort, our health and safety, or any worldly treasure. Loving God in this manner doesn't impoverish us, but enriches, as Jesus has reassured: "Seek ye first the kingdom of God [the kingdom of Love], and his righteousness; and all these things shall be added unto you."[128]

THE SECRET OF SECRETS

For those who have read this far, I will reveal the *Secret of Secrets*. This will be your reward for your persistence. I discovered this *Secret of Secrets* purely by chance, or so it appeared. Although I've shared the secret with just a few others, I don't think that those with whom I shared it, believed me when I said it was the *Secret of Secrets*, or agreed to the challenge I issued. I implore you not to make the same mistake. Believe me, I've saved the best for last. Throughout the book, I gave you a glimpse of the *Secret of Secrets* without identifying it as such, nor indicating the tremendous power hidden away in the *Secret*.

Here's what I discovered, the *Secret of Secrets* is hiding in plain sight. The Secret is revealed in the 91st Psalm, in Jesus's answer to a question posed, which of the commandments is the *Great Commandment* in the law, and in John the Evangelist's (considered the author of the First Epistle of John) awesome revelation regarding the Nature of God:

God is love; and he that dwelleth in love dwelleth in God, and God in him.[129]

This statement constitutes the whole secret, but a portion of it needs to be highlighted before the whole of it becomes practical, the part that directs us to dwell in God. I found that if you love God, as Jesus advised,

---

128 Matt 6:33
129 I John 4:16

"with all thy heart, and with all thy soul, and with all thy mind,"[130] not just occasionally, but daily, and not just daily, but hourly, and not just hourly, but minute by minute and second by second throughout the day and night, you'll dwell in Love and Love in you. The secret, then, is to send God your love continuously, and to send your neighbor your love, if your neighbor—singularly or collectively—comes to mind during your dwelling. It's not enough to say, "I love God," you have to spend the seconds of each day actually loving Him, actually directing the whole of your love to Him. When I did this, the promise of the 91st Psalm came to life:

> *Because he hath set his love upon me, therefore will I deliver him: I will set him on high, because he hath known my name.*
>
> *He shall call upon me, and I will answer him: I will be with him in trouble; I will deliver him, and honour him.*
>
> *With long life will I satisfy him, and shew him my salvation* (Ps 91:14-16).

Having sought first the Kingdom of God, the Kingdom of Love, the "added unto you" things manifested themselves without a direct effort on my part, but merely by desiring them. Problems I encountered resolved themselves quickly, usually in the most unexpected ways. My human needs were met in a similar manner, in ways that might be considered miraculous. Those who attempted to take advantage of me, or sought to hurt or damage me in other ways, found that they couldn't, compelled to acknowledge their misdeeds and offer a remedy. Usually, what's done to me, whether good or bad, is, in short order, revisited upon those who committed the act. To fully discuss the amazing events that ensued as a result of dwelling within God, within in Love, would require the writing of another book. This I can say with certainty: When I have dwelled in Love, the following

---

130 Matt 22:37

assurance has been mine, "For he [God, divine Love] shall give his angels charge over thee, to keep thee in all thy ways."[131]

We're instructed to "pray without ceasing."[132] We may not think of it as such, but to love God and one's neighbor is a prayer. I can't think of a more perfect prayer. Therefore, pray, that is, love God and all others, without ceasing. Remember, love is more an active verb, something that acts upon an object, than it is just a noun, or a characteristic, or a quality, or an attribute as in "God is love." As Love, God is the Eternal Expression of that characteristic, quality, or attribute, as we should be—the quality as well as an expression of that quality. I shared the *Secret of Secrets* (that is, to love God ceaseless) with another, a skeptic, who dismissed love as just a human emotion, not realizing the full potential and potency that come with the elevation of that human love to the fullness of the divine expression, and to do so through the simple, and transformative act of loving without ceasing.

To "dwell in love" is to cling to it, especially in difficult times, during trials and tribulations, through hardships, and against the fear that outcomes might be negative, hurtful, damaging, or insurmountable. That's the challenge before us. Although ancient prophets passed the *secret* down to us, we have, individually and collectively, failed to implement it, owing to our failed insight, reducing the *Secret of Secrets*, yet again, to a secret.

Notwithstanding the worldly illusions that appear to contradict the Allness of God, there's only one God, one power. When we recognize, finally, our oneness with God, the All-in-all, the illusion of more than one power will disappear, as the sun's radiance at its zenith dispels the morning mist. Our recognition of God's Allness doesn't usually come without trials and tribulations, as the illusions are obstinately assertive. Living out this lifetime, I wish I could say I lived it without regrets, that I routed the *opposition*, that I lived it without committing acts of which I'm ashamed. That's

---

131 Ps 91:11
132 I Thess 5:17

not to say that I haven't done things of which I'm proud, things which, to recall, still bring warmth to my heart, and a glow to my spirit.

For those I may have hurt during this lifetime, I ask for your forgiveness, as I now forgive you for the wrong that you may have directed towards me. In all of these instances, we created the perfect opportunity to advance the understanding of the other, allowed for greater insight into the depth of our being, so that we might use that insight to progress spiritually. And I have progressed, have advanced the interest of my Soul. Yet, despite my spiritual progress, I was tempted in this lifetime no less than many of you, sometimes succeeding in avoiding the temptation, but all too often failing in my effort. If you haven't lived life at the pinnacle of your ideal, take heart in my failures, and know that, despite them, you can still live a spiritual-foundational life and bring good to a world so desperately in need of it. It's not just a cliché, but a profound truth: "Omnia vincit amor." Love conquers all.

IV

Again, the kingdom of heaven is like unto treasure hid in a field; the which when a man hath found, he hideth, and for joy thereof goeth and selleth all that he hath, and buyeth that field.[133]

We humans spend a great deal of our earthly time, our brief sojourn in the material realm, pursuing the treasures without, the treasures of the exterior world, rather than the one within, the Kingdom of Heaven, "where neither moth nor rust doth corrupt, and where thieves do not break through nor steal."[134] If we're to develop our spiritual acumen, our spiritual sense, it behooves us to know where our heart resides, "For where your treasure is, there will your heart be also."[135] If we search the *fields* of the mind, the

---

133 Matt 13:44
134 Matt 6:20
135 Matt 6:21

heart, and the Soul, as assiduously as we search earthly fields in an effort to amass the goods of this world, we could amass, with the same industry, the goods of Spirit. It is there, in Spirit, in our *Father's House,* where our true abundance resides, our spiritual treasure, existing in such copiousness that there's little need to fear its depletion. And why would we fear, when our Father's Treasure is an infinite treasure, one that's always available to his Sons, and Daughters.

Throughout Jesus' teachings, we find the theme of reunification again and again. Of himself, Jesus said, "I and *my* Father are one."[136] When we reunite with the "true vine," the Christ, we unite with the "husbandman,"[137] the Father, God. Once we know ourselves as "branches," we learn that we're connected to the "vine," as the branches can't exist without the vine: "I am the way, the truth, and the life: no man cometh unto the Father, but by me."[138]

Unless we're searching in the field of the Soul, we can't find, inadvertently or on purpose, what's hidden there: a treasure of untold wealth. Even as my message will be embraced gladly by some, others, with equal fervor, will attempt to denounce it, stating roundly that my experiences in the astral realm are nothing more than hallucinations. Such denouncers have targeted the out-of-body experience, the near-death experience, as well as those experiences that are described as paranormal, or other-worldly.

Each reader of this book will have to make up his or her own mind regarding my experiences, as I can't definitively validate them, nor can I convince you beyond your natural skepticism. Therefore, I encourage each of you to "know thyself," to look within for the answers, for the truth, for the evidence of your own eternal, unlimited selfhood. Each of us has a *treasure*, a treasure within our own backyard, a *you* in you, waiting to be discovered.

---

136 John 10:30
137 John 15:1
138 John 14:6

I have unveiled for you the riches of that treasure, the riches of the *you* in you, the *you* that's hidden from view. Now, I invite you: "Go, and do thou likewise."[139]

---

139 Luke 10:37

REFERENCE BOOKS

Soul Traveler—Albert Taylor

The Projection of the Astral Body—Sylvan J. Muldoon

Astral Projection—Oliver Fox

Journeys Out of the Body—Robert A. Monroe

Far Journeys—Robert A. Monroe

Ultimate Journey—Robert A. Monroe

Proof of Heaven—Eben Alexander

Conversations with God, Book 1—Neale Donald Walsch

Dancing in the Light—Shirley MacLaine

The Nature of Personal Reality—Jane Roberts & Robert F. Butts

Communion: A True Story—Whitley Strieber

Leaving the Body—D. Scott Rogo

CONTACT INFORMATION

To reach Wilbert Hunt, email him at TheUNU@aol.com, or write him at Charlton Park LLC, P.O. Box 904, Hemet CA, 92546